Mastering
FCAT

Reading • Grade 10

AMSCO

AMSCO SCHOOL PUBLICATIONS, INC.
315 HUDSON STREET, NEW YORK, NY 10013

Contributing Writer: Cristina Rivas
Interior and Cover design: A Good Thing, Inc./Dianne Rubin
Cover Illustration: Seth Jabour
Compositor: A Good Thing, Inc.

When ordering this book, please specify either **R728W** or
Mastering FCAT Reading, Grade 10

ISBN 1-56765-085-6

PRINTED IN THE UNITED STATES OF AMERICA

10   08 07 06

About the Author

Karen Spigler is a reading specialist for Miami Dade County Public Schools. She writes curriculum for the district and conducts teacher workshops for FCAT preparation at the middle and senior high school levels. She holds a Master of Science in Education from the University of Miami and has taught English, French, and English to speakers of other languages.

About the Consultants

Ann Foster has taught for 20 years in Florida schools, spending her last 12 years in Brevard County. She served on the DOE FCAT Range-Finding Committee for short and extended responses in 1999 and has helped to prepare 10th graders for the FCAT since the examinations began. Ms. Foster currently teaches at West Shore Junior/Senior High in Melbourne, Florida.

Marla Ross is a CRISS trained teacher of Language Arts and Special Education at North Miami Beach Senior High School. She holds a Masters of Education from the University of Houston and has taught for over 13 years. Ms. Ross currently serves as her school's FCAT Resource Teacher and conducts in-service training for teachers.

Bonnie Valdez is a master CRISS trainer and currently coordinates *Project CRISS* for Pinellas County School District. She holds a Masters of Arts in Reading Education from Florida State University and taught middle school in Florida for 15 years before becoming involved in middle and high school teacher training.

Nancy Klores Welday is the Language Arts department head, as well as the reading resource teacher at Hialeah-Miami Lakes Senior High School. She has provided numerous in-service training classes for teachers. Mrs. Welday is a certified CRISS trainer and in 1998 was the recipient of the Dade Reading Council's Miami-Dade Secondary Reading Teacher of the Year award.

Contents

Introduction: To the Student

About This Book

This book will help you prepare for the reading portion of the grade 10 FCAT. It does not take the place of what you learn in a regular reading or English class. Instead, the explanations, strategies, and questions in this book should help you remember the reading skills you have already learned, making your skills stronger.

The book begins with a **Pretest,** so that you (and your teacher) can assess your skills. The Pretest is modeled on the FCAT. It has the same types of questions as the FCAT, at about the same level of difficulty. There is an answer sheet that indicates sections of the book you may need to review based on which multiple-choice questions you answered incorrectly.

This book has nine content chapters, and each one corresponds to the benchmarks tested on the 10th grade FCAT in Reading. The content of each benchmark, the essential knowledge and set of skills as listed in the Sunshine State Standards, is reviewed in each chapter. What you need to know to do well on the FCAT is explained and illustrated in each chapter through the use of examples. Read on to learn about the five major sections of each chapter in the book.

The section titled *Understanding the Benchmark* introduces the content of each benchmark at the beginning of a chapter. We have provided suggestions for activities that you can explore in the classroom or at home to help you better understand how important FCAT skills are—even in non-academic situations. These activities help reinforce what you learn in the classroom, and provide "real-world" relevance to what is being taught.

The next section of the book is called *Making the FCAT Connection.* Here you will find a brief review of how this benchmark will be presented on the FCAT. The kinds of questions that will assess a benchmark and the kinds of selections you will be expected to read are listed.

The third part, called *Taking a Closer Look,* introduces the important ideas and concepts imbedded in that chapter's benchmark. Here, examples and activities help you review the concepts you should be familiar with when taking the FCAT.

The *Try It Out* section of the book plays a crucial role in helping you become skilled at answering FCAT questions. Each includes a short reading selection followed by FCAT-style questions. What makes this section unique is that a gray sidebar appears along with the reading selection, prompting you to question as you read. This "questioning" practice will help you learn how to engage with a reading selection. This is an important step to becoming an active reader. Another important feature of *Try It Out* is the answer explanation that follows the questions. Each multiple-choice answer is explained, and model answers for any short- or extended-response questions are provided and explained.

Finally, the last section of each chapter is called *On Your Own.* In this section, longer readings—more like those found on the FCAT—are provided for you to read and respond to. Each of the readings is followed by a set of FCAT-like questions assessing your understanding of the benchmarks covered in the book so far.

Scattered throughout the book are two other important features:

The *FCAT 411* usually appears in the *Making the FCAT Connection* section of a chapter and provides important information about the exam.

The *FCAT EXTRA* appears in various sections of the book and alerts readers to important bits of "extra" information. The *FCAT EXTRA* usually provides helpful hints about the FCAT itself, or about strategies to use when reading a selection or answering questions on the test.

At the end of the book, we have included two full-length **Practice Tests.** Like the Pretest, these exams are modeled on the FCAT in style and difficulty.

As you have probably heard before, "Practice makes perfect." This statement couldn't be truer of the FCAT. The more you practice, the more prepared and comfortable you will be taking the test.

We wish you the best of luck!

About The FCAT

The Sunshine State Standards, adopted by the State Board of Education in 1996, identify the skills and essential knowledge that students should learn. To judge whether students are meeting these standards for learning, the Florida Comprehensive Assessment Test (FCAT) was developed.

The reading portion of FCAT is given in grade 4, and the mathematics portion is given in grade 5. Both sections are given during grade 8 and again in grade 10. This book is about the reading portion of the grade 10 FCAT.

The grade 10 FCAT for reading tests content based on eleven benchmarks:

Grade 10 Benchmarks

LA.A.1.4.2 Selects and uses strategies to understand words and text, and to make and confirm inferences from what is read, including interpreting diagrams, graphs and statistical illustrations.

LA.A.2.2.7 Recognizes the use of comparison and contrast in a text.

LA.A.2.4.1 Determines the main idea and identifies relevant details, methods of development, and their effectiveness in a variety of types of written material.

LA.A.2.4.2 Determines the author's purpose and point of view and their effects on the text. (Includes LA.A.2.4.5 Identifies devices of persuasion and methods of appeal and their effectiveness.)

LA.A.2.4.4   Locates gathers, analyzes, and evaluates written information for a variety of purposes, (including research projects,) real-world tasks, and self-improvement. (Includes LA.A.2.4.6 Selects and uses appropriate study and research skills and tools according to the type of information being gathered or organized, including almanacs, government publications, microfiche, news sources, and information services.)

LA.A.2.4.7 Analyzes the validity and reliability of primary source information and uses the information appropriately.

LA.A.2.4.8 Synthesizes information from multiple sources to draw conclusions.

LA.E.2.2.1 Recognizes cause-and-effect relationships in literary text. (applies to fiction, nonfiction, poetry, and drama.)

LA.E.2.4.1 Analyzes the effectiveness of complex elements of plot, such as setting, major events, problems, conflicts, and resolutions.

Test Specifics

There will be two types of questions on the test:

- **Multiple choice** The majority of the questions will be in multiple-choice format.

- **Performance tasks** Students write answers to two types of questions:

 Short response This requires a short written answer. Students should take about five minutes to complete a short answer response which is worth up to two points.

Extended response This requires longer written answers and more thought. Students may have to combine information from more than one passage in order to complete the answer. Students should take approximately ten minutes to answer an extended response question which is worth up to four points.

The FCAT reading test is divided into two parts, with 40-45 multiple-choice questions and ten performance tasks on the total test. After the test is completed, it will be sent to a team of educators for scoring.

Multiple-Choice Questions

On the FCAT, a multiple-choice question will have four possible answers, and only one of them will be considered the best answer. The four choices will be labeled A, B, C, D or F, G, H, I.

Here are some strategies for choosing the right answer to a multiple-choice problem:

- Think of the answer to the question before looking at the answer choices. Then look to see if your answer is one of the four choices.

- Eliminate answers you know are incorrect.

- Organize the information in a short outline or list.

- Try to find a clue in the question that will lead you to the answer.

- If a problem seems too complicated, skip it and move on to other questions for that reading. After you finish answering the remaining questions, return to the one you skipped. Sometimes later questions and answers give you insight into the more difficult ones you may have skipped.

- Don't panic if you feel you have spent too long on a question. Some questions are more difficult than others and will require more time. The questions that are less difficult and can be answered quickly will help make up for lost time.

Performance Tasks

As mentioned before, there are two types of performance tasks: short-response and extended-response. The answer to a performance task must be written in the proper place in the FCAT answer booklet.

Your answer to a performance task will be scored with a rubric, a guideline that tells the scorer how many points to award.

Short-Response Questions

On the FCAT, the short-response questions are identified by a symbol that says: "Read, Think, Explain." Each short-response problem is expected to take about 5 minutes and is worth 2 points. A complete, correct response earns the full 2 points. A response that is partly complete or partly correct may earn you 1 point. A response that is totally wrong or missing earns 0.

Two-Point Scoring Rubric

2 points   The response indicates that the student has a complete understanding of the reading concept embodied in the task. The student has provided a response that is accurate, complete, and fulfills all the requirements of the task. All necessary support and/or examples are included, and the information given is clearly text-based.

1 point   The response indicates that the student has a partial understanding of the reading concept embodied in the task. The student has provided a response that may include information that is essentially correct and text-based, but the information is too general or too simplistic. Some of the support and/or example may be incomplete or omitted.

0 points   The response is inaccurate, confused, and/or irrelevant, or the student failed to respond to the task.

In this type of question, you must do more than simply answer the question accurately and completely. You will also be asked to support your answer with details and information from the passage.

Extended-Response Questions

Extended-response questions are identified by the "Read, Think, Explain" symbol plus several little lines (which look like ruled paper or answer blanks). Each extended-response problem is expected to take 5 to 15 minutes and is worth 4 points. You will earn the full 4 points for a complete, correct response. You may earn partial credit (3 points, 2 points, or 1 point) for a partially correct or partially complete response. If you response is totally incorrect or missing, you will earn 0 points.

Four-Point Scoring Rubric

4 points   The response indicates that the student has a thorough understanding of the reading concept embodied in the task. The student has provided a response that is accurate and fulfills all the requirements of the task. All necessary support and/or examples are included, and the information is clearly text-based. Any extensions beyond the text are relevant to the task.

3 points   The response indicates that the student has an understanding of the reading concept embodied in the task. The student has provided a response that is accurate and fulfills all the requirements of the task, but the required support and/or details are not complete or clearly text-based.

2 points   The response indicates that the student has a partial understanding of the reading concept embodied in the task. The student has provided a response that may include information that is essentially correct and text-based, but the information is too general or simplistic. Some of the support and/or examples and requirements of the task may be incomplete or omitted.

1 point   The response indicates that the student has a very limited understanding of the reading concept embodied in the task. The response is incomplete, may exhibit many flaws, and may not address all the requirements of the task.

0 points   The response is inaccurate, confused, and/or irrelevant, or the student failed to respond to the task.

Extended-response questions often ask you to think beyond the information provided. As with the short-response questions, you must usually do more than just give an answer for each part. You must support your answer with details and information from the passage.

Because the extended-response questions require more writing, they can seem intimidating. However, answering one of these questions is not that complicated if you pay attention and follow the general guidelines provided in the following section.

Performance Task Success

Writing a top-scoring response requires that you *pay attention* to the question, to how you construct your answer, and to the space allotted for your answer.

- **The first sentence should provide focus to your answer,** summarizing your main point or claim that you will be making. Each sentence after the first one should work to prove this statement, pointing to specifics in the text that support your point. For a short response you should follow with at least two details from the text. For extended responses you should include more support, making sure to use more than two details from the text.

- **Answer the *whole* question.** In other words, make sure that you read and understand the question completely. Sometimes, a question may have more than one part. For instance, you might be asked a question like, "What can you conclude about the attitudes of the two speakers?" To score well, you would have to make sure you discuss the attitude of both speakers.

- Make sure to **use details and information from the text** to support your answers. You will have to go back to the story, essay, and also any accompanying charts, graphs, or maps, to find *details* that prove the point you are making. In one question you may be asked about the actions of the main character in a story. If you believe that his actions were mean and uncaring, your answer should state this opinion along with several points supporting this claim. A well-written answer might begin something like this: "In the story, Thomas was uncaring and mean. First, on the day of the party, he opened up all the beautifully wrapped gifts even though he knew they were for his sickly younger sister." Short responses should include *at least two details* to support your answer and extended responses should include *several details* (more than two).

- You should *not* copy all your supporting details straight out of the text. You will earn more points if you **paraphrase,** or put most or all of your answer into your own words. If you feel it is important to use a quotation from the text, make sure that you surround the word or sentence with quotation marks. Also make sure to comment on why that quotation is important in explaining your answer. What follows is an example of the proper way to use material copied directly from the text.

- Another important point to remember is that you are allowed to use only the lines provided inside the answer box. No writing in the margins of the test or outside the box is allowed. For this reason, it is important to practice writing responses in answer spaces like those provided in this book.

- Finally, make sure that you use complete sentences in your answers. You will not, however, be judged harshly for incorrect grammar. You should also make sure that your writing is legible—able to be read. Keep in mind that even the most correct answer cannot receive points if graders cannot read it.

Example Response

Below is an extended-response question about a story that most people are familiar with. Read the question, answer, and explanation carefully.

1 How does Pinocchio's personality change from the beginning of the story to the end? Use details and information from the story to support your answer.

After carefully reading the question, you know that you should focus on Pinocchio's personality. Since behavior is what demonstrates personality, the answer should describe Pinocchio's actions. Because the question asks about "change" that occurred from the beginning to the end of the story, it is important to use details that point to Pinocchio's behavior at the beginning, the middle, and end of the story. You should explain how and what changes take place.

> Pinocchio changes a lot during the story. In the beginning, he is an innocent, somewhat timid boy who is amazed at being able to talk, move, and think. Then, as he grows curious about the world, Pinocchio gets into trouble because he believes that everybody he meets is just as good-hearted as Gepetto. Later, Pinocchio begins to behave badly and act selfishly. He hangs out with delinquents and tells lies. Soon, he realizes how bad behavior hurts himself and others, and he focuses on Gepetto's feelings. In the end, Pinocchio is loyal, brave, loving, and unselfish. He proves this by sacrificing himself to save Gepetto.

How do you think this student response would score? Read the explanation below to see how the answer follows the guidelines listed above.

✔ This answer **focuses on Pinocchio's behavior, which demonstrates his personality.** Maintaining such focus is key to scoring well on the FCAT extended or short responses.

✔ The paragraph also **answers the whole question** by showing how Pinocchio behaves in the beginning, in the middle, and at the end of the story. It shows how he "changes" over time.

✔ Important **details and information from the story** are used to support the main point of the answer. If you reread the answer you'll notice that it lists several specific details, including behaviors and events from the story that show how Pinocchio changes.

✔ Also, the important details in the story are **paraphrased** and not copied from the actual story.

✔ Finally, we make sure that **our answer fits** into the number of lines in the box.

So, based on this analysis, this extended response would score high on the rubric earning four points.

Checking Your Answers

When you are practicing for the exam—with this book, in class, or on your own—make sure you make an effort to recall the guidelines provided in this introduction. Becoming familiar with them will help to ensure that you will do well when its test time. Below is a checklist you can use to make sure that you have answered short- and extended-response questions thoroughly.

Response Checklist	
Did I create a well focused first sentence that answers the question and summarizes my main point?	❏

Did I use details and information from the text to support my answer?
 	
    At least two for the short response?
    More than two for the extended response?
	❏

Did I try to paraphrase all of my main points from the text?	❏
When I have used lines taken directly from the text, did I use quotation marks and explain why the quote was important?	❏
Did I use complete sentences and write legibly?	❏
Did I address all parts of the question, making sure I answered it completely?	❏

FCAT Pretest

PART 1
Read the article "DNA Detectives" and answer Numbers 1 through 10.

DNA Detectives

By Julie Richard

Move over, Phillip Marlowe. Take a hike, Sam Spade. A new breed of gumshoe has hit the streets. And this one is armed with more than a trench coat and a cigarette when staking out his man. Or, in this case, his animal.

They've been called genetic gumshoes or molecular detectives. Whatever their label, science and technology have merged to create a new "police force" that is helping endangered animals.

In Japan, a four-star business hotel is transformed into a mini DNA lab. Night tables double as lab benches. The mini-bar becomes a fridge to store chemicals, the bathroom is transmogrified into a darkened laboratory where strands of DNA are being extracted under an ultraviolet light from a sample of whale meat procured at a local fish market. The scientists who extract the DNA are Westerners. They keep a low profile in the hotel. They don't shop the markets themselves, sending instead a "cover"—local Japanese who can blend in the crowd and seem like regular shoppers. The less questions the better in this search. And the results they're turning up are surprising.

"We immediately found lots of species that shouldn't have been there," explains Harvard University's Steve Palumbi, who was one of the Tokyo Project's originators. "We found humpback, fin whales, and large numbers of toothed whales and dolphins. That pattern has shown up over and over again in Japan."

The International Whaling Commission (IWC) established a moratorium on commercial whaling in 1986, but taking whales for scientific research was still permitted. Japan's legal harvest was limited to a few hundred minke whales annually. No other whales were supposed to appear on the market. But they did.

International law prohibits the movement of endangered species and their products. Ironically, that includes DNA, which is an animal product. "So we couldn't just go get the meat and bring the sample back to the U.S.," Palumbi explains. "The only thing we could do was take a mini laboratory to Japan."

At the mini lab, DNA strands are unraveled through meat, and a bacterial enzyme constructs a replica. It is this genetic replica, rather than the original sample, that can be transported over international borders for analysis.

The research, which began in 1993, wasn't immediately given credence by the IWC, nor was it welcomed by the Japanese government. "Nobody was checking on this other than us," says Frank Cipriano, one of Palumbi's partners on the project. "The Japanese government doesn't care about endangering animals; they care about domination of marine resources. It's about domination of marine resources. It's about fish. Whales are just a market."

For their part, the Japanese claim that any illegal products come from mammals inadvertently caught rather than hunted, or from meat that was caught before the ban and that had been in storage freezers for years and was therefore still legal to sell.

"They claimed they had a DNA inspection system in place and that's just not true," says Cipriano. "They did two surveys that have never been peer reviewed and they presented them to the Commission as a done deal."

It was difficult for the detectives to get the IWC's attention in the early years. The committee refused to hear it the first agenda. But the team kept returning. Cipriano made half a dozen trips to Japan and Korea, continuing to gather data.

Last year, for the first time, DNA evidence was included as a permanent part of the IWC's scientific committee agenda.

The effort has definitely paid off for the whales. "When we started, 25 percent of whale meat on the market was illegal," says Palumbi. "It's now under five percent," While the Japanese won't admit that the Tokyo Project's research had anything to do with it, they've increased enforcement of permits and have begun confiscating illegal whale meat imports.

Marine mammals aren't the only animals to benefit from the developments in DNA identification. Hundreds of Galapagos tortoises are being held at the Charles Darwin Research Station here, confiscated from tourists who try to smuggle them home in their luggage. Their DNA will be tested to identify what population they belong to. The results may enable each of them to be returned to their own native islands.

Wildlife products used in traditional Chinese medicines are being scrutinized for the illegal use of endangered species. Amazon parrots and monkeys are being tested in the hopes that dwindling numbers will be increased by breeding.

Even one of the world's delicacies, caviar, has come under the microscope. Dr. Rob Lasalle of the American Natural History Museum and his colleague, Dr. Vadim Birstein, began a project to

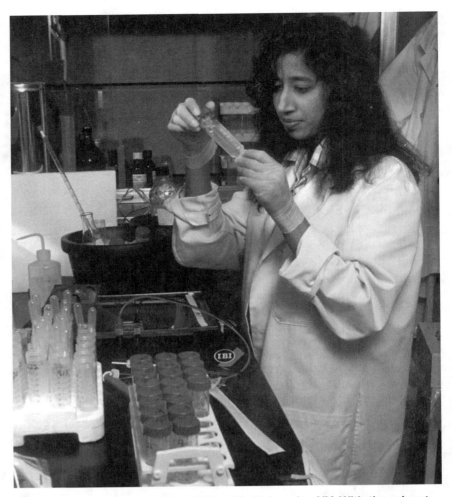

A researcher performs tests at Columbia University, NY. With the advent of genetic markers, DNA fingerprinting is extending the reach of forensic investigation and revolutionizing crimefighting as much as fingerprinting did one hundred years ago.

identify each of the 25 species of sturgeon, many of which are endangered, through DNA sequencing. Only a few of the species can legally be fished for caviar. Just like the Tokyo Project, the "Caviar Project" gathered samples from stores around New York, were labeled as caviar coming from legally fished sturgeon when they were, in fact, from protected species.

Birstein and DeSalle believe that most retailers are not to blame and that the real culprits are the poacher—and the Russian bureacracy that supports them.

"When the Soviet Union fell, poaching popped up and continued," explains Birstein. "Hundreds of different groups of the Russian Mafia jumped on it." There was uncontrolled poaching and fishing in the Caspian Sea. International law enforcement is not working at all. It's in the hands of bureaucrats."

Birstein and DeSalle created a method by which caviar could be tested quickly and simply at its export point. A certificate could then accompany the shipment, identifying its source both by species and by geography.

Go On ▶

Having completed his database of sturgeon species, DeSalle set out to solve the problems of other species, like endangered white and black ruffled lemurs in Madagascar, which are being bred in captivity. "Our DNA work tells us which individuals are most likely to be genetically or evolutionarily good to mix."

He is also using genetics to monitor tiger beetles. And he's working with the Bronx Zoo to identify Cayman crocodiles, which are big business in the illegal pet trade. "The main thing is that we can diagnose the species. It enables us to make sure that what's coming in is legal food or that a pet is really legal."

DeSalle never takes part in live animal experiments. "Animals are trapped and tagged in the wild," he explains. "Then a hair, blood, or fecal sample is brought back to be analyzed. We don't destroy or harm the animals."The IWC has now adopted testing standards and controls over the Norwegian and Japanese whaling industries— a direct result of Palumbi's and Cipriano's research. For their part, the two men have turned their attention to helping other marine animals.

One of Palumbi's latest projects is helping to establish marine parks in Indonesia. "We need these parks in order to keep biological diversity in the sea and to set aside areas where people can fish. Even if they're just 100 yards across, it still works."

Indonesia has established 36 parks so far. Palumbi's work is discovering if they are, indeed, protecting the animals. There are lots of mantis shrimps in Indonesia but in each marine park they act separate populations that don't migrate to other parks.

"That means you can't count on being able to wipe one with an oil spill or something and expect it to come back," says Palumbi. "The ocean currents aren't strong enough to move egg and larvae around. The only way to make them work is to have networks scattered throughout the sea."

Cipriano is working on identifying dolphin populations. "I've been studying how many species there really are. There are more than are recognized," he says. "We need to know how distinct the separate populations of dolphins are. If a particular animal that is being taken is distinct and divergent from other members of the species, we may be depleting a genetic resource. We're using genetics to identify management units and then we can take the data to the authorities."

With genetic detectives working to save animals the world over, Palumbi says there's still a lot that individuals can do to join the effort, even if they're not particularly handy with a DNA sequence. "Our experience with IWC is that individual efforts do make a difference," says Palumbi. "The whale stuff started because Don White, the head of the Earth Trust, walked into our office."

White had approached Palumbi because he was looking for proof that the Japanese whaling industry was violating international law. "[The project] was paid for by the contributions of people who donated money to his organization. Small amounts of money in individual efforts do help. People think that nothing they can do matters, but that's not true.

"It won't take a huge time for the ocean to begin to recover because we're in the early stages of damaging it. The trouble is we have no idea when we're going to flip over to the late stages. "Simply valuing the oceans is something that politicians and policymakers need to know that people care about. Everybody knows that people who live by the ocean like it. But changes depend on people who *don't* live by the oceans saying, 'Yes, I value that. And I want to know that the ocean is in good shape.'"

"If they're willing to stand up for that, then the message will be that there is economic value in healthy oceans. Simply value the oceans and tell people you do."

Answer questions 1 through 10. Base your answers on the article "DNA Detectives."

1 Read the following sentence from the article.

> The mini bar becomes a fridge to store chemicals; the bathroom is transmogrified into a darkened laboratory where strands of DNA are being extracted under an ultraviolet light from a sample of whale meat procured at a local fish market.

What does *transmogrified* mean?

A. changed

B. inserted

C. labeled

D. remodeled

2 What is the most important reason that the Tokyo Project's investigation had to be conducted in Japan?

F. The IWC was headquartered in Japan.

G. Scientists who participated were from Japanese universities.

H. The IWC feared moving the specimens would damage the DNA.

I. International law did not allow the DNA of a whale to be transported.

3 How does the Bronx Zoo benefit from testing animal DNA?

A. DNA helps to identify healthy species for breeding.

B. The tests help establish regulations for importing animals.

C. DNA testing helps control the irresponsible behavior of officials.

D. The tests help the zoo identify animals that are illegally sold as pets.

4 What is the main idea of the article "DNA Detectives"?

F. Illegal whaling has been reduced thanks to DNA detectives.

G. DNA detectives persisted until the IWC accepted their reports.

H. DNA detective work has benefited many different endangered species.

I. Japan is more interested in profiting from endangered species than protecting them.

Go On ▶

5 According to the article, how can individuals help the efforts of genetic detectives?

    A. They can contribute large sums of money to the IWC.

    B. They can voice concern about the oceans and endangered species.

    C. They can write to Congress in support of changing DNA testing laws.

    D. They can question governments violating international endangered species laws.

6 What problems do Birstein and DeSalle face in limiting the use of illegally fished sturgeon used in Russian caviar?

    F. Most of the caviar on the market comes from protected species.

    G. International laws cannot control poaching and involvement of the Russian Mafia.

    H. There is no quick way to test caviar at its export point so illegal caviar is on the market.

    I. The "Caviar Project" lost financial support and scientists are no longer able to test caviar.

7 READ THINK EXPLAIN   How do the statements of the Japanese government concerning illegal whale products differ from the statements of the Tokyo Project's scientists? Use information from the article to answer your question.

```
_____

_____

_____

_____

_____

_____

_____

_____
```

8 According to the article, the ocean

    A. needs to be monitored by DNA detectives.

    B. can be saved by efforts of concerned individuals.

    C. is in the final stages of damage caused by human error.

    D. has strong enough currents to move egg and larvae populations.

9 The author's purpose in writing the article was to

   F. persuade readers to help raise money and offer support for the IWC.

   G. persuade readers to help protect ocean dwelling endangered species.

   H. inform readers of DNA use in identifying and solving problems facing protected species.

   I. inform readers about a police force of scientists dedicated to ending commercial whaling.

10 READ THINK EXPLAIN If you were an animal activist, how would you use the information in the article to convince the government to continue the support of scientists working with animal DNA? Use details and information from the article to support your answer.

Go On

Read the articles "Diablo Country" and "Nuclear Energy" and answer Numbers 11 through 20.

Diablo Country
By Art Buchwald

Anti-nuclear demonstrators stand above the Satstop Nuclear Power Plant Site with arms raised in protest.

I pride myself on having a very open mind on things such as nuclear energy as long as they don't build a plant near my home.

So when I saw the Diablo Canyon demonstration in California a while ago, I watched it with the calm impartiality which I reserve for all things that don't affect me personally.

On one side were scruffy, unshaven, unshod protestors. On the other were well-dressed state troopers and clean, good-looking spokesmen for the power company. The dispute as I understand it, was the scruffy unbathed people claimed that the people in the white hats didn't know what they were doing. They had built a billion-dollar nuclear plant near the San Andreas fault, which everyone says is going to cause an earthquake in California sooner or later.

My wife, who doesn't know the first thing about nuclear energy, asked me one evening as we watched the scruffies being hauled off in sheriffs' vans, "Why would they build a nuclear plant next to an earthquake center?"

"Because it obviously makes sense. The people who construct those plants know what they're doing. If you had been listening to the nice, clean-cut men in white shirts, ties, and dark suits, you would know that the power company has done exhaustive tests, and the nuclear plant can withstand any earthquake shock known to man. Besides, we have a Nuclear Regulatory Commission that has the last word on whether a plant is safe or not. They would never have given their OK to open one if there was the slightest question that building a nuke plant next to an earthquake fault could hurt the environment."

"Then why are the people in the scruffy clothes willing to be arrested for trying to close down the plant?" she asked.

Go On

"Because they have an unrealistic fear of nuclear power. They don't understand it, and therefore they're against it. Many of them are students who enjoy getting involved in civil disobedience. But they're willing to go to jail for their beliefs."

"Whose side are you on?"

"I'm afraid I have to be on the side of those wearing the ties and coats. After all, they've been dealing with nuclear power all their lives and they should know if it's safe or not."

"A few years ago, you would have been on the side of the unwashed."

"I guess age does that to you. At some point in time you have to say that just because a person needs a shave doesn't make him right-and just because a person has short hair and dresses properly doesn't make him wrong."

"That's a stupid reason for taking one side over the other."

"There's more to it than that. The people who build nuclear plants are scientists, trained in our finest technical institutions. They work with computers and consult with famous experts who have an answer for every problem. The engineers and designers take extraordinary steps to see that not one bolt is put in wrongly. If they say a nuclear plant can survive an earthquake, I have to accept their word for it."

"This is not to say I am unsympathetic with the poor souls who are willing to go to jail because they lack faith in our great scientific establishment. But in this case, I believe they're making a mountain out of a molehill. I would bet my All Savers Bank Account that they are wrong."

Well, you can imagine my surprise when a week later the evening news announced that the Diablo Canyon nuclear reactor could not go into service because someone had gotten the drawings all mixed up, and the wrong pipes had been installed in the wrong sections of the plant. It meant that every pipe had to be personally inspected and replaced if it was discovered that it didn't belong there.

A man from the power company in a nice white shirt, tie, and blue suit explained it wasn't a very serious mistake and could have happened to anybody.

Another well-dressed man from the Nuclear Regulatory Commission said he was appalled at the sloppy engineering and was ordering an immediate investigation.

They didn't put on any scruffy people for comment. I wish they had, because I wanted to find out where to send them my All Savers Bank Account.

Go On ▶

Nuclear Energy

From *Environmental Science*

The Nuclear Age began on July 16, 1945, when the first atomic bomb exploded over the New Mexico desert. The technology that created the bomb led to the development of nuclear reactors. By 1953, nuclear reactors were powering electric generators. At that time, a future was envisioned in which the world was freed from its dependence on fossil fuels by the new "cheap" source of energy provided by splitting the atom. Nuclear power plants were soon under construction or planned for construction throughout the United States and in many other industrialized nations. However, unforeseen problems have diminished the dream of a future powered by nuclear energy.

At first, electricity produced by nuclear energy was much cheaper than energy derived from fossil fuel. But operating costs have risen rapidly, and electricity from nuclear power plants is now more that twice as expensive as that produced by other fuels. From 1970 to 1975, in the United States, plans were filed to build an average of 12 nuclear power plants per year; from 1975 to 1978, the number dropped to 9 plants per year. Since 1978, no new plants have been planned and several that had been planned were canceled.

Several factors have contributed to the decline of the nuclear industry in the United States. The main drawbacks to nuclear power are increased construction costs, public opposition to nuclear power, and concerns about safety and disposal of spent fuel. There are 110 nuclear plants in operation in the United States, most of them located in the eastern part of the country. Approximately 29 percent of our energy production comes from nuclear power.

By 1985, nuclear power generated 18 percent of the electrical power in the world. In some industrialized nations, the use of nuclear energy is very high. France, for example, generates more that 65 percent of its electrical energy with its 60 nuclear reactors. However, developing nations cannot afford this expensive power source. Fewer nuclear plants are now being constructed, and attention is focused on other means of electrical energy generation.

Nuclear reactor in the Loire Valley, France. The reactor is a device for producing a controlled release of nuclear energy. The fission of atomic nuclei produces a chain reaction.

The following charts show power usage for the states of New York and Ohio as well as averages for the entire United States.

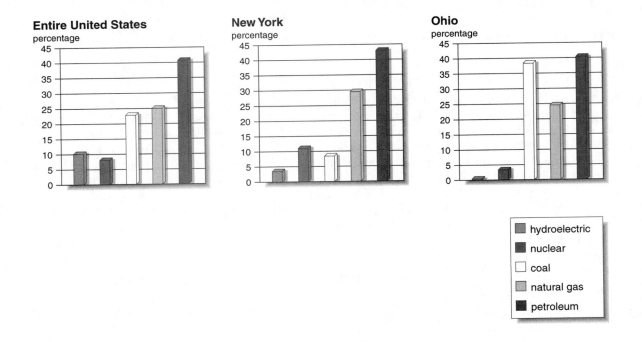

Go On ▶

Answer questions 11 through 20. Base your answers on the articles "Diablo Country" and "Nuclear Energy."

11 According to the second article's graphs, what can we infer about the type of energy used in different locations?

    A. Ohio prefers nuclear power to any other source.

    B. New York has more nuclear power plants than Ohio and the U.S. in general.

    C. Coal is more available in New York than in many other parts of the United States.

    D. Hydroelectric power and nuclear power are used in equal amounts in most parts of the United States.

12 What would be another good title for the "Diablo Country" essay?

    F. San Andreas Power Plant Under Scrutiny

    G. Diablo Goes Nuclear: Is It A Good Idea?

    H. Inside Information on Nuclear Power Plants

    I. An Old Man's Perspective on Nuclear Power

13 READ THINK EXPLAIN   What details support the idea that nuclear power plants may sometimes be the wrong choice for supplying power? Use details and information from both articles to support your answer.

Go On ▶

14 Which statement best supports the idea that nuclear power is an expensive source of energy?

   A. The same technology that created the atomic bomb helped develop nuclear power, making it costly.

   B. Public opposition to nuclear power and concerns about safety has driven up the cost of nuclear power.

   C. High operating costs of nuclear power plants and the high cost of the electricity it produces make them expensive.

   D. Lawsuits resulting from nuclear accidents make insuring nuclear plants an almost impossible and expensive undertaking.

15 Read the following sentences from "Diablo Country."

> On one side were scruffy, unshaven, unshod protestors. On the other were well-dressed state troopers and clean, good-looking spokesmen for the power company.

What does *scruffy* mean?

   F. immaculate

   G. untidy

   H. violent

   I. well-groomed

16 In the first article, what is the author's opinion of the protestors?

   A. They were clean, well-spoken and therefore right about power plant.

   B. They were messy, looking for trouble, and had no basis for their fears.

   C. They were young and irresponsible, and therefore had no concern for others.

   D. They were well-educated scientists who understood the world of nuclear power.

17 What method does the author use to organize the second article?

   F. spatial order

   G. cause and effect

   H. comparison and contrast

   I. argument and support

Go On

18 What evidence exists to support the statement that the nuclear industry is on the decline in the United States?

    A. No plants have been built since 1978.

    B. Protests against power plants have escalated.

    C. Unforeseen problems have caused nuclear accidents.

    D. People prefer fossil fuels as their main source of energy.

19 How did the first atomic bomb contribute to the development of nuclear power?

    F. It provided the funding necessary to develop nuclear reactors.

    G. Underdeveloped nations were able to support the development of the bomb.

    H. Nuclear power developed from the technology that created the atomic bomb.

    I. The bomb helped scientists understand the need to reduce dependency on fossil fuels.

20 READ THINK EXPLAIN   In the article, "Diablo County," how does the speaker's opinion about the nuclear power plant change from the beginning to the end of the passage? Use details and information from the article to support your answer.

Go On ▶

Read the story "Marigolds" and answer Numbers 21 through 28.

Marigolds
By Eugenia Collier

The half-dawn light was more eerie than complete darkness, and in it the old house was like the ruin that my world had become—foul and crumbling, a grotesque caricature. It looked haunted, but I was not afraid because I was haunted too.

"Lizabeth, you lost your mind?" panted Joey.

I had indeed lost my mind, for all the smoldering emotions of that summer swelled in me and burst—the great need for my mother who was never there, the hopelessness of our poverty and degradation, the bewilderment of being neither child nor woman and yet both at once, the fear unleashed by my fathers' tears. And these feelings combined in one great impulse toward destruction.

"Lizabeth!"

I leaped furiously into the mounds of marigolds and pulled madly, trampling and pulling and destroying the perfect yellow blooms. The fresh smell of early morning and of dew soaked marigolds spurred me on as I went tearing and mangling and sobbing while Joey tugged my dress or my waist trying, "Lizabeth stop, please stop!" And then I was sitting in the ruined little garden among the uprooted and ruined flowers, crying and crying, and it was too late to undo what I had done. Joey was sitting beside silent, frightened, and me not knowing what to say. Then, "Lizabeth, look."

I opened my swollen eyes and saw in front of me a pair of large calloused feet; my gaze lifted to the swollen legs, the age-distorted body clad in a tight cotton nightdress, and then the shadowed Indian face surrounded by stubby white hair. And there was no rage in the face now, now that the garden was destroyed and there was nothing any longer to be protected.

"M-miss Lottie!" I scrambled to my feet and just stood there and stared at her, and that was the moment when childhood faded and womanhood began. The violent, crazy act was the last act of childhood. For as I gazed at the immobile face with sad, weary eyes, I gazed upon a kind of reality that is hidden to childhood. The witch was no longer a witch but only a broken old woman who had dared to create beauty in the midst of ugliness and sterility. She had been born in squalor and had lived in it all her life. Now at the end of that life she had nothing except a falling-down hut, a wrecked body, and John Burke, the mindless son of her passion. Whatever verve there was left in her, whatever was of love and beauty and joy that had not been squeezed out by life, had been there in the marigolds she had so tenderly cared for.

Of course I could not express the things that I knew about Miss Lottie as I stood there awkward and ashamed. The years have put words to the things I knew in that moment, and as I look back upon it, I know that that moment marked the end of innocence... . Innocence involves an unseeing acceptance of things at face value, and ignorance of the area below the surface. In that humiliating moment I looked beyond myself and into the depths of another person. This was the beginning of compassion and one cannot have both compassion and innocence.

The years have taken me worlds away from that time and that place, from the dust and squalor of our lives and from the bright thing that I destroyed in a blind, childish striking out at God-knows-what. Miss Lottie died long ago and many years have passed since I last saw her hut, completely barren at last, for despite my wild contrition she never planted marigolds again. Yet, there are times when the image of those passionate yellow mounds returns with a painful poignancy. For one does not have to be ignorant and poor to find that one's life is barren as the dusty yards of one's town. And I too have planted marigolds.

Go On ▶

Answer questions 21 through 28 . Base your answers on the story "Marigolds."

21 The mood created by the author in the first paragraph of the story is one of

    A. fear and darkness.

    B. evil and witchcraft.

    C. pleasantness and light.

    D. mystery and unpleasantness.

22 Why does Miss Lottie grow marigolds?

    F. She wants the admiration and respect of others in the community.

    G. She wants to have something beauty in her otherwise depressing surroundings.

    H. She hopes to make people curious about her decisions about to keep a flower garden.

    I. She needs to feel the satisfaction that comes from planting flowers and watching them grow.

23 What is the author's purpose in writing the story "Marigolds"?

    A. to convince readers that absolutely anything is possible for young girls.

    B. to inform readers of the emotional problems caused by growing up poor.

    C. to encourage readers to beautify their surroundings by planting marigolds.

    D. to share with readers an event marking the beginning of a girl's maturity.

24 | READ | THINK | EXPLAIN | Why are Miss Lottie and the marigolds important to Lizabeth later in life? Support your answer using details and information from the story.

_____

_____

_____

_____

_____

_____

_____

_____

Go On ▶

25 Read the following sentence from the story.

> The years have taken me worlds away from that time and that place, from the dust and squalor of our lives and from the bright thing that I destroyed in a blind, childish striking out at God-knows-what.

What does *squalor* mean?

A. depression

B. filth

C. luxury

D. poverty

26 What led Lizabeth to destroy the marigolds in the garden?

F. her hatred for Miss Lottie

G. a need to accept a dare by Joey

H. the need for revenge against her family

I. her frustration and complicated emotions

27 How does the author convey the idea that Lizabeth realizes she is no longer innocent?

A. Lizabeth plants marigolds of her own.

B. Lizabeth feels compassion for Miss Lottie.

C. Lizabeth is no longer afraid of Miss Lottie.

D. Lizabeth decides she will replant the flowers.

28 What do the marigolds most likely represent to Miss Lottie?

F. the link to a better life she will never have

G. the only joy and beauty she is able to attain

H. the sentiments of her youth and lost memories

I. the remembrance of her father before his death

Part 2

Read the article "World is Skating on Thin Ice" and answer Numbers 29 through 39

World is Skating on THIN ICE

From *National Life Magazine*

If any explorers had been hiking to the North Pole this summer, they would have had to swim the last few miles. The recent discovery of open water at the Pole by an icebreaker cruise ship has surprised many in the scientific community.

This finding, combined with two recent scientific studies, confirms that the Earth's ice cover is melting at an accelerating rate. A study by two Norwegian scientists projects that within 50 years the Arctic Ocean could be ice-free during the summer. The other study, by a team of four U.S. scientists, reports that the vast Greenland ice sheet is melting.

An earlier study reported that the thickness of the ice sheet has been reduced by 42 percent over the last four decades. The area of the ice sheet has also shrunk by six percent. This thinning and shrinkage has reduced the Arctic Ocean ice mass by nearly half.

Meanwhile, Greenland is gaining some ice in the higher altitudes, but it is losing much more at lower elevations, particularly along its southern and eastern coasts. The huge island of 2.2 million square kilometers is experiencing a net loss of some 51 billion cubic metres of water each year, an amount equal to the annual flow of the Nile River.

The Antarctic is also losing ice. In contrast to the North Pole, which is covered by the Arctic Sea, the South Pole is covered by the Antarctic continent, a land mass roughly the size of the United States. Its continent-sized ice sheet, which is on average 2.3 kilometers thick, is relatively stable. But the ice shelves, the portions of the ice sheet that extend into the surrounding seas, are fast disappearing.

A team of American and British scientists reported in 1999 that the ice shelves on either side of the Antarctic Peninsula are in full retreat. From roughly mid-century through 1997, these areas lost 7,000 square kilometers. Huge icebergs that have broken off are threatening ships in the area. Scientists attribute the accelerated ice melting to a regional temperature rise of some 2.5 degrees Celsius since 1940.

These are not the only examples of melting. Lester Brown of the World watch Institute, in an Issue Alert released today says, "My colleague, Lisa Mastny, who has reviewed some 30 studies on this topic, reports that ice is melting almost everywhere—and at an accelerating rate. The snow/ice mass is shrinking in the world's major mountain ranges: the Rocky Mountains, the Andes, the Alps, and the Himalayas. In Glacier National Park in Montana, the number of glaciers has dwindled

Antarctica landscape with icebergs that have broken off due to accelerated ice melting. They are a threat to ships in the area.

Go On

from 150 in 1850 to fewer than 50 today. The U.S. Geological Survey projects that the remaining glaciers will disappear within 30 years."

Scientists studying the Quelccaya glacier in the Peruvian Andes report that its retreat has accelerated from 3 meters a year between roughly 1970 and 1990 to 30 metres a year since 1990. In Europe's Alps, the shrinkage of the glacial area by 35 to 40 percent since 1850 is expected to continue. These ancient glaciers could largely disappear over the next half-century.

Brown notes that shrinkage of ice masses in the Himalayas has also accelerated alarmingly. In eastern India, the Dokriani Bamak glacier, which retreated by 16 metres between 1992 and 1997, drew back by a further 20 meters in 1998 alone.

This melting and shrinkage of snow/ice masses should not come as a total surprise. Swedish scientist Svente Arrhenius warned at the beginning of the last century that burning fossil fuels could raise atmospheric levels of carbon dioxide (CO_2), creating a greenhouse effect. Atmospheric CO_2 levels, estimated at 280 parts per million (ppm) before the Industrial Revolution, have climbed from 317 ppm in 1960 to 368 ppm in 1999-a gain of 16 percent in only four decades.

As CO_2 concentrations have risen, so too has Earth's temperature. Between 1975 and 1999, the average temperature increased from 13.94 degrees, a gain of 0.41 degrees in 24 years. The warmest 23 years since record keeping began in 1866 have all occurred since 1975.

Researchers are discovering that a modest rise in temperature of only one or two degrees Celsius in mountainous regions can dramatically increase the share of

precipitation falling as rain while decreasing the share coming down as snow. The result is more flooding during the rainy season, a shrinking snow/ice mass, and less snowmelt to feed rivers during the dry season.

These "reservoirs in the sky," where nature stores fresh water for use in the summer as the snow melts, are shrinking and some could disappear entirely. This will affect the water supply for cities and for irrigation in areas dependent on snowmelt to feed rivers.

The Worldwatch Institute warns that if the massive snow/ice mass in the Himalayas—which is the third largest in the world after the Greenlandic and Antarctic ice sheets—continues to melt, it will affect the water supply of much of Asia. All of the region's major rivers—the Indus, Ganges, Mekong, Yangtze, and Yellow—originate in the Himalayas. The melting in the Himalayas could alter the hydrology of several Asian countries, including Pakistan, India, Bangladesh, Thailand, Vietnam, and China. Less snowmelt in the summer dry season to feed rivers could exacerbate the hydrological poverty already affecting so many in the region.

As the ice on land melts and flows to the sea, sea level rises. Over the last century, sea level rose by 20 to 30 centimeters. During this century, the existing climate models indicate it could rise by as much as one meter. If the Greenland ice sheet, which is up to 3.2 kilometers thick in places, were to melt entirely, sea level would rise by 7 meters.

Even a much more modest rise would affect the low-lying river floodplains of Asia, where much of the region's rice is produced. According to World Bank analysis, a one-meter rise in sea

level would cost low-lying Bangladesh half its Riceland. Numerous low-lying island countries would have to be evacuated. The residents of densely populated river valleys of Asia would be forced inland into already crowded interiors. Rising sea level could create climate refugees by the million in countries such as China, India, Bangladesh, Indonesia, Vietnam, and the Phillippines.

Even more disturbing, ice melting itself can accelerate temperature rise. As snow/ice masses shrink, less sunlight is reflected back into space. With more sunlight absorbed by less reflective surfaces, temperature rises even faster and melting accelerates.

Brown says that we don't have to sit idly by as this scenario unfolds. He says there may still be time to stabilize atmospheric CO_2 levels before continuing carbon emissions cause climate change to spiral out of control. "We have more than enough wind, solar, and geothermal energy that can be economically harnessed to power the world economy. If we were to incorporate the cost of climate disruption in the price of fossil fuels in the form of a carbon tax, investment would quickly shift from fossil fuels to these climate-benign energy sources."

The leading automobile companies are all working on fuel cell engines. Daimler Chrysler plans to start marketing such an automobile in 2003. The fuel of choice for these engines is hydrogen. Even leaders within the oil industry recognize that we will eventually shift from a carbon-based energy economy to a hydrogen-based one. The question, notes Brown, is whether we can make that shift before Earth's climate system is irrevocably altered.

Go On ▶

Answer questions 29 through 39. Base your answers on the article "World is Skating on Thin Ice."

29 What information led scientist to discover that the Earth's ice cover is diminishing rapidly?

A. the discovery of the greenhouse effect by a Swedish scientist about 30 years ago

B. the fact that mountainous areas of the world are experiencing more precipitation

C. the discovery by the British that the ice shelf in Antarctic is stable and predictable

D. a discovery of open water at the North Pole and evidence from two scientific studies

30 What effects would the rising sea level have on Bangladesh?

F. The rainfall would increase and the ice mass would diminish.

G. The country would lose much of its farmland forcing residents to move inland.

H. Mountainous areas would experience less rainfall, depleting summer water reserves.

I. The temperature of low-lying areas would rise forcing people to move to cooler coastal areas.

31 READ THINK EXPLAIN — If you were an environmentalist how could you use this information to convince the public to look at fuel sources other than fossil fuels? Support your answer with details and information from the article.

32 What evidence best supports the author's claim that people have been aware of the changes in the earth's climate for a very long time?

   A. The warmest 23 years have all taken place in the last 30 years.

   B. Over the last century, sea levels rose significantly in all parts of the world.

   C. The glaciers in the Alps have shrunk about 40 percent in the last fifty years.

   D. At the beginning of the last century a Swedish scientist recognized effect of increased CO_2 levels on the earth's temperature.

33 What is the author's purpose in writing this article?

   F. to explain how scientists became aware of the reduction of the polar ice cover

   G. to convince readers to help fund research to learn the causes of the melting ice cap

   H. to illustrate effects of global warming on the world, especially the Asian population

   I. to convince readers that the melting ice cap illustrates a need for alternate sources of power

34 What evidence supports the idea that the glaciers in Europe's Alps may disappear over the next fifty years?

   A. The shrinkage of ice masses has been consistent over time so this mass will follow the same pattern.

   B. In the past 150 years, they have shrunk to almost one half their original size.

   C. The shrinking ice mass in the Himalayas has accelerated by 36 meters since 1992.

   D. The US Geological Survey projects that the remaining glaciers will disappear soon.

35 How will the melting snow/ice masses in the Himalayas affect the water supply of Asia?

   F. The floodplains will overflow and people would have to learn flood control farming.

   G. As the snowmelt that feeds rivers diminishes, many countries will become even drier.

   H. The amount of precipitation will increase causing more flooding during the dry season.

   I. As the snowmelt decreases, area rivers will change course, no longer flowing into countries that need water the most.

36 How do some scientists suggest we control the use of fossil fuels?

   A. develop alternate sources of fuel

   B. replace fossil fuel with wind and solar power

   C. tax the use fossil fuel to offset climate disorders

   D. use only hydrogen based-based fuel in automobiles

Go On ▶

37 What possible hope does hydrogen offer to the global warming crisis?

F. Hydrogen is a less expensive source of energy, allowing more funding for research of alternate fuel sources.

G. Automobile manufactures find hydrogen to be the most efficient fuel for the engines of the future.

H. Hydrogen-based fuel will help reduce the amount of carbon dioxide in the atmosphere, reducing the greenhouse effect.

I. Hydrogen will help balance the amount of carbon emission in the atmosphere, changing the Earth's climate system.

38 What is the relationship between carbon dioxide levels in the atmosphere and the Earth's temperature?

A. As carbon dioxide levels increase, there is a decrease in ice shrinkage.

B. As the Earth's temperature decreases, carbon dioxide levels rise.

C. Rising carbon dioxide levels cause an increase in earths temperature.

D. Lower carbon dioxide levels in the atmosphere causes heat waves.

39 READ THINK EXPLAIN Why does the author feel man can control the earth's rising temperature? Use details and information from the article to support your answer.

Read the article "The Boom of the 1880s" and answer Numbers 40 through 47.

The Boom of the 1880s

The hard times of the late 1870s did not last in California. Prosperity returned to California and to the nation in the 1880s. In fact, southern California experienced a boom in these years similar to what had happened to San Francisco and the Bay Area during the gold rush era. Suddenly, thousands of people from out of state wanted to live in the sunny, dry climate of southern California. Why, all of a sudden, was this region "discovered" and settled by so many newcomers in the 1880s?

The Railroad Rate War

A major factor was the coming to California of a railroad company strong enough to challenge the Southern Pacific's monopoly. The Atchison, Topeka, and Santa Fe Railroad managed to obtain the right of way for laying tracks through a strategic pass in the San Gabriel and San Bernardino mountains. The Santa Fe's new line into southern California from Arizona was completed in 1886.

The competing railroad companies now entered into a savage rate war. Each company attempted to offer a lower passenger rate than its rival. Ticket prices to southern California plummeted. At one point, a passenger paid little more than a dollar to ride from Kansas City all the way to the West coast. The Santa Fe and Southern Pacific publicized both their low fares and the attractions of southern California. People took advantage of the rate war to travel west and see what the excitement was all about. Promoters of southern California real estate were overwhelmed by the number of visitors to their region—120,000 in 1886 alone.

Advertising the Golden State

Even before the boom time of the mid-1880s, many Easterners had heard about the unusual attractions of California. Popular guidebooks to the state promoted its pleasures. One by Charles Nordhoff, *California:*

For Health, Pleasure, and Residence, was published in 1872. It ran through many editions and sold three million copies. True but slightly exaggerated tales of instant success and happiness were told throughout the book. For example, an orange grower is quoted as saying:

Last year my trees paid the whole of my family expenses for the year; that was my first crop. This year I shall make over 5,000 clear; after next year I am planning to take my family for six months to Europe, and I expect thereafter to have four or five months for travel every year with sufficient means from my 20 acres to go where my wife and children may wish to go.

Although there were other boosters of California, Nordhoff may be considered the state's more famous advertiser.

Among the many other books that followed Nordhoff's was J. W. Hanson's *The American Italy,* published in 1896. According to this book's subtitle, California was the "Scenic Wonderland of Perfect Climate, Golden Sunshine, Ever-Lasting Flowers, and Always-Ripening Fruits." Magazines also promoted the joys and wonders of California living. There was *Sunset* magazine, for example, originally created by the Southern Pacific as promotional literature for its passengers.

Go On ▶

A Healthful Climate

About 15 percent of the people who came to California in the 1880s did so for health reasons. Doctors advised patients with respiratory illnesses to breathe the fresh, dry air of the Southwest. At this time, many people believed that healthful air alone could cure diseases. They even had a name for the treatment-climatotherapy. Boosters told stories of miraculous cures, of dying patients restored to new life, and health in California. Newspapers reported that wounds healed more quickly there. Mark Twain joked that Lake Tahoe could restore an Egyptian mummy to life.

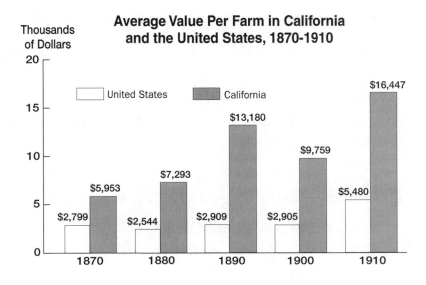

Average Value Per Farm in California and the United States, 1870-1910

Thousands of Dollars

United States | California

1870: $2,799 / $5,953
1880: $2,544 / $7,293
1890: $2,909 / $13,180
1900: $2,905 / $9,759
1910: $5,480 / $16,447

Scenic Attractions

By the 1880s, a growing number of people had become aware of he natural wonders of California. The state had established the Yosemite area as a park as early as 1864. After the building of the transcontinental railroad, more and more vacationers came to Yosemite to marvel at its massive rocks (El Capitan, Half Dome) and towering waterfalls (Bridalveil Falls, Yosemite Falls). The foremost spokesperson for conserving Yosemite and the surrounding region was John Muir, a self-educated natural scientist. Muir's books and his articles in *Century* magazine made people aware of the importance of California's mountain wilderness.

Other parts of the Sierra also attracted visitors. Mount Whitney, 14,494 feet high, was nationally famous as the highest mountain in the United States (except for the mountains in the Alaska territory). Three men first scaled this mountain in 1873, and a group of four women accomplished the feat in 1878. Mountain hiking was a popular sport in the 1880s. At this time, however, few roads led to the Sierras, so most vacationers would choose to climb in the San Gabriel Range to the south. From the 1880s until the depression of the 1930s, the San Gabriels offered a variety of mountaintop hotels, resorts, and campgrounds.

The Boom in Real Estate

Some Easterners came to California only to hike in the mountains, breathe the healthy air, and then leave. Thousands of others, however, came to settle permanently in the country of orange groves and bountiful living described in Nordhoff's guidebook. Real estate developers were eager to greet these newcomers and point out all of the advantages of buying land "cheap" before its price doubled and tripled. Many developers sincerely believed in southern California's future, but others were less than honest in their methods of selling land. One unscrupulous promoter tied oranges to Joshua trees in the Mojave Desert and told ignorant customers that his property was a prime citrus-growing area!

As developers hoped, land prices in the Los Angeles area climbed higher and higher in the mide-1880s. Between 1884 and 1888, plans went forward for building 100 new towns in Los Angeles County alone. Out of the dusty, brawling frontier town of the past, Los Angeles grew quickly into a true city. Surrounding communities (Pasadena, Glendale, Burbank, Pomona, San Diego, Santa Ana) also changed overnight from rural villages into urban centers. As towns grew and land prices soared, few people seemed to notice that southern California lacked adequate water to support a large population.

By 1885, the real estate boom was in full swing. Buyers bought at one price, sold at a higher price, and bought again and sold again. The small number of old-timers who witnessed the excitement could hardly believe what was happening. In just two years, the price of town lots and agricultural lands skyrocketed. In Los Angeles, a 22-acre lot that cost $12,000 in 1883 sold for $40,000 in 1887. Farmland priced at $100 an acre in 1886 brought $1,500 an acre the next year. ∎

Answer questions 40 through 47. Base your answers on the article "The Boom of the 1880s."

40 What was the effect of the "savage rate war" among railroads in California?

   A. Lower rates ended the boom in California.

   B. Lower rates brought more people to California.

   C. Lower rates made the railroads compete for right of way.

   D. Lower rates made the Southern Pacific go out of business.

41 How were Nordhoff's guidebook and Hanson's book alike?

   F. They both over-glorified California.

   G. They both sold over a million copies.

   H. They both told tales of instant success.

   I. They both described California's natural wonders.

42 Which statement best reflects the main idea of the article?

   A. The 1880s boom in California happened for several reasons.

   B. The 1880s boom was caused by promoters in southern California.

   C. The 1880s boom had many negative effects on the state of Caliornia.

   D. The 1880s boom had both positive and negative effects on California.

43 READ THINK EXPLAIN   What happened to land prices in southern California as a result of the 1880s boom? Use details and information from the chart and article to support your answer.

Go On

44 Which detail in the article does the chart support?

    A. The price of town lots skyrocketed in Los Angeles.

    B. The prices of farms in California rose sharply in the late 1880s.

    C. Communities around Los Angeles quickly became urban centers.

    D. Developers sometimes exaggerated the value of agricultural lands.

45 What does *unscrupulous* mean as used in the following sentence from the article.

    One unscrupulous promoter tied oranges to Joshua trees in the Mojave Desert and told ignorant customers that his property was a prime citrus-growing area!

    F. imaginative

    G. intelligent

    H. unethical

    I. unknown

46 What problem did people fail to realize as the population of California grew?

    A. the loss of open spaces

    B. the lack of urban centers

    C. the inadequate water supply

    D. the lack of quality farmland

47 READ THINK EXPLAIN What factors led to the 1880s boom in southern California? Support your answer with details and information from the passage.

Read the poem "Oranges" and answer Numbers 48 through 54.

Oranges

By Gary Soto

The first time I walked
With a girl, I was twelve,
Cold, and weighted down
With two oranges in my jacket.
December. Frost cracking
Beneath my steps, my breath
Before me, then gone,
As I walked toward
Her house, the one whose
Porch light burned yellow
Night and day, in any weather.
A dog barked at me, until
She came out pulling
At her gloves, face bright
With rouge. I smiled
Touched her shoulder, and led
Her down the street, across
A used car lot and a line
Of newly planted trees,
Until we were breathing
Before a drugstore. We
Entered, the tin bell
Bringing a saleslady
Down a narrow aisle of goods.
I turned to the candies
Tiered like bleachers,
And asked what she wanted-
Light in her eyes, a smile
Starting at the corners
Of her mouth. I fingered

A nickel in my pocket,
And when she lifted a chocolate
That cost a dime,
I didn't say anything.
I took the nickel from
My pocket, then an orange
And set them quietly on
The counter. When I looked up,
The lady's eyes met mine,
And held them, knowing
Very well what is was all
About.

Outside,
A few cars hissing past,
Fog hanging like old
Coats between the trees.
I took my girl's hand
In mine for two blocks,
Then released it to let
Her unwrap the chocolate.
I peeled my orange
That was so bright against
The gray of December
That, from some distance,
Someone might have thought
I was making a fire in my hands.

Go On ▶

Answer questions 48 through 54. Base your answers on the poem "Oranges."

48 What is most likely the author's purpose in the poem?

    A. To express his memories of his first date

    B. To convince the reader not to be afraid of love

    C. To show the embarrassment he felt in the store

    D. To emphasize the importance of oranges in his life

49 What contrast does the author make in the last section of the poem?

    F. He makes a distinction between fog and rain.

    G. He contrasts the girl's candy bar and his orange.

    H. He states the fog looks like old coats hanging between trees.

    I. He contrasts the dismal weather and the glow of his orange.

50 The speaker in the poem can best be described as

    A. an older man looking back at his youth.

    B. a teenager who wants to have more money.

    C. a young boy who is nervous about his date.

    D. an older man who loved oranges and chocolate.

51 What is the central problem in the poem?

    F. The boy is afraid of asking out a girl and meeting her family.

    G. The speaker does not have enough money to buy the chocolate.

    H. The girl's parents do not allow her to walk with the boy to the store.

    I. The cold weather prevents the couple from spending much time outside.

52 In the last line *"a fire in my hands"* most likely represents

    A. a spirit of love the speaker feels for the young girl.

    B. a warm memory of a bright and wonderful first date.

    C. the nervous energy the speaker feels being on his first date.

    D. a childlike image of the magic that the oranges were able to create.

Go On ▶

53 What can the reader infer from the action of the woman in the poem?

    F. She was embarrassed for the young boy's situation.

    G. She liked the boy and wanted to give him the candy.

    H. She understood the boy's problem and wanted to help.

    I. She too was poor and wanted the girl to have her candy bar.

54 READ THINK EXPLAIN What is the setting of the poem? How does the author use the setting to help convey the poem's message? Support your answer with details and information from the poem.

FCAT Pretest Checklist

This checklist is designed for you to evaluate your FCAT Pretest. By using this checklist, you can determine which skills you may need more work on in preparation for the official FCAT. Check your answers against those in the first column of the checklist. If you miss an answer, mark the box next to the number of that answer. Once you have checked your answers to the FCAT Pretest, note which sections you need to review by referring to the sections listed in the third column. Page numbers in the fourth column provide the location of those sections in this book.

Answer	Check if missed	Review this section	Pages
1. A	☐	LA.A.1.4.2 Vocabulary	31-39
2. I	☐	LA.A.2.4.1 Details	79-80
3. D	☐	LA.A.2.4.1 Details	79-80
4. H	☐	LA.A.2.4.1 Main Idea	78-83
5. B	☐	LA.A.2.4.4 Gathering, Analyzing and Evaluating	119-125
6. G	☐	LA.E.2.2.1 Cause and Effect	177-183
7. Answers may vary	☐	LA.A.2.2.7 Comparing and Contrasting	99-102
8. B	☐	LA.A.2.4.1 Details	79-80
9. H	☐	LA.A.2.4.2 Author's Purpose	99-102
10. Answers may vary	☐	LA.A.1.4.2 Inference	31-32, 38-41
11. B	☐	LA.A.2.4.4 Gathering, Analyzing and Evaluating	119-125
12. G	☐	LA.A.2.4.1 Main Idea	78-83
13. Answers may vary	☐	LA.A.2.4.1 Details	79-80
14. C	☐	LA.A.2.4.8 Synthesizing Information	157-160
15. G	☐	LA.A.1.4.2 Vocabulary	31-39
16. B	☐	LA.A.2.4.2 Author's Purpose	99-102
17. G	☐	LA.A.2.4.1 Organizational Pattern	80-83
18. A	☐	LA.A.2.4.7 Details	79-80
19. H	☐	LA.A.2.4.1 Details	79-80
20. Answers may vary	☐	LA.A.2.4.2 Author's Purpose	99-102
21. D	☐	LA.E.2.4.1 Elements of Plot	202
22. G	☐	LA.A.2.4.1 Details	79-80
23. D	☐	LA.A.2.4.2 Author's Purpose	99-102
24. Answers may vary	☐	LA.A.2.4.8 Synthesizing Information	157-160
25. B	☐	LA.A.1.4.2 Vocabulary	31-39
26. I	☐	LA.E.2.2.1 Cause and Effect	177-183
27. B	☐	LA.E.2.4.1 Elements of Plot	202-203
28. G	☐	LA.A.2.4.8 Synthesizing Information	157-160
29. D	☐	LA.A.2.4.1 Details	79-80
30. G	☐	LA.E.2.2.1 Cause and Effect	177-183
31. Answers may vary	☐	LA.A.2.2.4 Gathering, Analyzing, and Evaluating	119-125
32. D	☐	LA.A.2.4.1 Details	79-80
33. H	☐	LA.A.2.4.2 Author's Purpose	99-102
34. B	☐	LA.A.2.4.8 Synthesizing Information	157-160
35. G	☐	LA.E.2.2.1 Cause and Effect	177-183
36. C	☐	LA.A.2.4.1 Details	79-80
37. H	☐	LA.A.2.4.8 Synthesizing Information	157-160
38. C	☐	LA.A.2.2.7 Comparing and Contrasting	99-102
39. Answers may vary	☐	LA.A.2.4.2 Author's Purpose	99-102
40. B	☐	LA.E.2.2.1 Cause and Effect	177-183
41. F	☐	LA.A.2.2.7 Comparing and Contrasting	99-102

42. A	☐	LA.A.2.4.1 Main Idea	78-83
43. Answers may vary	☐	LA.A.2.4.8 Synthesizing Information	157-160
44. B	☐	LA.A.2.4.8 Synthesizing Information	157-160
45. H	☐	LA.A.1.4.2 Vocabulary	31-39
46. C	☐	LA.A.2.4.1 Details	79-80
47. Answers may vary	☐	LA.E. 2.2.1 Cause and Effect	177-183
48. A	☐	LA.A.2.4.2 Author's Purpose	99-102
49. I	☐	LA.A.2.2.7 Comparing and Contrasting	99-102
50. A	☐	LA.A.2.4.1 Details	79-80
51. G	☐	LA.E.2.4.1 Elements of Plot	199-200
52. B	☐	LA.A.1.4.2 Inference	31-32, 38-41
53. H	☐	LA.A.2.4.8 Synthesizing Information	157-160
54. Answers may vary	☐	LA.E.2.4.1 Elements of Plot	201-202

Chapter one

Understanding What You Read

Benchmark LA.A. 1.4.2

Selects and uses strategies to understand words and text, and to make and confirm inferences from what is read, including interpreting diagrams, graphs, and statistical illustrations.

Think about how much you read everyday. Whether you are choosing items from a menu in a restaurant, or checking the performance of your favorite team in last night's game, you are *reading*.

Sometimes you might read the newspaper, a magazine, or a novel simply for enjoyment. However, as a student, you often find yourself reading to gather information about a topic. In your classes, or while doing research for school, you read textbooks and are expected to understand complex charts and graphs. If you come across words you do not understand, how do you find out what they mean? Your best bet is to use a reading strategy—a technique that helps you determine the meaning of unfamiliar words in a text.

Sometimes, you will have to understand only what is stated directly in a reading. But other times you will be required to go beyond stated information in search of deeper meanings. In these instances, you will need to combine information you read with your own knowledge to draw a conclusion. This process is called *inferring*.

What you read + your own knowledge = inference

This chapter will show you how to better make inferences, read charts and graphs, and determine word meanings. The strategies in this chapter will not only help you understand material in your textbooks or on the FCAT, they will also make it easier for you to understand information you encounter throughout your lifetime.

Understanding the Benchmark

Try using the suggestions below to practice learning unfamiliar words or to make inferences about information you gather. Practicing these strategies now will help you when you take the FCAT.

- Look for science or other technical articles in popular magazines. Notice how writers define words that are technical or unfamiliar to most readers.
- Watch television news magazine shows. Look for inferences that the reporters make based on the facts in a story.

Making the FCAT Connection

On the FCAT, questions testing this benchmark will require you to read texts as well as graphs, charts, and diagrams. You will make inferences about meanings, determine word meanings, and interpret statistical information presented in the form of charts and graphs. Sometimes you may be asked the meaning of a word that is unfamiliar to you. When this happens, take comfort in the fact that there will always be enough information in a passage to help you infer the meaning of the new word.

Expect to encounter multiple-choice and short-reponse questions based on informational and literary texts to measure your understanding of this benchmark.

Taking a Closer Look

Can you decipher the meaning of the word *decipher*? If you guessed that decipher means "figure out," then you probably used the *context clues* in the sentence to help you. Context clues are words that come before and after a particular word or phrase that can help you determine the meaning. In this case, the use of the word in the sentence helped you figure out its meaning. Using context clues is one of the best strategies for deciphering meanings of unfamiliar words.

Another strategy is to examine word parts. Words are built from smaller "parts" called roots. The meaning of a root is changed when a prefix and/or a suffix is added.

Prefixes are word parts added to the beginning of words. *Suffixes* are word parts added to the end of words. When a prefix or suffix is added to a word, it changes the word's meaning. Sometimes it changes the word's part of speech or use. Look at the examples below:

Word	Part of Speech	Meaning
certain	adjective	sure, known, proved to be true
certain**ty**	noun	the state of being clear, constant
uncertainty	noun	the state of being unclear, not constant, doubtful

Examine the chart below. It provides you with some of the more common prefixes, their meanings, and illustrates how they change word meanings.

COMMONLY USED PREFIXES AND THEIR MEANINGS

Number-Related Prefixes

prefix	meaning	example	explanation
semi-	half	semicircle	*half* of a circle
hemi-	half	hemisphere	*half* of a sphere
mono-	one	monotone	*one* tone of voice
uni-	one	unicycle	*one*-wheeled cycle
bi-	two	bicycle	*two*-wheeled cycle
di-	two	diverge	split *two* ways
tri-	three	tricycle	*three*-wheeled cycle
dec-	ten	decimal	system of tens
cent-	one hundred	centimeter	*hundredth* of a meter
mill-	one thousand	millimeter	*thousandth* of a meter
kilo-	one thousand	kilometer	*one thousand* meters
poly-	many	polygon	shape with *many* sides

Time-Related Prefixes

prefix	meaning	example	explanation
ante-	before	antecedent	coming *before*
fore-	before	forethought	think of something *before* it happens
pre-	before	predate	date *before*
post-	after	postdate	date *after*
re-	again	recycle	use *again*
retro-	past	retroactive	active after a *past* date

Position-Related Prefixes

prefix	meaning	example	explanation
ad-	toward	advance	move *toward*
circum-	around	circumnavigate	sail *around*
hypo-	under	hypodermic	*under* the skin
para-	beside	parallel lines	*beside* each other
peri-	around	periscope	tool for viewing *around* something
super-	over, above	supervise	look *over*

Other Commonly Used Prefixes

prefix	meaning	example	explanation
co-	together	coordinate	move *together*
contra-	against	contradict	argue *against*
de-	away, from	desert	abandon, move *away*
di-	apart	digress	move *apart*
ex-	away from	exclude	keep *away* from
extra-	additional	extraordinary	in *addition* to the ordinary
hyper-	extremely	hyperactive	*extremely* active
in-	into	insert	put *into*
in-	not	incapable	*not* able to
il-	not	illegal	*not* allowed
non-	not	nonessential	*not* important
pro-	forward	proceed	go *forward*
sub-	under	submarine	*under* the sea
syn-	together	synchronize	move *together*
trans-	across	transport	bring *across*
ultra-	extremely	ultramodern	*extremely* modern

Do you see how knowing different prefixes can help you understand unfamiliar words? Learning suffixes can be just as helpful. Examine the chart below to learn some common suffixes, their meanings, and how they change the meanings of root words.

COMMONLY USED SUFFIXES AND THEIR MEANINGS

Noun Suffixes (People)

suffix	meaning	example	explanation
-ant	person who	servant	*person who* serves
-ent	person who	student	*person who* studies
-ar	person who	beggar	*person who* begs
-er	person who	runner	*person who* runs
-ard	person who	coward	*person who* cowers
-ist	person who	dentist	*person who* works with teeth
-ster	person who	youngster	*person who* is young
-ee	person who	employee	*person who* is employed

Noun Suffixes (Places or Things)

suffix	meaning	example	explanation
-age	process	passage	*process of* passing
-ance	act of	acceptance	*act of* accepting
-ation	state of	starvation	*state of* starving
-cy	state of	literacy	*state of* being literate
-ery	act of	robbery	*act of* being robbed
-et	little	islet	*little* island
-ion	action, result	fusion	*act of* being fused together
-ism	state of	egotism	*state of* being self-involved
-ity	state of	nobility	*state of* being noble
-ment	state of	disappointment	*state of* being disappointed
-tude	state of	multitude	*state of* being numerous
-ty	state of	safety	*state of* being safe
-ure	state of	rupture	*state of* being broken

Adjective Suffixes

suffix	meaning	example	explanation
-able	able, likely	capable	*able* to do something
-en	made of	wooden	*made of* wood
-ful	full of	thankful	*full* of thanks
-ish	like	childish	*like* a child
-like	like	dreamlike	*like* a dream
-ly	like	motherly	*like* a mother
-less	without	hopeless	*without* hope
-ous	full of	joyous	*full* of joy
-some	showing	lonesome	*showing* signs of loneliness
-ward	in the direction	backward	*in the* reverse *direction*
-y	showing	wavy	*showing* waves

Now that you have seen how prefixes and suffixes create new words, practice deciphering the word meanings below using this strategy. Be sure to underline the prefixes and/or suffixes that provided clues to the word's meaning.

restate _____

monotone _____

transatlantic _____

motionless _____

diversity _____

postdated _____

inductee _____

unlikable _____

perimeter _____

proactive _____

Examine the brief list below of some common roots that words are built upon. Keep in mind that this list contains only a sampling of the many roots in use in the English language. Do you recognize any?

root	meaning	example	explanation
agr	field	agriculture	field cultivation
am, amor	love, liking	amicable	friendly
aud	hear	audible	able to be heard
bene	good, well	beneficent	producing good
chron	time	chronological	arranged in order of time
cred	believe	credence	acceptance as true
dem	people	democracy	government by the people
dic	speak, say	diction	choice of words
ego	I	egocentric	self-centered
fac	make, do	facilitate	to make easier
fin	end, limit	confine	keep within limits
fort	strong	fortitude	strength of mind
gen, genit	kind, birth	generate	bring into existence
greg	gather, flock	gregarious	sociable
here, hes	stick	adhere	stick, be attached
ject	throw	reject	cast off, throw back
liber	free	liberate	to set free
loc	place	dislocate	to put out of place
man, manu	hand	manual	done by hand
pod, ped	foot	pedestrian	going on foot
scrib, script	write	postscript	to write after
spec	look, appear	spectator	one who watches
vers	turn	reverse	to turn back
vid, vis	see, look, sight	revise	to look at again

While some of those words may be familiar to you, were any unfamiliar? Did you recognize some of the roots in the list above? Try creating your own examples of words containing roots listed above. For each word, provide definitions, and show the various parts that make up the word (root, suffix, prefix). Follow the example provided.

Root:	Example:	Parts:	Definition:
cred	incredible	in+cred+ible	not able to be believed
⎯⎯	⎯⎯	⎯⎯	⎯⎯⎯⎯⎯⎯
⎯⎯	⎯⎯	⎯⎯	⎯⎯⎯⎯⎯⎯
⎯⎯	⎯⎯	⎯⎯	⎯⎯⎯⎯⎯⎯
⎯⎯	⎯⎯	⎯⎯	⎯⎯⎯⎯⎯⎯
⎯⎯	⎯⎯	⎯⎯	⎯⎯⎯⎯⎯⎯

As you can see by now, knowledge of prefixes, roots, and suffixes is an important part of solving the word-meaning puzzle. However, there are other strategies that can be used to help you understand unfamiliar words you encounter while reading. Pay attention to how a word is used, the sentence it appears in, and other context clues that provide hints to the meaning of words.

The chart below provides a list of some helpful clues to look for in readings you encounter on the FCAT and beyond. Words to be defined or explained in the "example" column are shown in **boldface**. The information provided that helps us determine the word's meaning is underlined.

Clue	What to Look For	Example
Boldfaced or Italicized words	These words are oftentimes defined in the reading	Magellan was the first person to **circumnavigate,** or sail completely around, the earth.
Antonyms/Contrasts	Signal words such as *unlike, not, however,* can help you to look for contrasts	Not all molecules exist as **polar molecules;** some separate into positive and negative ions.
Synonyms or Restatements	A word or phrase that is similar to the difficult word will give you clues to its meaning	Scientists have discovered hot water **spewing,** discharging, and sending out ground rocks of salt from the ocean floor
Cause/Effect	The stated cause or effect will give you clues to the meaning of a difficult word	**Inflation** is often brought on by people wanting more goods than produced, thus causing prices to rise.
Example/Explanation	The explanation of a difficult word will appear in an example	The discussions are becoming increasingly **partisan;** neither the players union nor the owners will compromise.

Now let's practice using the different clues from the chart above to help you determine the meanings of the following words.

1. People often call Maria *exigent* because she is very demanding.

    Exigent probably means _____

2. After a slight *modification* of the recipe, her chocolate chip cookies tasted much better than they had before.

    Modification probably means _____

3. The *devastation* and destruction were evident as we walked through the area hit by the hurricane.

    Devastation probably means _____

4. Since MBJ Electronics secretly owned the other two companies producing 3-D video games, they *monopolized* the market.

    Monopolized probably means _____

5. Unlike her *incorrigible* sister, Teresa was a model student who did well in classes and was always well behaved.

    Incorrigible probably means _____

FCAT EXTRA!

Always reread the sentence before and after any unfamiliar word you encounter. Doing so may provide the additional information or clues you need to infer the meaning of the word.

In addition to understanding new words and phrases, it is important to be able to read charts and graphs. When you "read" a chart or graph, you are able to understand the information it presents and make inferences—draw conclusions—about it. Take a look at the chart below:

The Changing Face of Immigration to the United States		
From Where Did the Immigrants Come? Comparing 1891 and 1991		
Areas of the World	**1891 (Percent of Total Immigration)**	**1991 (Percent of Total Immigration)**
Europe	97.4%	8.0%
Asia	1.4%	18.7%
America (All areas of North and South America except the United States)	.9%	71.0%
Africa	.1%	1.8%
Oceania (Australia, New Zealand, Pacific Islands)	.1%	.4%
All other areas of the world	.1%	.1%

What inferences can you make from the information in this chart? Write down any conclusions you are able to come to using the information above to support your statements. One is provided for you.

- *A far greater percentage of immigrants came to the United States from Europe in 1891 than in 1991.*

_____

_____

_____

_____

_____

Now take a look at a different kind of informational graphic.

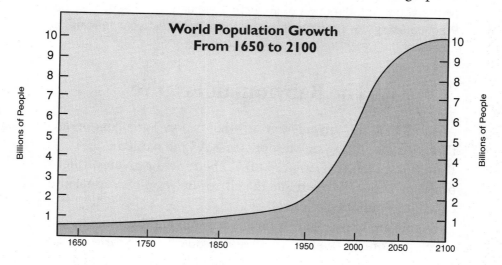

What does it tell you about its subject matter? Below is one conclusion you might draw from the chart. What other conclusions might you make? Again, write down any conclusions you are able to come to and be sure to use the information on the graph to support your statements.

• *The rate of population growth was much greater after 1950*

than before.

_____

_____

_____

_____

_____

_____

_____

Always examine titles, labels, and legends, and captions that appear with a graph, chart, or other informational illustration. These provide important information about what an author is trying to illustrate to readers.

This practice section aims to help you set a purpose for reading. It points you in the direction of important aspects of a reading selection. Practice using the prompts in the margins to direct your reading of a selection.

The Babylonian Empire

Around 2300 B.C., invaders from what is now Syria conquered the city-states of Lower Mesopotamia. A king named Hammurabi (ruled 1792–1750 B.C.) became the greatest ruler of this new empire. He made the city of Babylon his capital and called his empire Babylonia

Hammurabi was known for his wisdom and justice. He developed one of the first written law codes in the world. Hammurabi's Code had nearly 300 laws. It provided rules for settling problems that arose in the everyday lives of the Babylonians. These laws were designed to prevent the strong from oppressing the weak. For example, the code outlined the rules and punishments for dishonest business practices and nonpayment of debts. It also regulated the fees of doctors and protected the right of women to own certain types of property.

The code substituted legal penalties for personal revenge in dealing with crimes. In many cases, however, the required punishments were severe, such as cutting off a hand or putting out an eye.

Long after the end of the Babylonian Empire, Hammurabi's Code continued to influence the development of other legal systems.

The Babylonians made many other contributions to the development of a high level of civilization in Mesopotamia. Their astronomers, scholars who studied the stars and planets, developed a lunar calendar. The calendar provided for a 12-month year, a 7-day week, and a 24-hour day. Babylonian scholars created a system of arithmetic based on the number 60. They gave us the 60-minute hour and the 360-degree circle.

Predict:
What does the title tell you this passage will be about?

Define:
What context clues are there in this passage?

Now answer the questions that follow.

1. In the second paragraph, the word *oppressing* probably means
   A. protecting.
   B. joining with.
   C. giving assistance to.
   D. taking unfair advantage of.

2. What inferences can you draw from this passage about the lasting influence of the Babylonians?

_____

_____

_____

_____

_____

_____

_____

Check your answers below.

For the first question, D is the correct answer. The sentence context suggests that *oppressing* has a negative meaning, because the laws were meant "to prevent the strong from oppressing the weak." The next sentence provides examples of taking unfair advantage: "dishonest business practices and nonpayment of debts." We can eliminate the other answers since they offer positive meanings for the word "oppressing."

For the second question, a top-score response would begin with a topic sentence that directly responds to the question. At least two supporting details would follow. An example might include:

There are several examples from the passage that show the lasting influence of the Babylonians. First, the author suggests that Hammurabi's Code helped shape the legal systems of other societies for many years. At the end of the passage, the author also underscores the Babylonian influence by referring to the "many other contributions to the development of a high level of civilization in Mesopotamia." He implies that "the 60-minute hour and the 360-degree circle" can be traced back to Babylonian scholars.

The following section includes reading selections that are similar to passages on the FCAT. Remember to stay actively involved while you read, using the reading strategies from this chapter.

Read the article "An Organic Farmer's Secret" before answering Numbers 1 through 8.

An Organic Farmer's Secret

By Robert E. Sullivan

KINDERHOOK, New York, — A young organic farmer has stolen an idea from some poor city dwellers, and turned it into a lifelong guaranteed job for himself. And everyone's happy about it—especially those interested in protecting farmlands.

Within a few weeks Jean-Paul Courtens, a native of Amsterdam and highly trained organic specialist who practices Community Supported Agriculture (CSA) for 600 Albany and Manhattan dwellers, will sign a contract not only guaranteeing him a lifelong lease on a beautiful farm in Hudson River Valley, but guaranteeing it too, to his three children, if they choose to be farmers—and theirs, too.

Courtens will sign an "inheritable" lease with Equity Trust, a conservation group concerned with the disappearance of farmland throughout the country. He won't own the land—140 rolling acres in the foothills of the Catskills—but he'll have a guaranteed lease to it for as long as he farms it. The deal wouldn't be possible without the contribution of another conservation fund, the Open Space Institute, which will buy the development rights for the land.

And therein lies the uniqueness of the deal. Conservation groups around America frequently make purchases of the development rights to farmlands—ensuring that they will be forever green.

But the system does not mean they will be forever farms. Far from it. "There are literally hundreds of these around the country," said Charles Matthei of Equity Trust. "And they effectively conserve the land and they conserve the integrity of the land, but they don't guarantee that the land will be usable to farmers."

"Take Merin County, in California, The agriculture Land Trust of California set aside thousands of acres. Then within three years the sale price doubled."

"That's because the rich people from Los Angeles and Seattle bought it for weekend 'farms' which they don't farm. The land is no longer affordable for farmers," Matthei said.

So Courtens, 40, and Equity Trust have borrowed an idea used by more than 100 communities across the United States to stop "gentrification." The communities have, with the help of foundations, incorporated whole neighborhoods, bought the land, and leased the homes back to their inhabitants and their heirs—and theirs too.

An organic farmer in a tractor plows his field with the Rocky Mountains in the background.

It stops the bulldozer, and the rent increases that can be as much as 1,000 percent in two or three years.

And it may just stop the bulldozer from some farmlands. Word of the agreement has gotten around, and it "has already had an impact around the country," Matthei said.

"We have received queries not only from farmers throughout the country, but also from other foundations and from public officials," he said. According to government statistics, in the five years ending in 1997 some nine million acres of farmland across the country were changed to commercial, industrial, or residential use.

The deal is particularly useful for Courtens because he is an organic farmer. It takes years to return to nature farms that have used chemicals. Courtens needs to build up the soil in the manner he learned in technical college in Holland, and for that he needs a guarantee that he can continue farming it.

"I don't want to own the land," he said, " I just want to farm. It is a lifestyle I have chosen."

He'll have to pay market rent—for a farm, not for rural estate—but he won't have to worry, ever, about a mortgage.

Courtens also has another guarantee. Some 600 farm "members" pay between $300 and $350 each to get weekly shipments of organic vegetables and fruit in Albany and the Upper West Side of Manhattan.

The arrangement guarantees Courtens a certain income, frees him from worrying about price fluctuations, and eliminates the middleman, as he brings the food to weekly meetings in his own truck.

The "members" get organic food at something akin to a third of the cost in health food stores, according to Courtens' figures, plus they get the good feeling of helping to support farmlands.

Manhattanites and Albany dwellers sometimes go to the farm to pick their own crops, or even volunteer to help, for no pay.

"Some drive up three hours just to work on the farm," Courtens said. "Can you imagine that?"

With two forms of guarantee, Courtens can do what he wants to do. Farm. And the farm should stay a farm.

Answer Numbers 1 through 8. Base your answers on the article "An Organic Farmer's Secret."

1 Why does Equity Trust lease the land to Courtens instead of selling it to him?

    A. Because in three years, the sale price could double.

    B. Because they want to make sure he uses the land for farming.

    C. Because they want to be able to increase the rent on the land.

    D. Because farmland is always worth more money when it is leased.

2 What can you infer from the passage about rich people from Los Angeles and Seattle?

    F. They buy land in order to farm it.

    G. They are interested in producing organic food.

    H. They want to preserve America's farming heritage.

    I. They want to own weekend, getaway homes in the country.

3 What does the author imply about farming families?

    A. They are usually a close-knit group.

    B. They pass down farms from one generation to the next.

    C. They are large due to the amount of work to be done on a farm.

    D. They are endangered since children don't wish to become farmers.

4 How can Courtens charge less for his organic food than a health food store?

    F. He leases his farmland.

    G. He transports his own food.

    H. He learned cost-cutting techniques in Holland.

    I. He has customers who buy weekly shipments.

5 What can you infer about the people who volunteer to help at the farm?

    A. They enjoy working at the farm.

    B. They like to earn extra money on the weekends.

    C. They want to make sure that the farm is a success.

    D. They want to guarantee they get their share of the crops.

6 Read the sentence from the passage.

> **So Courtens, 40, and Equity Trust have borrowed an idea used by more than 100 communities across the United States to stop "gentrification".**

What does *gentrification* mean?

    F. city land being turned back into farm land

    G. farm land disappearing because of urban sprawl

    H. poor people moving back into areas where they once lived

    I. rich people moving into areas where poor people once lived

7 READ THINK EXPLAIN Explain how different groups benefit from the farm-lease agreement that Courtens arranged with Equity Trust. Support your answer with details and information from the article.

_____

_____

_____

_____

_____

_____

_____

_____

8 What can you infer from the passage about the importance people place on the farming lifestyle? Support your answer with details and information from the article.

Read the article "Growth of a New Economic Order" before answering Numbers 1 through 8.

Growth *of a* New Economic Order

From
Global History

In the 1900s, the trend toward a new economic order started when the countries in Asia, Latin America, and Africa decided to industrialize. These countries became known as the Third World or developing nations.

The leaders of some developing countries adopted command economies. In a command economy, the government has complete control over the country's means of productions. The government usually sets production quotas for the manufacturers and determines what goods would be made and what price they would sell for. Leaders in third world countries felt that government-controlled decision-making would speed up the process of industrialization. Then, too, Communist countries gave financial and military aid to encourage them to do so. The developing countries also sold their goods profitably to Communist nations.

The new economic order took on shape when the Soviet Union and Eastern Europe abandoned communism for free-market economies, or capitalism, in the late 1980s and early 1990s. In capitalism, private individuals own the means of production. Capitalism is called free-market economy because it is controlled by the market, not by a government or even by the people who own the means of production. The forces that rule the marketplace are supply and demand and competition. These forces decide what products will be made, who will make them, and what their prices will be.

The changeover from command economics to free-market economy did not always go smoothly. The governments could no longer give financial and trade support to developing countries. These countries soon decided to improve their economies by adopting the free-market capitalistic system.

Integration of Developing Nations into the Global Economy

The industrialized nations encouraged Communist countries to adopt free-market economies. Unfortunately, when the change took place, the industrialized nations were having economic problems of their own. Although they continued to be the most prosperous nations in the world, the growth rates of the economies declined in the early 1990s. Britain, the United States, and Canada showed little growth. In France, unemployment soared. Japan's economy was weaker than it had been in the previous 40 years. As a group, the industrial countries had growth rates that stayed in the range of 2 to 3 percent per year.

New Competitors in the World Market

Many leaders of industrialized countries began to realize that their countries' high unemployment had a more serious cause than an economic slump. They began to see the developing nations as rivals in the world market. With more than 3 billon inhabitants hungry for a better life, new free-market countries stepped up their competition with the industrialized nations. Developing nations in Asia, for example, began to rival Japan. The Chinese Economic Area (CEA), which included China, Hong Kong, and Taiwan, dramatically increased its exports. It moved from eleventh place in world trade rankings in 1973 to fifth place in 1990. It rose even higher in the mid-1990s.

Figure I

Latin America and Caribbean
485.8 Million

High-Income Developed Nations-
N. America, Europe, Japan, Russia
919 Million

Sub-Saharan Africa
596.4 Million

Developing Europe and central Asia
477.9 Million

TOTAL 5.753 Billion

East Asia and Pacific
1,732.4 Million

South Asia
1,265.7 Million

Eastern Europe was slow to win a place in the world market. As time went on, however, some Eastern European countries began to export more goods to Western Europe. Poland, Hungary, the Czech Republic and Slovakia were the quickest to move toward free-market economies and to build trade with the West. Those nations agreed to create a free trade area by 1999.

In 1992, they signed trade agreements with the European Union (EU). The EU is a group of Western European nations that cooperate economically with one another. About 40 percent of Eastern European exports to the EU nations, such as food, textiles, steel, and chemicals, competed with similar Western European goods. Alarmed at this competition, some unhappy competitors in the EU called for trade barriers. Tariffs on products imported from non-EU countries would raise the prices of these goods, making them unattractive to consumers.

Competition for Investment

Developing countries began to edge out the industrialized ones in other areas besides trade. Investment, for example, began to shift away from the West. Regions such as Southeast Asia offered lower labor costs, greater productivity, and more rapidly growing markets than those in the West. As they privatized their industries, many countries in Eastern Europe and Latin America sold government-owned businesses to foreign as well as to domestic investors. Economists regard privatization as an important step in the transition from command to free-market economies. It usually results in more efficient and profitable industries.

As the developing nations attracted more investors, they sent new waves of goods and people to the nations of the West. To stay competitive, many Western business firms restructured or downsized. This means that they lowered their

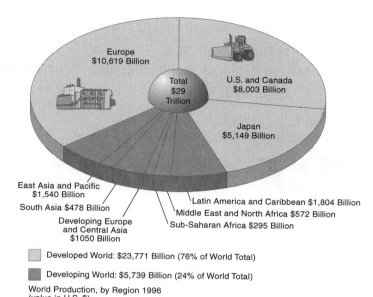

Figure 2

Developed World: $23,771 Billion (76% of World Total)

Developing World: $5,739 Billion (24% of World Total)

World Production, by Region 1996 (value in U.S. $)

expenses by eliminating jobs and asking senior employees to retire before age 65.

Some firms reduced costs by moving their factories to developing countries, where they saved vast sums of money on wages. Taiwanese workers earned one-fifth the wages of workers in industrialized countries. Brazilian and Mexican workers earned one-tenth.

Investment in technology also moved abroad. American and Japanese investors, for example, made India a center for the manufacture of computer microchips. When South Korea, Taiwan, Hong Kong, and Singapore—the Four Tigers of Asia—created high-tech industries, multinational corporations built factories there. Investors poured billions of dollars into the stock markets of India, Korea, Mexico, and other Third World nations.

Answer Numbers 1 through 9. Base your answers on the article "Growth of a New Economic Order."

1 Read the sentence below.

> **These countries became known as Third World or developing nations.**

What does the word *developing* mean?

A. emerging

B. limitless

C. powerless

D. underachieving

2 According to Figure 1, which two world regions have the greatest population?

    F. Developing Europe and Central Asia

    G. East Asia and Pacific and South Asia

    H. East Asia and Pacific and Latin American and Caribbean

    I. High Income Developed Nations and Latin American and Caribbean

3 READ THINK EXPLAIN   Why did many developing nations begin to build free-market economies in the 1980s and 1990s? Use details and information from the article to support your answer.

_____

_____

_____

_____

_____

_____

_____

4 Read the sentence from the passage.

    The leaders of some developing countries adopted command economies.

The phrase *command economies* can best be described as a:

    A. Capitalistic system that promotes the economy.

    B. Communist system where the people work for the government.

    C. government-controlled system where the government manages production.

    D. publicly-controlled system where supply and demand regulate production.

5 READ THINK EXPLAIN What inferences can you draw from Figure 2 about the Developed World and the Developing World in regard to world production? Use details and information from the article to support your answer.

_____

_____

_____

_____

_____

_____

_____

_____

6 When a country changes from a command economy to a free-market economy, what factor do economists feel is most important for success?

   A. government support

   B. privatization of industry

   C. investment by foreigners

   D. restructuring of companies

7 Western businesses that asked older employees to retire early called the process

   F. downsizing.

   G. competition.

   H. privatization.

   I. industrialization.

8 Developed nations probably decided to invest in Third World nations due to the fact that

    A. developed nations no longer had economic power.

    B. developed nations needed more space to produce products.

    C. Third World nations could offer workers at a much lower cost.

    D. Third World nations had more modern facilities in which to work.

9 READ THINK EXPLAIN Why did competition between developing and industrialized nations grow in the 1990s? Use details and information from the article to support your answer.

Read the article "Music on the Brain" before answering Numbers 1 through 7.

MUSIC ON THE BRAIN

Experts still don't know how and why tunes tickle our fancy—but new research offers intriguing clues

It's hard to exaggerate the effect music can have on the human brain. A mere snippet of a song from the past can trigger memories as vivid as anything Proust experienced from the aroma of his *petite madeleine*. A tune can induce emotions ranging from unabashed joy to deep sorrow and can drive listeners into states of patriotic fervor or religious frenzy—to say nothing of its legendary ability to soothe the savage beast.

Yet in spite of music's remarkable influence on the human psyche, scientists have spent little time attempting to understand why it possesses such potency. "We tend to think of music as an art or a cultural attribute," notes Robert Zatorre, a neuroscientist at McGill University in Montreal, "but it is a complex human behavior that is as worthy of scientific study as any other."

That's why Zatorre helped organize a conference, "The Biological Foundations of Music," sponsored last week by the New York Academy of Sciences, at which experts in disciplines ranging from neuroscience and neurology to brain imaging and psychology met to exchange notes about what's known—and more important, what remains to be learned—in this small but growing field.

What seems clear is that the ability to experience and react to music is deeply embedded in the biology of the nervous system. While music tends to be processed mostly in the right hemisphere of the brain, no single set of cells is devoted to the task. Different networks of neurons are activated, depending on whether a person is listening to music or playing an instrument, and whether or not the music involves lyrics.

Specific brain disorders can affect the perception of music in very specific ways. Experiments done on epileptics decades ago showed that stimulating certain areas of the temporal lobe on both sides of the brain awakened "musical memories"—vivid recreations of melodies that the patients had heard years earlier. Lesions in the temporal lobe can result

The Syracuse Symphony orchestra with conductor Grant Cooper, performing at Emerson park in Auburn, New York as part of their Summer Parks Concerts.

in so-called musicogenic epilepsy, an extremely rare form of the disorder in which seizures are triggered by the sound of music. Autism offers an even greater puzzle. People with this condition are mentally deficient, yet most are "musical savants" possessed of extraordinary talent.

The opposite is true of the less that 1% of the population who suffer from *amusia,* or true tone deafness. They literally cannot recognize a melody, let alone tell two of them apart, and they are incapable of repeating a song (although they think they are doing it correctly). Even simple familiar tunes such as *Frere Jacques* and *Happy Birthday* are mystifying to amusics, but when the lyrics are spoken rather than sung, amusics are able to recognize the song immediately.

"This goes way beyond an inability to carry a tune," observes psychologist Isabelle Peretz of the University of Montreal. "They can't dance and they can't tell the difference between consonance [harmony] and dissonance either. They all appear to have been born without the writing necessary to process music." Intriguingly, people with amusia show no overt signs of brain damage or short-term-memory impairment, and magnetic-resonance-imaging scans of their brains look normal.

There is evidently no way to help these unfortunate folks (though, admittedly, they don't know what they're missing). But for instrumentalists, at least, music can evidently trigger physical changes in the brain's wiring. By measuring faint magnetic fields emitted by the brains of professional musicians, a team led by Christo Pantev of the University of Muenster's Institute of Experimental Audiology in Germany has shown that intensive practice of an instrument leads to discernible enlargement of parts of the cerebral cortex, the layer of gray matter most closely associated with higher brain function.

As for music's emotional impact, there is some indication that music can affect levels of various hormones, including cortisol (involved in arousal and stress), testosterone (aggression and arousal), and oxytocin (nurturing behavior) as well as trigger release of the natural opiates known as endorphins. Using PET scanners, Zatorre has shown that the parts of the brain involved in processing emotion seem to light up with activity when a subject hears music.

As tantalizing as these bits of research are, they barely begin to address the mysteries of music and the brain, including the deepest question of all: Why do we appreciate music? Did our musical ancestors have an evolutionary edge over their tin-eared fellows? Or is music, as M.I.T. neuroscientist Steven Pinker asserts, just "auditory cheesecake," with no biological value? Given music's central role in most of our lives, it's time that scientists found the answers.

Answer numbers 1 through 7. Base your answers on the article "Music on the Brain."

1 What would probably trigger musicogenic epilepsy?

    A. singing a repetitive song

    B. listening to a recorded song

    C. playing a musical instrument

    D. reading music from a song sheet

2 Read the sentence from the passage.

> **Yet in spite of music's remarkable influence on the human psyche, scientists have spent little time attempting to understand why it possesses such potency.**

What does *potency* mean?

    F. emotion

    G. feeling

    H. frenzy

    I. strength

3 Read the sentence from the passage.

> **Some people with this condition are mentally deficient, yet some are proficient musicians; some are "musical savants" possessed of extraordinary talent.**

The phrase *musical savant* can best be described as a:

A. person who is autistic.

B. person of high intelligence.

C. child who is drawn to music.

D. person with advanced musical talent.

4 READ THINK EXPLAIN   Why might the author agree that music affects the emotions? Use details and information from the article to support your answer.

_____

_____

_____

_____

_____

_____

_____

_____

5 Read the sentence from the passage.

> **The opposite is true of the less than 1% of the population who suffer from amusia or true tone deafness.**

Which of the following statements is true about people who suffer from *amusia*?

A. They easily forget all the words of a song.

B. They can hum tunes exactly as they are written.

C. They show hearing loss when tested using music.

D. They are unable to distinguish one song from another.

6 What does Steve Pinker imply by saying that music is "auditory cheesecake"?

    F. Music has a strong influence on the auditory system.

    G. Scientists should study the impact of music on the brain.

    H. Music is pleasant but has no real biological importance.

    I. Playing an instrument causes brain matter to increase.

7 READ THINK EXPLAIN   Why does it seem probable that music is worthy of study by scientists? Use details and information from the article to support your answer.

_____

_____

_____

_____

_____

_____

_____

C h a p t e r   t w o

Comparing and Contrasting Text Elements

Benchmark LA.A. 2.2.7

Recognizes the use of comparison and contrast in a text.

Have you started thinking about life after high school? Should you go to college? Does the career that interests you require a college degree? If so, where will you go? Most of the time, we seek information to help us reach a decision or form an opinion. This information is sometimes organized by *comparing* (pointing out similarities) or *contrasting* (pointing out differences) two or more subjects.

Take a closer look at your local newspaper. In it, you will find examples of comparison and contrast in almost every section. If you turn to the sports pages, you are likely to see columns of statistics that compare and contrast teams' results, or articles that compare one team's performance to that of another. In the entertainment section, you will find that movie reviews often compare or contrast an actor's latest movie performance to his earlier ones.

What other examples of comparison and contrast can you think of? Think of places you have seen, heard, or read comparisons being made. Have there been times you recall comparing/contrasting different things, people, places, or ideas before making an important decision? Write a few examples from recent memory below.

_____

_____

_____

_____

Understanding the Benchmark

Below is a list of some places you can look for examples of comparison and contrast. Try some of these activities on your own. The more you practice recognizing comparisons and contrasts in everyday life, the better prepared you will be when taking the FCAT.

- Go to the travel section of your newspaper and look for an article that compares and/or contrasts two different locations. Which place would you prefer to visit and why?
- Look in your literature book for an essay that compares or contrasts two authors, characters, or settings in a novel. Look closely at the words the author chose to point out differences and similarities in the essay.
- Check the Internet for information about a dream product that you would like to buy (stereo, computer, car). Look for examples of comparisons and contrasts between brands.

Making the FCAT Connection

On the FCAT you will be asked questions that require you to explain how comparisons or contrasts are used in the passages you read. Often, you will be asked to read two different selections and compare or contrast a feature they share. You may be asked to compare and contrast any of the following elements:

Characters	Style	Tone	Point of View
Subjects	Main Idea	Setting	Author's Purpose

Multiple-choice and short-response questions from both informational and literary texts will be asked on the FCAT to measure your understanding of this benchmark.

Taking a Closer Look

Remember that a comparison points out the *similarities* between two or more subjects. In order to announce that a comparison is being made, writers often use *signal words*. Review the list of some common signal words below. Knowing these words will help you recognize when a comparison is being made in a text.

Comparison Words			
too	like	both	not only . . . but also
also	similar to	same as	in the same way
resemble	accordingly	likewise	

Read the examples listed below that show how these signal words are used in a comparison.

<u>Both</u> my mother and father have trouble understanding why I listen to hip-hop.

Exercising has <u>not only</u> improved my heath, but it has <u>also</u> changed my social life.

Now try practicing on your own. Write a sentence that shows a comparison. Remember to use one of the signal words from the list above in your sentence.

_____

_____

_____

_____

On the other hand, contrasts point out *differences* between two or more subjects. As with comparisons, there are signal words that point to a contrast being made. Some common signal words used by writers are listed below.

Contrast Words		
different from	but	however
on the contrary	instead	while
yet	differ	unlike

Here are some examples of sentences that contain signal words showing contrasts being made.

<u>While</u> my sister loves to go the movie theater, I am convinced that videos are the best way to see a film.

The Spartans have the best record in the league, <u>yet</u> statistics show that the Falcons may win the title.

Now try writing an example of a contrast on your own. Remember to use signal words from the list above.

_____

_____

_____

_____

Once you are able to recognize comparisons and contrasts within a work, or between two or more works, you will need to organize that information. A graphic organizer, such as a Venn diagram, can help you visually organize and understand the similarities and differences between the subjects.

Here is an example of a Venn diagram that compares and contrasts two different sports:

Baseball   **Basketball**

nine players

small ball

score by circling bases

usually nine innings

umpire

team sport

one ball in play

fun

active sport

coaches

five players

large ball

score by making baskets

usually four quarters

referees

indoors

Always place information that relates to *both* subjects in the overlapping area of the diagram, and information that relates to only one subject in the outlying areas.

Write on your test! It is important to remember that writing on the exam is allowed. When you read FCAT selections and recognize important compare/contrast signal words, make a note of it! Drawing a quick diagram, making notes in the margins, or underlining important information can help you focus on what you are reading. Spending a few moments to follow this advice *will save you time* when answering questions!

Read the article below and answer the questions that follow. Remember to use the reading strategies you have reviewed so far. Take time to reflect on the questions and suggestions listed in the column to the right.

Columbus and the Moon
By Thomas Wolfe

The National Aeronautics and Space Administration's moon landing 10 years ago today was a government project, but then so was Columbus's voyage to America in 1492. The government, in Columbus's case, was the Spanish Court of Ferdinand and Isabella. Spain was engaged in a sea race with Portugal in much the same way that the United States would be caught up in a space race with the Soviet Union four-and-a-half centuries later.

The race in 1492 was to create the first shipping lane to Asia. The Portuguese expeditions had always sailed east, around the southern tip of Africa. Columbus decided to head due west, across open ocean, a scheme that was feasible only thanks to a recent invention—the magnetic ship's compass. Until then, ships had stayed close to the great land masses even for the longest voyages. Likewise, it was only thanks to an invention of the 1940's and early 1950's, the high-speed electronic computer, that NASA would even consider propelling astronauts out of Earth's orbit and toward the moon.

Both NASA and Columbus made not one, but a series of voyages. NASA landed men on six different parts of the moon. Columbus made four voyages to different parts of what he remained convinced was the east coast of Asia. As a result, both NASA and Columbus had to keep coming back to the government with their hands out, pleading for refinancing. In each case the reply of the government became, after a few years: "This is all very impressive, but what earthly good is it to anyone back home?"

Predict:
What might Columbus and the moon have in common?

Compare/Contrast:
Circle any important signal words you see.

Main Idea:
What is the main idea of each paragraph?

Analyze:
Use a diagram to help organize information.

Did you circle the signal words you saw in the reading? Take a few moments to complete the Venn diagram on the next page to help you to organize the information you just read. After you have done this, answer the questions that follow.

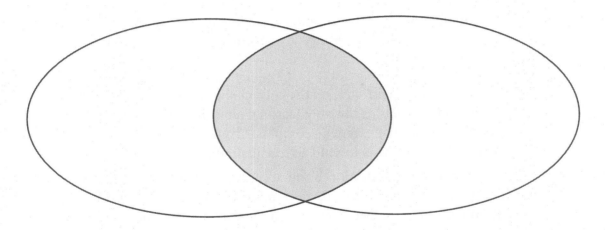

1. Why does the author compare the magnetic ship's compass to a high-speed electronic computer?

   A. Each invention was created to promote exploration.

   B. The compass and computer are important inventions.

   C. The government invented both to assist navigation.

   D. Both inventions made new forms of travel possible.

2. What are the similarities between Columbus's voyages and NASA's space program?

   _____

   _____

   _____

   _____

   _____

   _____

   _____

   _____

Looking for signal words and organizing the information should have helped you in answering the questions above. Check your answers below.

For the first question, D is the correct answer. The information in paragraph two tells us the only reason Columbus could sail across an open ocean was the magnetic compass. Likewise, it was the computer that enabled scientists to send astronauts out of Earth's orbit.

For the second question, a top-scoring response would begin with a clear topic sentence directly responding to the question. It would also include at least two details from the reading selection supporting the answer. An example of a top-scoring response follows:

There are several similarities between Columbus's voyages and NASA's space program. First, both the space program and the Spanish expeditions were government-funded. Also, the governments sponsoring each venture were competing with another country. Finally, Columbus's travels and the space program were made possible by newly invented technology and both resulted in a series of voyages.

When taking the FCAT, you will often be required to read two or more separate passages before answering any questions. When this happens, try to make connections between the selections as you read. Ask yourself: What do these have in common? How do they differ?

The following section includes reading selections that are similar to passages on the FCAT. Remember to stay actively involved while you read, using the reading strategies from this and previous chapters of the book.

Read "The Speech of Chief Seattle" before answering Numbers 1 through 8.

⋇ The Speech of ⋇
Chief Seattle

Detail from 20th century cast bronze statue of Chief Seattle in Pioneer Square, Seattle.

Yonder sky that has wept tears of compassion upon my people for centuries untold, and which to us appears changeless and eternal, may change. Today is fair. Tomorrow it may be overcast with clouds. My words are like the stars that never change. Whatever Seattle says the great chief at Washington can rely upon with as much certainty as he can upon the return of the sun or the seasons. The White Chief says the Big Chief at Washington sends us greetings of friendship and goodwill. This is kind of him for we know he has little need of our friendship in return. His people are many. They are like the grass that covers vast prairies. My people are few. They resemble the scattering trees of a storm-swept plain. The great—and I presume—good White Chief sends us word that he wishes to buy our lands but is willing to allow us enough to live comfortably. This indeed appears just, even generous, for the Red Man no longer has rights that he need respect, and the offer may be wise also, as we are no longer in need of an extensive country.

There was a time when our people covered the land as the waves of a wind-ruffled sea cover its shell-paved floor, but that time long since passed away with the greatness of tribes that are now but a mournful memory. I will not dwell on, nor mourn over, our untimely decay, nor reproach my paleface brothers with hastening it as we too may have been somewhat to blame. Youth is impulsive. When our young men grow angry at some real or imaginary wrong, and disfigure their faces with black paint, it denotes that their hearts are black, and that they are often cruel and relentless, and our old men and old women are unable to restrain them. Thus it has ever been. Thus it was when the white man first began to push our forefathers westward. But let us hope that the hostilities between us may never return. We would have everything to lose and nothing to gain. Revenge by young men is considered gain, even at the cost of their own lives, but old men who stay at home in times of war, and mothers who have sons to lose, know better. To us the ashes of our ancestors are sacred and their resting place is hallowed ground. You wander far from the graves of your ancestors and seemingly without regret. Your religion was written upon tables of stone by the iron finger of your God so that you could not forget. The Red Man could never comprehend nor remember it. Our religion is the traditions of our ancestors—the dreams of our old men, given them in the solemn hours of night by the Great Spirit; and the visions of our sachems, and is written in the hearts of our people.

Your dead cease to love you and the land of their nativity as soon as they pass the portals of the tomb and wander way beyond the stars. They are soon forgotten and never return. Our dead never forget the beautiful world that gave them being. They still love its verdant valleys, its murmuring rivers, its magnificent mountains, sequestered vales and verdant lined lakes and bays, and ever yearn in tender, fond affection over the lonely hearted living, and often return from the Happy Hunting Ground to visit, guide, console and comfort others.

Answer questions 1 through 5. Base your answers on "The Speech of Chief Seattle."

1 Read the sentences from the passage.

> **Today is fair. Tomorrow it may be overcast with clouds.**

What do the sentences suggest about Chief Seattle's view of change?

A. The weather is unpredictable.

B. The chief is dishonest but hopeful.

C. The sky is an indicator of what is to come.

D. The chief believes the future of his people is uncertain.

2 Which statement best describes the view of Chief Seattle's people regarding revenge?

F. Older people want revenge, while younger men have more to lose.

G. Young men want revenge and older people want to help them get it.

H. Young men think revenge is worthwhile, while older people know better.

I. Both the old and young among Chief Seattle's people believe that the time for revenge has past.

3 Read the sentence from the passage.

> **To us the ashes of our ancestors are sacred and their resting place is hallowed ground.**

What does *hallowed* mean?

A. common

B. expensive

C. holy

D. precious

4 READ THINK EXPLAIN How does Chief Seattle describe the contrasting views that cultures have of the dead? Use details and information from the speech to support your answer.

_____

_____

_____

_____

_____

_____

_____

_____

5 READ THINK EXPLAIN How are Chief Seattle's people different from the way they were in the past? Use details and information from the speech to support your answer.

_____

_____

_____

_____

_____

_____

_____

Read the article "Three Styles of Farming" before answering Numbers 1 through 8.

Three Styles of
FARMING

From *Global Geography*

In crowded East Asia, farmers must squeeze crops into every possible patch of ground. Southeast Asia is different. It has room to breathe—and room to farm. In some places there is land suitable for farming that has not yet been cleared. A few parts of Southeast Asia do, however, suffer from overcrowding. For example, Indonesia's island of Java has one of the highest population densities in the world—while the next-door island of Sumatra is trying to attract new settlers.

The people of Southeast Asia practice three main styles of farming. One is called slash-and-burn farming. Villagers who use this style move from place to place as the soil wears out. A second style involves permanent cultivation of small plots of land. The third is plantation farming—the growing of commercial crops on large estates with the use of hired labor.

Slash-and-Burn Farming   Phu Noc is a farmer in the mountains of northern Thailand. His village of some 450 people is perched on a ridge that overlooks a deep valley. Stands of tall teak trees dot the hilltops, mixed with sections of low-growing vegetation.

The people in Phu Noc's village live in one spot for several years, until the soil wears out. Then they take down their simple huts and move them to a new patch of trees and other growth to clear new fields. And they *burn*—

set fire to piles of trunks and branches. The ashes from the fires help to make the soil more fertile. The soil will give several years of service before it too wears out.

Phu Noc tends a small patch of corn near his hut. Farther away he raises dry rice—rice that is grown without irrigation. He also raises a few vegetables, such as yams. Phu Noc's village raises only enough food to feed its people, with no surplus for sale. This practice is called subsistence farming.

When done carefully, slash-and-burn farming can use soil resources without destroying them. But such methods provide only a shaky existence for Phu Noc and his fellow villagers. When crops fail, the villagers often hunt for nuts and berries in the woods. What is more, slash-and-burn methods waste a valuable resource —the sturdy teak trees that could be cut and sold for lumber. Thailand's government wants villagers like Phu Noc to settle on permanent farms in nearby valleys. But many, like Phu Noc, prefer the way of life they know—the one their ancestors followed.

Permanent Cultivation   Ramón grows paddy rice in a plain near Manila, in the Philippines. His family owns a farm of about four acres. Because the farm is a permanent one, it pays Ramón to build and maintain irrigation ditches. It also pays him to buy fertilizer. With irrigation and fertilizer, he can grow far more rice than Phu Noc does in the hills of Thailand.

Ramón keeps some of his rice and sells some to provide a cash income. He also makes money from the sale of small amounts of sugarcane that he grows near his house. In a garden behind the

Thailand-Mai Salong area Akha women cultivating a tea field.

house, he and his wife raise vegetables, pigs, and chickens to help balance their diet.

For Ramón, as for most Southeast Asian farmers, the chief crop is rice. Secondary crops vary from corn or beans to sugar or rubber. Some farmers, like Ramón, own their land. Others rent land and share their crops with the landowner. Farms such as Ramón's grow most of the food that Southeast Asians eat.

Plantation Farming Shiva works on a rubber plantation in the low hills near the western shores of the Malay Peninsula, in Malaysia. The plantation covers almost 2000 acres (nearly 3 square miles). It belongs to a corporation—a large company with many stockholders.

A commercial rubber plantation like this one represents a major investment. First, the land had to be bought and cleared. Next, rubber seedlings that were brought originally from South America had to be planted. After that, 5 to 10 years had to pass before any rubber could be harvested. Processing plants had to be built. Finally, the trees were ready to tap.

Workers like Shiva went to work. Walking between rows of trees, Shiva makes a careful V-shaped cut in each trunk. Beneath the cut he places a cup to catch the milky white sap that begins to ooze out. Later in the day he returns to the plantation's processing plant, where it is thickened, dried, and bound into large solid bales. Then it can be shipped to factories to be turned into rubber products.

Shiva is one of several hundred workers employed on the plantation. Some are single men who live in barracks. Others, like Shiva, live with their families in neat one-story homes.

Two women working in the rice fields near Manila, Philippines.

Large plantations play a key role in the economics of several Southeast Asian countries. Malaysia and Indonesia are the world's leading producers of natural rubber. They have exactly the warm, rainy climate that rubber trees require. Much of the rubber they produce is exported. It provides money that can be used to buy imported machinery and other goods.

Other plantation crops grown in Southeast Asia include sugar, oil palms, coconuts, pineapples, tobacco, and spices. Many of these products are also grown by small farmers like Ramón.

Traditional and Modern Agriculture in Southeast Asia is a mixture of traditional and modern practices. Farmers like Phu Noc use only simple tools—digging sticks, hoes, and the like. Farmers like Ramón may plow with water buffaloes, or they may use small tractors. Workers on large

plantations use both hand tools and mechanized equipment.

Many Southeast Asians combine farming with fishing. Ample supplies of fish are provided by the seas (sardines, tuna, sharks) and rivers (smelts, carp, catfish). Fish are the main source of animal protein in the region's diet.

In the past, few of the countries of the region were *self-sufficient* in food. That is, few of them produced all the food they needed. Many depended on imports of rice from countries like Myanmar and Thailand, which have often had surpluses. In recent years, however, countries of the region have made major efforts to boost rice production. With the help of new varieties of rice that give higher yields, these efforts have been paying off. The new rice varieties are part of a Green-Revolution that is raising food yields in many parts of the world.

Answer questions 1-8. Base your answers on the article, "Three Styles of Farming."

1 How is farming in Southeast Asia different from farming in East Asia?

A. Southeast Asia has more rainfall.

B. There is more room in Southeast Asia.

C. There are more people in Southeast Asia.

D. There are more plantations in Southeast Asia.

2 How does the island of Java differ from its neighbor Sumatra?

F. Java has more people.

G. Java has fewer subsistence farmers.

H. Sumatra has less room to grow crops.

I. Sumatra has more slash-and-burn farmers.

3 In which of these ways does plantation farming differ from the other two types of farming?

A. Crops are tended by the entire village.

B. Crops are harvested by traditional methods.

C. Crops are moved to new land once soil is worn out.

D. Crops are grown for profit rather than for personal use.

4 Why is Ramón in the Philippines able to grow more rice than Phu Noc in Thailand?

F. Ramón uses a tractor.

G. Ramón uses irrigation and fertilizer.

H. Phu Noc grows yams as well as rice.

I. Phu Noc uses old-fashioned methods.

5 READ THINK EXPLAIN How is plantation farming different from the other two farming methods? Support your answer with details and information from the article.

_____

_____

_____

_____

_____

_____

_____

_____

6 In what way are most Southeast Asian farmers alike?

A. Their main crop is rice.

B. Their farms are overcrowded.

C. They are completely self-sufficient.

D. They use the same farming methods.

7 How are Phu Noc's farming tools different from those used by workers on large plantations?

F. Phu Noc uses simple tools.

G. Phu Noc uses small tractors.

H. Phu Noc uses water buffaloes.

I. Phu Noc uses mechanical tools.

8 READ THINK EXPLAIN   Is slash-and-burn a better or worse farming method than permanent cultivation? Explain your response using details and information from the article.

_____

_____

_____

_____

_____

_____

_____

Read "The New Colossus" and "A Nation of Immigrants" before answering Numbers 1 through 7.

THE NEW COLOSSUS
by Emma Lazarus

Not like the brazen giant of Greek fame,

With conquering limbs astride from land to land;

Here at our sea-washed, sunset gates shall stand

A mighty woman with a torch, whose flame

Is the imprisoned lightning, and her name

Mother of Exiles. From her beacon-hand

Glows world-wide welcome; her mild eyes command

The air-bridged harbor that twin cities frame.

"Keep, ancient lands, your storied pomp!" cries she

With silent lips. "Give me your tired, your poor,

Your huddled masses yearning to breathe free,

The wretched refuse of your teeming shore.

Send these, the homeless, tempest-tossed to me.

I lift my lamp beside the golden door."

A Nation of Immigrants

From *Global History*

In the last half of the 19th century, the U.S. population increased more than threefold, from about 23.2 million in 1850 to 76.2 million in 1900. A significant portion of the growth was fueled by the arrival in these years of some 16.2 million immigrants. An additional 8.8 million more arrived during the peak years of immigration, 1901-1910.

Growth of Immigration

In every era, the motives for emigration from one country to another are a combination of "pushes" (negative factors from which people are fleeing) and "pulls" (positive attractions of the adopted country). The negative forces driving Europeans to emigrate in the late 19the century included (1) the poverty of displaced farmworkers driven from the land by the mechanization of farmwork, (2) overcrowding and joblessness in European cities as a result of a population boom, and (3) religious persecution of Jews in Russia. Positive reasons for choosing to emigrate to the United States included this country's reputation for political and religious freedom and the economic opportunities afforded by the settling of the Great Plains and the abundance of industrial jobs in U.S. cities. Furthermore, the introduction of large steamships and the relative inexpensive one-way passage in the ships' "steerage" made it possible for millions of poor Europeans to emigrate.

"Old" Immigrants and "New" Immigrants

Through the 1880s, the overwhelming majority of immigrants came from northern and western Europe: the British Isles, Germany, and Scandinavia. Most of these "old" immigrants were Protestants, although a sizable minority were Irish and German Catholics. Their language (mostly English-speaking) and high level of literacy and occupational skills made it relatively easy for these immigrants to blend into a mostly rural American society in the early decades of the 19th century.

Beginning in the 1890s and continuing to the outbreak of World War I in 1914, there was a notable change in the national origins of most immigrants. The "new" immigrants came from southern and eastern Europe. They were Italians, Greeks, Croats, Slovaks, Poles, and Russians. Many were poor and illiterate peasants, who had left autocratic countries and therefore were unaccustomed to democratic traditions. Unlike the earlier groups of Protestant immigrants, the newcomers were largely Roman Catholic, Greek Orthodox, Russian Orthodox, and Jewish. On arrival, most new immigrants crowded into poor ethnic neighborhoods in New York, Chicago, and other major U.S. cities. An estimated 25 percent of them were "birds of passage," young men contracted for unskilled factory, mining, and construction jobs, who would return to their native lands once they had saved a fair sum of money to bring back to their families.

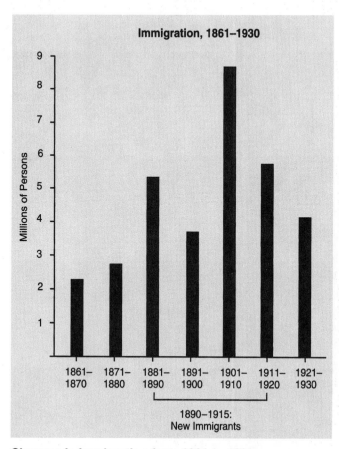

Changes in immigration from 1861 to 1930.

Answer the questions 1 through 7. Base your answers on "The New Colossus" and "A Nation of Immigrants."

1 What contrast is used in the first stanza of "The New Colossus"?

A. sunset and sunrise

B. conquering arms and lit torches

C. Greek sea and an American harbor

D. a menacing image and a welcoming image

2 According to the poem, what is the torch held in the statue's hand most like?

F. a political symbol

G. a conquering giant

H. a welcoming beacon

I. a sun drenched harbor

3 READ THINK EXPLAIN According to the article, how did the "new immigrants" differ from the "old immigrants?" Use details and information from the article to support your answer.

4 Based on the information in the article and graph, which statement is correct?

A. The immigration rate increased steadily from 1901 to 1930.

B. The highest immigration rate of the period was from 1911–1920.

C. The immigration rate from 1901–1910 was almost triple the rate from 1871–1880.

D. A total of about 16 million immigrants entered the U. S. every year from 1871 to 1910.

5 How are the poem and article alike?

    F. Both encourage people to immigrate.

    G. Both explain the history of immigration.

    H. Both tell why people wished to immigrate.

    I. Both name the countries from which people immigrated.

6 What does the author of the article suggest was an important "push" factor in immigration?

    A. The immigrants had low literacy rates.

    B. The United States was underpopulated.

    C. People in Europe suffered religious persecution.

    D. The United States offered political and religious freedom.

7 READ THINK EXPLAIN How does the tone of "The New Colossus" differ from the tone of "A Nation of Immigrants"? Use details and information from the passages to support your answer.

Main Idea, Details, and Patterns of Organization

Benchmark LA.A. 2.4.1.

Determines the main idea and identifies relevant details, methods of development, and their effectiveness in a variety of types of written material.

Think about the last research project you were asked to do for school. How hard was it to narrow down the information to *just* the amount you needed? Today, in a time of internet search engines and online publicly accessed databanks, it is very easy to become overwhelmed with the amount of information available. It's possible to obtain thousands of pieces of text on almost any given subject. The better you understand how a text is organized, the easier it will be for you to gather and use information.

Writers usually have a plan they follow to organize their writing. They will focus on one *main idea* and support that idea with *details*. Working through this chapter will provide you practice and strategies for recognizing the main idea, identifying facts and details that support the main idea, and recognizing organizational patterns and how they affect a reading selection.

Understanding the Benchmark

Most articles or books that are intended to inform the reader will present their main idea clearly. If you practice some of the suggestions below, you'll be able to spot main ideas on the FCAT in a flash!

- Listen to news clips on television that preview coming stories. These short excerpts usually contain the central idea of the news event.

- Remember that newspaper articles usually present the topic or main idea in the first or second paragraph of the story. Read at least one story a week from your favorite section of the newspaper. Notice how articles—and even information within each paragraph—are ordered.

- Pay attention to graphs or pictures and their captions. These often help to illustrate the most important ideas of a reading selection.

- Look at an instruction manual or a "how-to" article or book. How is the information organized to help you understand the directions? What key words or illustrations are used? How does the organization of the writing help you follow directions?

Making the FCAT Connection

On the FCAT, you can expect questions that ask you to determine the main idea and identify important details in the reading. In addition, you will be asked how the author organizes the details in the reading and how this organization helps to support the main idea.

Multiple-choice, short-response, and extended-response items from both informational and literary texts will be used to evaluate this benchmark.

Taking a Closer Look

Main Idea and Details

The main idea of a work is the most important thing the writer wants to say. It is the idea that holds a paragraph or text together, expressing what it is all about. In an essay, the main idea is often expressed concisely at the beginning and sometimes at the end of the writing. This is a *directly stated main idea*. However, the main idea is not always stated directly—in some writing it is implied. An *implied main idea* requires you to "read between the lines," to figure out what main idea is suggested in a passage. You may have to combine or synthesize the details in a passage to determine its implied main idea. In works of fiction, the main idea is almost always implied.

How can you identify the main idea of a piece of text? One good question to ask yourself while you are reading is "What is the most important point the author wants to communicate about the subject?" The answer to this question will help you identify the main idea.

Examine a selection's title. Often, but not always, the title of a work can help you predict what the piece will be about. Examine titles from newspaper articles everyday and practice predicting what stories will be about.

Once you have identified the main idea of a piece of writing, you will notice that the author supports it with *details*. Details may be descriptions, facts, examples, or statistics, that support the main idea. Each detail will not be as important as the main idea, but when put together, they should present a compelling argument, opinion, mood, or plot.

One helpful way to analyze the main idea and details in a selection is to create a simple chart. An example of one that you might use to identify the main idea and details is shown here for an article about college life, below:

Main Idea	There's more to college than taking classes.
Details	• Talking to professors • Socializing with other students • Experiencing a career through internships • Living on your own for the first time • Exposure to new ideas

Using a chart like this can help you when you *see* the main idea and details clearly in relationship to each other.

Patterns of Organization

In order to convey the main idea, details need to be *organized* in a way that readers will recognize. There are some very common patterns of organization that many writers often follow. A few of the most common patterns are:

Cause and Effect—The main idea is supported by an explanation of why something happened and the result of its happening. (See Chapter Eight)

Comparison and Contrast—The main idea is supported by indicating how subjects are the same or different. (Review Chapter Two)

Descriptive—The main idea is supported by concrete details such as facts, examples, statistics, or vivid descriptions that illustrate the topic.

Problem/Solution—The main idea discusses a problem and the conclusion of the passage describes how the problem was or was not resolved. This can also take a question/answer form, where a question is posed as the main idea and the conclusion of the passage works to answer the question.

Time Order—The main idea is supported by a series of events occurring in time. (See Chapter Nine)

In order to make it easier for readers to recognize an organizational pattern, good writers often use key words or phrases called *transitions*. These transitional words and phrases help *connect* the ideas and details of a story or article. This creates an easy-to-follow and reader-friendly format.

Some common organizational patterns and the transitional words that are used to signal them are identified in the chart below.

Organizational Pattern	Transitional Words and Phrases
Cause and Effect	as a result, because, for this reason, hence, since, so that, therefore, then, thus
Comparison and Contrast	*comparison*—like, likewise as, as if, in addition, as though, in the same way *contrast*—although, however, but, instead, nevertheless, in contrast, on the other hand
Descriptive	*adjectives*—filthy, shadowy, magnificent *concrete nouns/verbs*—thunderbolt, firefly, hawk, soar, peel, exclaim *directional words*—above, behind, next to
Problem/Solution	is resolved, the cause, the problem, the effect, one solution, the result, question
Time Order	afterward, all the while, as soon as, before, during, eventually, finally, first, meanwhile, second, then, thereafter, while

After reviewing the chart, look at the short passages that follow. Are there transitions used to signal a specific pattern of organization? Determine the main idea and the organizational pattern of each passage and circle any transitional words and phrases you recognize as you read.

Getting to class on time is almost impossible. First, I have to allow myself enough time to take care of the cat's breakfast as well as my own. Then I have to consider the unpredictable buses that never run on schedule. Finally, I'm faced with the crowded halls at school and a locker that is always stuck!

Main idea _____

Organizational Pattern _____

For three days and nights torrid rains pummeled the coast, flooding neighborhoods and destroying roads. The water-soaked land became a swamp floating with twisted debris. Never in the history of the city had a hurricane caused so much destruction.

Main idea _____

Organizational Pattern _____

Even though we were only gone a little while, Cleo had gotten out. Because she was still such a small cat, the few inches the window was open was plenty of room for her to work her way to freedom. Had we repaired the torn window screen earlier that week, the whole mess could have been avoided.

Main idea _____

Organizational Pattern _____

Maintaining our national hiking trails is a growing concern. Lack of funding and a dwindling interest in environmental issues are contributing to the problem. I suggest that a national organization be formed from local community movements to save the trails.

Main idea _____

Organizational Pattern _____

Which organizational pattern from the chart isn't included above? Write your own example of a paragraph that utilizes that pattern of organization. Be sure to use transition words to signal which pattern of organization you are using.

_____

_____

_____

_____

_____

_____

_____

There are additional patterns of organization not described earlier in the chapter. Review the chart below to learn about the other ways authors organize their writing. Can you think of examples for each?

Flashback	usually used in literary texts. The author starts with a situation and then "flashes-back" to earlier events.
Spatial order	used to describe how something looks or its location. The details in a spatial order description might proceed from botton to top, from left to right, or from nearby to far away.
Bulleted lists	usually used in informational texts to make important points. • point one • point two • point three
Degree order	often used in informational texts. The author presents ideas in order of importance, usefulness, familiarity, etc.
Foreshadowing	usually used in literary texts. Early on, the author gives subtle hints of things that will happen later in the text.
Argument/Support	usually used in informational texts. The author takes a stand on an issue then supports it with details.

FCAT EXTRA!

As a reader, it's important to be aware of transitions and how they are used. But why stop there? Utilize this helpful set of tools when you write! Use transitions to point out to the reader when you are moving from one thought to another, most commonly, at the beginning of new paragraphs.

Now try using the methods you have reviewed in this chapter to help you identify main idea, details, and patterns of organization in the reading below. Follow the strategies provided in the margins to guide your reading and help you answer the questions that follow.

Three Passions I Have Lived For

By Bertrand Russell

Three passions, simple but overwhelmingly strong, have governed my life: the longing for love, the search for knowledge, and unbearable pity for the suffering of mankind. These passions, like great winds, have blown me hither and thither, in a wayward course over a deep ocean of anguish, reaching to the very verge of despair.

I have sought love, first, because it brings ecstasy—ecstasy so great that I would often have sacrificed all the rest of my life for a few hours of this joy. I have sought it, next, because it relieves loneliness—that terrible loneliness in which one shivering consciousness looks over the rim of the world into the cold unfathomable lifeless abyss. I have sought it, finally, because in the union of love I have seen, in a mystic miniature, the prefiguring vision of the heaven that saints and poets have imagined. This is what I sought, and though it might seem too good for human life, this is what—at last—I have found.

With equal passion, I have sought knowledge. I have wished to understand the hearts of men. I have wished to know why the stars shine.... A little of this, but not much, I have achieved.

Love and knowledge, so far as they were possible, led upward toward the heavens. But always, pity brought me back to earth. Echoes of cries of pain reverberate in my heart. Children in famine, victims tortured by oppressors, helpless old people a hated burden to their sons, and the whole world of loneliness, poverty, and pain make a mockery of what human life should be. I long to alleviate the evil, but I cannot, and I too suffer.

This has been my life. I have found it worth living, and would gladly live it again if the chance were offered me.

Before going further, use a chart to help you identify the main idea, details, and organizational structure in the essay you just read. Use the reading strategies provided in the margin to help you build your chart.

Predict:
Try to predict what the main idea will be.

Identify:
Look in the first paragraph to find the main idea.

Analyze:
Look for the key words that signal the organization of the piece.

Stop and Reflect:
Notice key points in each paragraph as you read.

Summarize:
Sum up each paragraph as you read.

Main Idea	
Details	•
	•
	•

Now answer the questions that follow.

1. Which statement best expresses the main idea of the essay?

   A. The author is content with the way he lived his life.

   B. The author's life was guided by his deep personal concerns.

   C. Love is the most significant value to shape the author's life.

   D. Each of the author's passions was equally important to him.

2. How does Russell develop the idea that he lived his life for certain passions?

_____

_____

_____

_____

_____

_____

_____

_____

_____

_____

_____

Focusing on the main idea and looking for the organizational pattern of Russell's essay should have helped you in answering the questions. Now, check your answers.

B is the correct answer to the first question. Answer choice C is too specific and choice D is too general. Choice A isn't supported by the *details* in the essay. While each of the other answers expresses a true statement about the reading, B is the statement that best summarizes the main idea of the article.

Did you recognize the second question as one that asks you how the author organizes his ideas? If you refer back to the list of organizational patterns earlier in this chapter, you will notice that the pattern used here is descriptive; the author makes a statement in the first paragraph and develops that idea through vivid descriptions and examples. Recognizing the pattern will help you in organizing your answer to the question.

A top-scoring response would begin with a clear statement that directly responds to the question. That statement would be followed by at least two supporting details from the passage. An example of a top-scoring response follows:

The author uses description to organize his work and develop the idea that he lived his life for three passions. He describes love as important because it brought him happiness and kept him from being lonely. The author also details how his desire for knowledge drove him to pursue it, and his compassion for mankind kept him striving to help his fellow man.

Use the strategies from this chapter in future readings. Remember to "Predict" what the reading will be about, "Summarize" paragraphs as you read, "Reflect" on key points of each section or paragraph, and "Analyze" the text for key words! If you do this while reading, answering questions will be a snap!

The following section includes reading selections that are similar to passages on the FCAT. Remember to stay actively involved while you read, using the reading strategies from this and previous chapters of the book.

 **Read the article "The Southwest Tradition" before answering Numbers 1 through 5.**

The Southwest Tradition

During the past century, investigators have been solving one of the great mysteries of the North American continent: who built the spectacular, prehistoric cliff dwellings and the other ancient structures scattered throughout the American Southwest?

The key to this mystery, curiously enough, involves farming, and how this simple activity fosters the growth of civilization. We know that agriculture first evolved in the world's harsh, hot, arid deserts, then spread to more temperate climates . . . not the other way around, as one might expect. All civilizations first took root in the deserts of the world, including the deserts of the American Southwest.

A century ago, few would believe that ancestors of the American Indians could be responsible for the magnificent structures of the Desert Southwest. Today, after a century of fieldwork in archeology, the best evidence suggests that ancient farmers built these great civilizations and were the grandparents of the present-day, Native American Pueblo people as well.

We know that, although farming was introduced into the southwestern deserts as early as 4000 years ago, hunting and gathering remained an important means of acquiring food until about 500 BC, when the agricultural revolution flourished with the regular cultivation of corn, beans, and squash. The evolution of corn or maize was itself a critical element in this process. As with everywhere else in the world, this led to a sedentary lifestyle, the adoption of cooperative, organized social structures and, in turn, to the formation of urban settlements, including, in this case, spectacular cliff dwellings.

The prehistoric peoples of the Four Corners region shared common archaic roots, but different adaptation to regional variations in environment, climate, and resources, together with different levels of Mesoamerican influence, resulted in formation of the three primary cultures known today as the Southwest Tradition: the Mogollon, the Hokakam, and the Anasazi. Other, possibly related prehistoric cultures interspersed in this region included the Sinagua, Salado, and Hakataya.

The Southwest's arid desert climate has been very effective in preserving many of the cities, towns and cultural remains of these prehistoric peoples. Tree-ring dating has provided very accurate dates from 500 BC to about 1500 AD. There are 28 federal areas existing or proposed in Arizona, Utah, Colorado, and New Mexico, designed to protect and display this treasury of spectacular artifacts. Thousands of other archeological sites are under the protection of state and local entities throughout the Four Corners region.

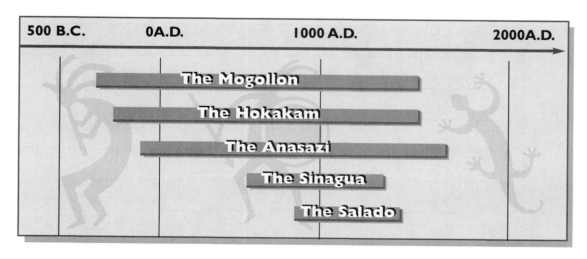

Answer questions 1-5. Base your answers on the article "The Southwest Tradition."

1 Which suggestion below would be the best alternate title for this article?

   A. The Four Corners
   B. The Cliff Dwellers
   C. The American Southwest
   D. Native American Pueblos

2 Which activity most promoted the growth of civilization?

   F. agriculture
   G. building
   H. trading
   I. warfare

3 READ THINK EXPLAIN   How does the author's use of chronological order support the main idea of the story? Use details and information from the story to support your answer.

_____

_____

_____

_____

_____

_____

_____

_____

_____

_____

_____

_____

4 Which cultures were the most influential in forming the ancient civilizations of the Southwest?

    A. Pueblo, Salado, and Sinagua

    B. Anasazi, Mogollon, and Salado

    C. Pueblo, Mogollon, and Anasazi

    D. Hokakam, Anasazi, and Mogollon

5 What is the connection between farming and the ancient buildings in the American Southwest? Use details and information from the article to support your answer.

Read the article "Critters Vex People as Habitats Collide" and answer Numbers 1-8.

Critters Vex People as
HabitatsCollide

By Andrew Alderson

LOS ANGELES—The uninvited daytime guest, weighing nearly 400 pounds, was hungry when he climbed into Rick Marrone's lakeside home through an open window. His mood deteriorated when he took a bite out of some fruit and found it was artificial.

The black bear then went to the refrigerator, cleared the contents onto the floor and enjoyed an impromptu picnic. The identity of the intruder would have remained a mystery if a neighbor in New Jersey had not seen him escaping across the garden.

This particular clash of interests between man and beast ended—as it often does these days—in a victory for the animal. As American urban development spreads, a war is gathering pace between humans and wildlife. People are increasingly ending up second best.

Recently, the Insurance Information Institute estimated that animal-related damage to property was running at more than $1.2 billion a year across the United States—and rising. "You have so many people living in areas not designed for human habitation," said Steve Goldstein, a spokesman for the New York-based organization. "Sometimes people find themselves cohabiting with creatures they never planned to cohabit with."

While armadillos are a menace in Oklahoma, where they are destroying gardens, there are tales of wolves roaming near Minnesota homes, a cougar prowling an estate in Colorado and feral chickens pecking out at people in California. Even when man loses patience and takes the law into his own hands, he is in danger of making a fool of himself. In Michigan, one local tried to shoot a possum invading his kitchen, but hit a gas pipe. The consequent explosion caused $18,000 worth of damage.

Raccoons top the trouble-makers' list. One group did tens of thousands of dollars worth of damage to a property in Ohio when they entered through the chimney as the owner wintered in Florida. They ate all the food in the cupboards, clawed their way through hardwood floors and soiled furniture.

Ask Sean and Lisa Rankin how they fared when a raccoon with an attitude invaded their kitchen, fought their pet cat for food and used their boat as a lavatory. When it made unfriendly advances toward their 11-month-old son, Sydney, the Rankins fought back.

"I started throwing fruit from the tree at him," said Mrs. Rankin. "He caught it. I pictured him going back to his raccoon friends and saying, 'You won't believe these stupid humans—they're throwing me breakfast.'"

A raccoon feeds from a garbage can in a residential area.

Unable to win their own war, the Rankins turned to one of an estimated 5,000 U.S. firms now helping homeowners deal with unwanted pests. Business is booming for Joe Felegi, whose Critter Control Company handles 200 calls a day. He usually traps his prey in cages using bait. Then, depending on the species, he either kills them or releases them into the wild. Yet urban sprawl means that his release spots have dwindled from 30 to three over the years. "I'm trapping where I used to release," he said.

A generation ago, animal intruders might have been shot and eaten. Today, gun laws are tighter and animal-welfare groups are on the side of the assailants. Stephanie Boyles, a wildlife biologist for People for the Ethical Treatment of Animals in Norfolk, Va., urges homeowners not to harm "innocent, defenseless" creatures. "The animals were there first," she said.

Many residents now resort to more humane deterrents, supporting a $250 million-a-year industry supplying everything from homemade traps to warning devices with intriguing names such as MoleBlaster and The Garden Cop. Disastrous tales of these critter-controllers abound. A Fort Lauderdale, Fla., man who tried to exterminate a land crab by pouring gasoline down its hole and lighting it had a much closer brush with death than his intended victim.

Others have tried more old-fashioned measures, but with little success. Patrick Christmas, a lawyer, resorted to squirrel bashing when they invaded the attic of his home in the District and chewed through electric wiring. He dressed for battle, donning a hockey helmet, mask, gloves and padded jacket. He then pursued the pests on the roof of his three-story house and started swatting. "All I could think of was being found dead at the bottom of my house, wearing a hockey mask and a ski parka in August," he said. The squirrels are still there.

Answer questions 1-8. Base your answers on the article "Critters Vex People as Habitats Collide."

1 What is the main idea of this reading passage?

   A. Animals are winning in conflicts over habitats.

   B. Humans are living in places that were once wild.

   C. Animals are becoming a serious menace to humans.

   D. Humans are learning to live peaceably with animals.

2 Why is business booming for Joe Felegi's Critter Control Company?

   F. His company uses humane methods for removing animals.

   G. His company is the only one that addresses problem animals.

   H. Homeowners are afraid to try to get rid of animals themselves.

   I. Homeowners need help removing animals that invade their homes.

3 Which of the following would be another good title for this passage?

   A. "Critters: 20, Humans: 0, At Half-Time!"

   B. "Getting the Upperhand on Animal Pests"

   C. "How to Attract Wildlife to Your Backyard"

   D. "Another Victory for Human Rights Activists"

4 Which animal has caused the most problems recently for homeowners?

    F. bears

    G. wolves

    H. raccoons

    I. armadillos

5 What can you infer from the passage about people's attempts to remove animal pests themselves?

    A. People's attempts at removing animal pests often backfire.

    B. People's attempts are most successful when humane methods are used.

    C. People are more capable than experts when it comes to taking care of pests.

    D. People have grown tired of animal-welfare groups telling them what to do.

6 What is the best definition of the word "intruder" as used in the following sentence?

> **The identity of the intruder would have remained a mystery if a neighbor in New Jersey had not seen him escaping across the garden.**

    F. return visitor

    G. overnight guest

    H. unknown visitor

    I. unwelcome guest

7 READ THINK EXPLAIN How does the last story in the passage about the lawyer who "resorted to squirrel-bashing" support the main idea of the article? Support your answer with details and information from the article.

_____

_____

_____

_____

_____

_____

_____

8 READ THINK EXPLAIN How does the author organize or present the main idea of this passage? Support your answer with details and information from the article.

Read the article "Animal Reaction" and answer Numbers 1 through 8.

Animal Reaction

By Lisa Gutierrez

Pets suffer from allergies, too—sometimes to humans

All dogs scratch themselves. But Laura Sutherland had never seen her dogs Casper and Boomer put on such a show.

About a year ago her 3-year-old Shih Tzus began rubbing up against the furniture, sawing their silky, furry flanks back and forth under chair rungs. Outside on the patio they scraped their bodies against the coarse bricks. Then came the constant paw licking.

"It kept them up at night," recalled Sutherland, a former registered nurse and Kansas City mother of three sons. "They'd get up at night and lick. It was way too over the top."

Veterinarian Dan Hecker at Hecker Animal Clinic examined and tested the siblings and discovered they are allergic to house dust, leaf mold and goldenrod. "And various and sundry weeds, all of which are on the golf course where I walk my dogs every day," Sutherland said.

At this time of year animal allergies send pet owners to local veterinary clinics in "bucket loads," as one local vet said.

The same tree pollen and molds that fell their owners can drive dogs and cats wild. These companion pets are the most likely to fall victim to allergies, which are treatable with

antihistamines, steroids and allergy shots. Dogs seem more genetically wired to develop allergies than cats.

Sometimes—and we're not pulling your tail—pets can even be allergic to humans. "It is kind of a man-bites-dog kind of thing," said veterinarian Bohdan L. Thompson in Olathe, who has seen more than a few such cases.

The usual suspects

Animals don't sniffle and suffer the way we do. We sneeze; they scratch. And pet owners may not recognize the symptoms.

"The vast majority of cats and dogs that have inhalant allergies don't have any respiratory signs," said Jean Greek, veterinary dermatologist with Veterinary Specialists of Kansas City in Overland Park.

Veterinarians often see owners "at wit's end," Thompson said. "If they come to us, that dog is

driving them crazy. Those are the ones who come in with all their (dog's) tags taped together because the dog is scratching loudly at night. They say, `I think he has fleas.' "

Fleas are the most common cause of pet allergies. The saliva of just one flea can cause a reaction, though not all dogs and cats are allergic to fleas. Like humans, animals can also be allergic to certain foods (like beef, corn and soybeans) or environmental particles that cause "canine hay fever."

The list of possible allergens is long; some tests look for as many as 63. If your eyes itch as you read this, you'll recognize the culprits: grasses, trees, feathers, house dust, cats, secondhand smoke and the icky one no one likes to talk about—cockroaches.

Zito, a 2-year-old Border collie owned by dog trainer Melissa French of Shawnee, began scratching like mad last summer. His red-toned coat didn't fill out like it usually does. A blood test showed that Zito was allergic to weeds. Too bad for Zito.

"This is primarily what our yard is made of," said French, who gives Zito an allergy shot every two weeks. "That's why he has issues."

Getting their dander up

Weeds weren't the issue for Maggie, a 9-year-old Yorkie owned by Lisa and Peter Arnold of Olathe.

A few years ago Maggie inexplicably began licking and chewing her feet obsessively, mostly in the summer when the lawn greened up. She rubbed her itchy nose on the carpet so often that her once-black nose now glows pink.

Thompson, Maggie's veterinarian, tested her for allergies and—surprise!—the blood test revealed human dander among the allergens giving her fits. Human dander—the dead, dandruff-like skin that humans shed every day—is a major ingredient of house dust.

Vets don't always test for human dander allergies because it happens so rarely. Some don't do it for philosophical reasons: How do you tell a loving owner that she gives her puppy the itches?

But Maggie's owner, Lisa Arnold, laughed over the diagnosis and still tells people about it. "Nobody believes it because it's supposed to be the other way around," said Arnold, a customer service representative for John Deere Co.

Pinpointing the cause of a pet allergy can be tricky. No allergy test is 100 percent accurate. And it's not as though the patient can say, "It hurts here, doc."

If fleas don't appear to pose a problem, and if the animal's symptoms don't appear seasonal, a vet may change the pet's diet for a while to rule out a food allergy. "It's easier to prove an allergy if you avoid what is causing the reaction," said Catherine Outerbridge, a clinical fellow in dermatology in the University of California-Davis School of Medicine.

"When we believe that the only reason they're itching is a pollen mold, we try antihistamines, which work in about a third of dogs. They're not as helpful as for people, and there's no way to know which ones work well for dogs."

People cures, animal cures
Veterinarians recommend oral antihistamines such as Benadryl designed for humans. But some of the newer drugs, such as Claritin and Allegra, "are not acceptable," Bob Kennis said.

"Most of the newer generation are non-sedating. Drugs like Benadryl have some sedative properties and give them (animals) some relief in that way," said Kennis, a veterinary dermatologist and assistant professor in the College of Veterinary Medicine at Texas A&M.

"The newer ones have not been researched, nor are they approved for usage in dogs. I don't know a standard dosage in dogs."

Veterinarians also prescribe low-dose, anti-inflammatory steroids to control the itchiness. But steroids have side effects, especially in dogs because they can't tolerate high doses like cats can.

"They can cause hormonal problems, increase their appetite, lead to more frequent urination," Outerbridge said. "We use it like a fire extinguisher, as a short-term relief."

Veterinarians typically use one of two animal allergy tests; sometimes they use both. One is a blood test, the other an intradermal skin test. The skin test is like that used on humans: Small amounts of allergens are injected into the animal's skin to identify which ones cause a reaction.

Some vets consider allergy testing overkill if an animal exhibits seasonal symptoms that are easily treated. The tests can be pricey — less than $200 for a blood test and up to $400 and more for the skin test.

Vets also debate the merits of blood testing. Some criticize it for giving too many false-positive results while others say newer tests have worked out those early kinks.

"One of the things I find most upsetting about the blood test is you need to be pretty certain that that's the dog's problem," dermatologist Greek said.

"I see animals all the time, and the owners have been dutifully

tested positive for human dander allergy, takes shots.

So does 4-year-old Nathan Arnold. He's allergic to dogs.

And then there was the dog that was allergic to, uh, dogs.

Jim Humphrey, a veterinarian at the Johnson County Animal Clinic in Overland Park, saw it a few years back. A dog tested positive for allergies to dog dander.

The dog's owner laughed that "Sally is allergic to herself."

Pet allergies

Look for "pathological scratching." Pets may stop eating or playing or may wake up during the night to scratch.

- Other clues: Biting, licking or scratching their paws, face, ears, underarms, groin and front

legs. Cats may break out in an almost undetectable rash, develop large skin lesions or pull out so much hair that it creates bald spots.

- Before you buy or adopt, look at the parents. This stuff runs in families. Purebreds are particularly prone, vets say.

Allergy-prone breeds include:
Dalmatians
Golden retrievers
Cocker spaniels
Terriers
Labrador retrievers
Bichons frises
Shih Tzus
Lhasa apsos

giving the dog allergy shots for a year or two, waiting for it to kick in. But that was never the problem. Maybe the dog was hypothyroid ... or has scabies."

Now there's a pleasant thought.

Animal allergies aren't pretty, and sometimes they create downright strange situations.

In the Arnold home, for instance, Maggie the Yorkie, who

Answer questions 1 through 8. Base your answers on the article "Animal Reaction."

1 What is the main idea of the reading passage?

A. Pets can have allergies just like humans.

B. Vets are finding new ways to treat pet allergies.

C. Pets sometimes become allergic to their owners.

D. Pet owners are learning how to deal with allergies.

2 Why is it hard for pet owners to realize their pet has an allergy?

F. The symptoms are seasonal.

G. The symptoms suggest a more serious problem.

H. Pets show no symptoms when they have an allergy.

I. Pets scratch instead of sneeze when they have an allergy.

3 What is the most common cause of pet allergies?

A. fleas

B. grass

C. weeds

D. house dust

4 READ
   THINK
   EXPLAIN How does the story about the Arnold's dog Maggie support the article's main idea? Support your answer with details and information from the article.

---

5 What can you infer from the passage about the Arnold family?

A. They put their son's needs over the well-being of their dog.

B. They put their dog's needs over the well-being of their son.

C. They are concerned about their son's and their dog's well-being.

D. They are concerned about the expense of caring for an allergic dog.

6 Which of the following is a major ingredient of house dust?

F. mold

G. pollen

H. human dander

I. environmental particles

7 What do vets prescribe for short-term relief of a pet's itching?

    A. steroids

    B. skin tests

    C. blood tests

    D. antihistamines

8 READ THINK EXPLAIN   How are dogs and humans alike and different, when it comes to allergies? Support your answer with details and information from the article.

_____

_____

_____

_____

_____

_____

_____

_____

Purpose, Point of View, and Persuasive Appeal

Benchmark LA.A. 2.4.2

Determines the author's purpose and point of view and their effects on the text. (Includes LA.A.2.4.5 Identifies devices of persuasion and methods of appeal and their effectiveness.)

The ability to develop and express a strong argument is important to everyday life. You can use persuasion techniques to talk a teacher into giving you extra time to complete an assignment. If you are convincing, you might be able to get your parents to allow you to stay out past curfew. As you learn more about persuasive techniques, you will be able to recognize and differentiate between strong and weak arguments in advertisements, editorials, and campaign speeches.

Keep in mind that every time an author writes, he or she has a purpose in mind. Writers usually write to explain, to persuade, or to entertain. Understanding an *author's purpose* will help you interpret what he or she has to say.

In addition to a purpose, an author will usually have a *point of view*. Everyone approaches a topic from a personal perspective. This perspective is called a point of view. It helps to understand what point of view an author is writing from as it can color, or influence, the facts of a piece of writing.

Understanding the Benchmark

Everyday life is filled with writing that embodies purpose and particular points of view. Here are some suggestions for practice in identifying these elements of writing. Being alert to purpose and point of view in the things you read will give you an edge when it comes to the FCAT.

- Read the editorials in your newspaper. They are written to express the author's point of view. Authors will also use persuasion to influence the minds of his/her readers.

- Remember that all advertisements are trying to sell products or services. Notice the language in the ads and think about how advertisers try to connect their products to a set of feelings that appeal to you.

- Scan movie and restaurant reviews. Notice how the authors of these articles try to persuade you that their opinions and points of view are valid.

- Listen to political ads and speeches. You will be sure to hear many persuasive techniques used.

Making the FCAT Connection

On the FCAT you will be asked questions that require you to identify an author's purpose for writing something or an author's point of view. You will also need to analyze an author's purpose as well as the power of any persuasive devices an author uses.

Multiple-choice, short-response, and extended-response items from both informational and literary texts will assess this benchmark.

Taking a Closer Look

Author's Purpose

The author's purpose is the goal or aim a writer expresses in his/her work. Often, if you can recognize the type of writing, figuring out the author's purpose becomes easier.

TYPE OF WRITING	AUTHOR'S PURPOSE
Narrative	to tell a story
Descriptive	to illustrate a person, event, or place; to convey a mood
Expository	to explain, illustrate, or present information
Persuasive	to express an opinion and convince readers to think/feel/act a certain way.

Some works involve more than one purpose. For example, a persuasive work may contain expository sections. While a narrative tells a story, it may also contain sections that are descriptive. Try to look for the main idea of a reading when you are determining the author's purpose.

Just as the title of a piece can help you predict the main idea, it can also help you predict the author's purpose. Look at the titles below. What do you think the author's purpose might be for each piece? The first one is done for you.

Childhood Fears

I think the author will probably explain and illustrate what kids are

afraid of

Learning to Make the Grade

_____

_____

Careless Rainforest Destruction Must End

_____

_____

My Favorite Place to Visit

_____

_____

When you use the title to make predictions about a selection, you should go back after you finish reading to check whether your prediction was correct. Doing this will help you improve your predicting abilities.

Author's Point of View

Along with a purpose, the author will usually have a point of view about the subject he or she is writing on. The point of view is the author's perspective or position on a subject. The chart below illustrates how an author's point of view is expressed differently in different kinds of writing.

TYPE OF WRITING	ELEMENTS OF POINT OF VIEW
Fiction (including short stories, poems, and novels)	The author may use characters or a narrator to express attitudes in the story.
Non-fiction (including informative news accounts, articles, biographies, and documentaries)	The author's point of view is primarily neutral. Informative writing is used to explain, describe, or instruct.
Persuasive pieces (including editorials and advertisements)	The point of view clearly reflects the author's attitude about a subject. Sometimes the opinion is directly stated and other times it is implied. The author may try to convince readers to believe something, feel a certain way, or take action by appealing to their feelings, and/or values.

Read the excerpts below. How would you summarize the author's point of view for each? The first one is completed for you.

> "If teenagers work long hours after school, they may miss out on important study time and after-school clubs and activities."

This author doesn't think kids should work after school.

> "Jack was terrified as he walked through the vacant parking lot. He immediately sped up, knowing that the quickly approaching footsteps behind him spelled trouble. He thought back to the many times his mother reminded him about walking alone late at night."

_____

> "The cobalt blue waters, immaculate white sandy beaches, and fabulous hotels make Castle Island a must for any serious vacationer."

_____

As you continue reading articles, poems, and stories, in this book, in your classes, or on the FCAT, remember to "read between the lines" as any good reader does. Ask yourself: "Why did the author write this?" (author's purpose) and "Where is he/she coming from?" (author's point of view).

FCAT EXTRA!

Questions on the FCAT about point of view will usually ask you to identify the author's perspective. They may also ask you about opposing points of view or to discuss the methods of persuasion an author uses to get the reader to take some action or adopt an opinion.

You are about to read the poem *Alabama Centennial* by Naomi Long Madgett. Use the reading strategies discussed in this lesson to help you answer the questions that follow.

Alabama Centennial
by Naomi Long Madgett

They said, "Wait." Well, I waited.
For a hundred years I waited
In cotton fields, kitchens, balconies,
In bread lines, at back doors, on chain gangs,
In stinking "colored" toilets
And crowded ghettos,
Outside of schools and voting booths.
And some said, "Later."
And some said, "Never!"

Then a new wind blew, and a new voice
Rode its wings with quiet urgency,
Strong, determined, sure.
"No." It said. "Not 'never,' not 'later,'
Not even 'soon.'
Now.
Walk!"

And other voices echoed the freedom words,
"Walk together, children, don't get weary,"
Whispered them, sang them, prayed them, shouted them.
"Walk!"
And I walked the streets of Montgomery
Until a link in the chain of patient acquiescence broke.

Then again: Sit down!
And I sat down at the counters of Greensboro.
Ride! And I rode the bus for freedom.
Kneel! And I went down on my knees in prayer and faith.
March! And I'll march until the last chain falls
Singing, "We shall overcome."

Not all the dogs and hoses in Birmingham
Nor all the clubs and guns in Selma
Can turn this tide.
Not all the jails can hold these young black faces
From their destiny of manhood,
Of equality, of dignity,
Of the American Dream
A hundred years past due.
Now!

Predict:
What do you already know about Alabama?

Analyze:
At this point, how does the author create a new mood?

Summarize:
Put this idea into your own words.

Point of View:
How does the author feel about African Americans?

Purpose:
What emotion is portrayed here?

Now answer the questions that follow.

1. Which statement best reflects the author's purpose?

   A. to persuade the reader to be open-minded

   B. to explain to readers examples of discrimination

   C. to describe the history of the Civil Rights Movement

   D. to illustrate the courage and determination of African Americans

2. What is the author's opinion about the African Americans' fight for freedom?

   _____

   _____

   _____

   _____

   _____

   _____

   _____

   _____

   Identifying the purpose of the poem and the author's point of view about the subject should have been helpful in answering the questions. Check to see if you answered the questions correctly below.

   The first question asks you to select the statement which best reflects the author's purpose in the poem. To find the author's purpose, ask yourself, "Why did the author write this poem?" The best response to that question is answer choice D. The author wants to illustrate for readers the courage and determination of African Americans. Even though we don't see "I would like to inform readers ..." anywhere in the poem we can listen to *what* and *how* the message of the poem is written to figure out what the author's purpose was in writing it.

For the second question, a top-scoring response would begin with a complete sentence that directly responds to the question. It would also include at least two supporting details from the text. A top-scoring response follows:

The author of the poem admires and respects African Americans for their courage and determination in gaining freedom. She discusses the "new voice" that encouraged people to break free of injustices of the past. Also, the author describes the courage it took for African Americans to walk in and "sit-in" in restaurants that were segregated. Finally, the author praises people who did not back down, even when faced with physical violence and imprisonment.

The following section includes reading selections that are similar to passages on the FCAT. Remember to stay actively involved while you read, using the reading strategies from this and previous chapters of the book.

Read the following two articles before answering Numbers 1 through 6.

Excerpt from

A THOUSAND DAYS:
John F. Kennedy in the White House

By Arthur Schlesinger

Yet he had accomplished so much: the hope for peace on earth, the elimination of nuclear testing in the atmosphere and the abolition of nuclear diplomacy, the new policies toward Latin America and the third world, the reordering of American defense, the emancipation of the American Negro, the revolution in the national economic policy, the concern for poverty, the stimulus to the arts, the fight for reason against extremism and mythology. Lifting us beyond our capacities, he gave his country back to its best self, wiping away the world's impression of an old nation of old men, weary, played out, fearful of ideas, change and the future; he taught mankind that the process of rediscovering America was not over. He transformed the American spirit— and the response of his people to his murder, the absence of intolerance and hatred, was a monument to his memory. The energies he released, the standards he set, the purposes he inspired, the goals he established would guide the land he loved for years to come. Above all, he gave the world for an imperishable moment the vision of a leader who greatly understood the terror and the hope, the diversity and the possibility, of life on this planet and who made people look beyond nation and race to the future of humanity. So the people of the world grieved as if they had terribly lost their own leader, friend, brother.

On December 22, a month after his death, fire from the flame burning at his grave in Arlington was carried at dusk to the Lincoln Memorial. It was fiercely cold. Thousands stood, candles in their hands; then, as the flame spread among us, one candle lighting the next, the crowd gently moved away, the torches flaring and flickering, into the darkness. The next day it snowed—almost as deep a snow as the inaugural blizzard when I went to the White House. It was lovely, ghostly and strange.

It all ended, as it began, in the cold.

President John F. Kennedy in the White House Oval Office.

MARTIN LUTHER KING, Jr.

by Henry Abraham and Irwin Pfeffer

Dr. Martin Luther King Jr. speaks in a church, 1967.

You are Martin Luther King, Jr., and you have a dream for America. It is a dream of a future in which race no longer matters, in which blacks and whites live as equals—full equals. In your preacher's voice, with rich sentences rolling off your tongue, you have tried to describe this dream to others.

"I have a dream," you have said, "that one day this nation will rise up and live out the true meaning of its creed: '...that all men are created equal.' I have a dream that one day on the red hills of Georgia the sons of former slaves and the sons of former slave owners will be able to sit down together at the table of brotherhood."

You have traveled around this nation telling others of your dream. But you don't just talk. You also act. You lead your supporters in defying laws that you believe to be unfair.

What sort of laws? Laws that allow a restaurant to serve whites but not blacks, for example, and that allow restaurant owners to have blacks arrested for trespass. For years it was common for Southern "white" restaurants to refuse to let blacks sit down to eat a meal. Blacks might buy food at a take-out counter, but they could not sit down and eat it there.

The sit-in was one technique used to fight such customs. Blacks would sit down at a restaurant or lunch counter, order a meal or a cup of coffee, and wait. They would not be served. They would keep their seats and wait. Sometimes all the seats would fill up with blacks waiting to be served. Often the restaurant owners would call the police and have the blacks arrested.

It was college students who first used sit-ins, in 1960, but you soon joined in. In 1962, you were sentenced to four months at hard labor for refusing to leave a restaurant in a department store in Atlanta, Georgia. You appealed and were released on bail.

The next year you went to Birmingham, Alabama, to lead several hundred people in street marches and sit-ins. You said Birmingham was the most segregated city in the United States, and you wanted to bring change. The police used snarling dogs and fire hoses against your supporters. Pictures of these activities were printed in newspapers around the world. Again you were arrested and put in jail. Again you were released. Seeing the pictures from Birmingham, President Kennedy declared, "I can well understand why the Negroes of Birmingham are tired of being asked to be patient."

That was your point, after all. By your method of civil disobedience—breaking the law to court arrest, then submitting quietly to the police—you were trying to show that black Americans were suffering under unjust laws. You believed that nonviolent protest was the way to convince white Americans to change those laws. And many whites, including President Kennedy, came to agree.

In August 1963, you and other civil rights leaders walked at the head of a "march on Washington." Some 200,000 or more people joined the march through the streets of the nation's capital. It was a peaceful parade, with whites and blacks walking arm in arm. The march ended at the Lincoln Memorial. It was from the steps of this monument that you declared, "I have a dream."

Answer questions 1-6. Base your answers on the articles "Martin Luther King, Jr." and "A Thousand Days: John F. Kennedy in the White House."

1 What are the authors' main purpose in writing these articles?

    A. to explain the ideas behind civil unrest

    B. to persuade the reader to promote racial equality

    C. to positively portray two American political figures

    D. to give examples of American civil unrest in the 1960s

2 The authors in both passages would agree that

    F. John F. Kennedy never met Martin Luther King, Jr.

    G. each man was committed to his beliefs about racial equality.

    H. the public believed that both men needed to stop civil disobedience.

    I. both Kennedy and Martin Luther King, Jr. were loved by all Americans.

3 READ THINK EXPLAIN How does the author of "A Thousand Days" support the idea that Kennedy was able to bring about change in the country? Use details and information from the article to support your answer.

_____

_____

_____

_____

_____

_____

_____

4 According to the second article, which sentence best describes a "sit-in"?

    A. A demonstration that took place on busses.

    B. A group who sat holding the American Flag as a symbol of freedom.

    C. Black Americans who would sit in a restaurant that would not serve them.

    D. Police officers using dogs and hoses to stop protesters from sitting in front of government buildings.

5 READ THINK EXPLAIN   How do the authors of "Martin Luther King, Jr." support the idea that King "had a dream?"

_____

_____

_____

_____

_____

_____

_____

_____

_____

_____

_____

_____

_____

_____

_____

_____

6 READ THINK EXPLAIN   What is the first author's opinion of John F. Kennedy? Use details and information from the article to support your answer.

_____

_____

_____

_____

_____

_____

_____

_____

Read the article "The New Enemies of Journalism" and answer Numbers 1 through 6.

The New Enemies
of JOURNALISM

By Charles Kuralt

On the television news programs now, bells ring, pictures flip and tumble, and everybody seems to be shouting at me. This may be the way to do it, but I don't think so.

The news is bad enough without added jingle and flash. I think it would be better to tell it calmly, with as many of the details as possible, and not to try to make it more exciting than it is. I even think viewers would appreciate that, and tune in.

This runs contrary to the prevailing opinion at the networks. One of my bosses said of a program I used to work on, "We want to keep it a news broadcast, but one that is more interesting, rapidly paced, with more spontaneity and serendipity, almost like all-news radio. We want a news program that better serves the needs of people who don't have time to watch television for long periods ... and need to get information quickly."

I respect this man, but I respectfully disagree with his judgment. I don't see how a news broadcast can be quick without also being cheap and shallow. Almost any story worth mentioning is worth an additional word of explanation. The story told in a few seconds is almost always misleading. It would be better not to mention it at all. And all those electronic beeps and bells and flashy graphics designed to "grab" the viewer and speed the pace along only subtract a few seconds that could be used to explain the events of the day in the English language.

The "quick news" idea has been preached for years by the shabby news consultants who have gone about peddling their bad advice to small television stations. They have never given a thought to the needs of the viewer, or to the reason the news is on the air in the first place— namely that this kind of country cannot work without an informed citizenry. The ninety-second news story does not serve the people, neither do the thirty- and twenty-second stories, and that's where we're headed. Fast. With bells and graphics.

In this sort of journalism there is something insulting to the viewer, the man or woman who sits down in front of the television set in the wistful hope of being informed. We are saying to this person, "You are a simpleton with a very short attention span," or, "You are too much in a hurry to care about the news anyway." Sooner or later, this viewer, who is *not* a simpleton and *not* too much in a hurry to care, will get the message and turn the dial. The networks are in a news-rating race. The one that wins it will be the one that stays calm and intelligent and reliable—the most responsible, not the most excitable.

(I offer an analogy from the newspaper world. When I first came to work in New York, such sensational newspapers as the *Journal-American*, the *Mirror*, the *News*, and the *Post* nipped at the heels of the solid, reflective *New York Times*. The *News* is on its uppers, the *Post* is a joke and the

A behind-the-scenes look at how a television director and technician edit and bring together different images to create a "rapidly paced" newscast.

others are memories. The *Times* may be the only one of them all to survive.)

Even if I am wrong, even if it turns out that a network news department can achieve high ratings by putting red slashes on the screen and shouting out the headlines and jangling people's nerves, does that mean it should?

Right now, more Americans are out of work than at any time since the Great Depression. The President is asking that the country spend more dollars on military hardware than the government possesses. Meanwhile, many dollars for the unemployed, the poor, the blind, and the disabled, may be taken away. How can any discussion of these matters be carried out in short, loud bursts on television?

In Geneva, negotiators for the United States and the Soviet Union are meeting to seek some way out of the terrible nuclear confront-ation. Our country seems to be sliding into a bog of Central American quicksand. The Congress has on its agenda a sweeping revision of the federal criminal law. These subjects also call for much explanation and public debate.

They will inevitably slow the pace of any news program that takes them up. but they are the stuff of our national life. The people expect us to inform them about these things, and if we don't, who will? If the people are given baby food when they are hungry for a meal of information, they will be undernourished and weakened—and then what will

become of the country that is the last, best hope of man?

The best minds in television news are thinking more about packaging and promotion and pace and image and blinking electronics than about thoughtful coverage of the news. I have worked in the field for twenty-five years, and every year I thought we were getting better. Suddenly, I think we're getting worse.

Answer questions 1-6. Base your answers on the article "The New Enemies of Journalism."

1 With which statement would the author agree?

    A. Television news coverage needs to be in depth.

    B. Television news is more effective when told quickly.

    C. Newspapers rather than television should report news.

    D. Promotion and image are the most important parts of the news.

2 What is the author's main purpose in writing the article?

    F. to state his opinion of television news

    G. to explain the concept of network news

    H. to explain different styles of presenting news

    I. to convey a positive picture of television news

3 What is the opinion of the management of television networks regarding the news?

    A. People want more detailed news coverage.

    B. The news is what creates an informed citizenry.

    C. The public is concerned about conflicts in Central America.

    D. News should be kept short since most people don't have much time to watch.

4 READ THINK EXPLAIN What is the author's opinion about television news coverage? Use details and information from the article to support your answer.

_____

_____

_____

_____

_____

_____

_____

_____

5 Which statement best describes the author's opinion about television news viewers?

A. People only want "quick news."

B. Viewers appreciate the flashy coverage.

C. American viewers have short attention spans.

D. Viewers are probably insulted by news without any explanation.

6 READ THINK EXPLAIN What is the author's purpose in titling the article "The New Enemies of Journalism"? Use details and information from the article to support your answer.

_____

_____

_____

_____

_____

_____

_____

Read the article "Death of Privacy" and answer Numbers 1 through 8.

DEATH OF PRIVACY

By Christine Varney

Cyberspace security: Information technology can be a threat as well as a blessing. What rules do we need to prevent misuse of all the personal data that we trail behind us when we navigate the Web?

At the beginning of the last century, my grandparents sailed to America, leaving behind their Irish farming village. The people in their community knew my family's history, their opinions and personalities, friendships and feuds.

At the beginning of this century, we are in some ways returning to that village. On-line and at work, we are organizing ourselves as a series of tight knit communities where secrets are very hard to keep. We are, once again, becoming a transparent society—one where everyone knows everything about everyone else in real time. But today, the communities are digital and often global, and the information isn't in words but bytes. There also are some significant differences between today's electronic transparency and the personal familiarities of the rural agrarian village.

These differences, in fact, give rise to one of the most complex questions we face as we enter this new era: how do we reconcile our concerns about personal privacy with the massive new flow of readily available personal information? The decisions we are making today could determine whether we bequeath our children a society in which their lives are enhanced by modern information

A man browses at an online store.

technology, or one in which they feel themselves the victims of it.

In my ancestral village back in Ireland, people had the advantage of context. My grandparents knew most of the people they received information about; they were in a position to evaluate its accuracy. And more often than not, sharing information fostered a closer sense of community. In their village, knowing that someone was ill, for example, allowed others to lend a hand. The utter absence of privacy was sometimes annoying; every small town had

its gossips and its ruined reputations. But social sanctions—all the more powerful because everybody know everybody else—generally kept people from misusing personal information.

By contrast, in today's data-rich environment where information is free-floating and widely available, there is no context. Information is open to interpretation without first-hand knowledge of the individuals involved. There are few sanctions—legal, social or otherwise—against abusing or exploiting it.

This is the crux of the problem. When we shop often at a particular Web site, we don't mind if that site gives us discounts because we are good customers—it's called rewarding loyalty. But we are outraged to learn that information about us can be used to determine our "price flexibility"—marketing jargon for the maximum amount we might pay for an item based on our previous buying behavior.

Where do we draw the line? In the U.S. Congress and in the states, lawmakers are looking for ways to protect consumers and help guide the collection and use of personal information online. There is general agreement that sensitive information—regarding our health, our finances, our children—is entitled to the highest degree of protection. New laws now govern all three of those areas. But even here, in an area that seems relatively straightforward, the devil is in the details. Recently, for example, I went looking on-line for asthma medicine for an ailing relative. I was confronted with a variety of banner ads selling asthma-related products and services. The ads were helpful. With a simple click, I found informational sites I didn't know existed. But, I wondered, what electronic tracks had I left behind me? The ads enhanced my ability to sort through an enormous amount of relevant and irrelevant information. I am comfortable with that. I will be much less comfortable if my search is associated with my name or used for purposes like marketing products that I don't want.

Who owns information? That is the heart of the matter. In the United States, federal law has little to say about information in the private sector, but there is a wealth of law on the books restricting the government's ability to gather and keep information about us. Perhaps because Americans long ago fought for their independence from a foreign government, Americans have never been shy about passing laws—in addition to the Fourth and Fifth Amendments to the Constitution—to protect us from unwarranted government intrusion into our personal lives.

Europeans have taken a different approach. For many years in most of Europe, a citizen was "entered on the government rolls" at birth to record his religion, register him in the health-care system and for voting later on. Europe evolved a set of rules allowing virtually unrestricted government use of such information. However, a much stricter set of rules than in America developed regarding corporate abuse of personal data. The differences between these two views of privacy have led to protracted negotiations over the last few years about the flow of personal information between Europe and the United States. The Europeans want to see if the privacy practices of U.S. companies adequately meet their expectations: they are offering "safe harbor" to companies that do. U.S. companies are now reviewing what sorts of privacy practices will satisfy Europe's stricter data-protection laws. What is at stake here is the disruption of the flow of information between Europe and the United States. Much remains unclear.

In the U.S. Congress and the state legislatures, two opposing forces are lining up for a fight. On the one hand, there are those who say the private sectors efforts to create a framework for protecting privacy have failed and congress must step in. Others argue that industry efforts are sufficient and oppose legislation of any kind. Both are missing the point.

The point, in the Information Age, is to give consumers the power to protect their privacy. Whether obtaining medical or financial information on the Net or buying the latest CD on-line, consumers are entitled to know that their personal interests are not being stored in someone else's data bank. In some instances, the answer may lie in privacy-enhancing technologies that allow us to surf the Web anonymously. In the end, there may be loopholes in existing laws that need to be closed or a lack of law that needs to be filled. Always, there is need for an educated public.

Too often the privacy debate has been polarized between those who wish to fully prohibit the use of personal information and those who wish to fully exploit it. Most of us have a foot in both camps: we welcome the marvelous benefits of information technology, but we have an equally powerful desire for personal privacy. Perhaps the most that can be hoped for is a modus vivendi not unlike that reached in my grandparent's village. They may have chafed sometimes at their lack of privacy, but it gave them a sense of belonging to a larger community —as long as it was not abused. Common sense, in the end prevailed. That is what we should aim for today as well.

Answer questions 1-8. Base your answers on the article "Death of Privacy."

1 What is the author's purpose in writing this article?

    A. to compare the global community to an Irish village

    B. to share ways to protect personal information on-line

    C. to ease fears about sharing personal information on-line

    D. to complain about the abuse of personal information by companies

2 How does the author feel about companies gathering personal information for marketing purposes?

    F. She is angered by it.

    G. She is flattered by it.

    H. She is surprised by it.

    I. She is encouraged by it.

3 What is the author's opinion of European privacy practices?

    A. She disapproves of their practice of recording people's religions.

    B. She approves of the social services provided by those governments.

    C. She thinks they do a better job of keeping personal information from government.

    D. She thinks they do a better job of protecting private information from corporations.

4 What does the following excerpt tell you about the author's point of view?

> **Too often the privacy debate has been polarized between those who wish to fully prohibit the use of personal information and those who wish to fully exploit it. Most of us have a foot in both camps: we welcome the marvelous benefits of information technology, but we have an equally powerful desire for personal privacy.**

    F. She feels the Internet is a great threat, and should be used with care.

    G. She believes there will never be a solution that makes everyone happy.

    H. She thinks the new technology is good, but wants to protect her privacy.

    I. She imagines that many new laws will be needed to protect personal privacy.

5 Which of the following can you infer from the passage about European citizens?

    A. They are distrustful of privacy-enhancing technology.

    B. They fear exchanging personal information with anyone.

    C. They are wary of exchanging information with the United States.

    D. They are fearful of giving their personal information to the government.

6 How does the author's comparison between privacy practices in Europe and in the United States support her point of view? Support your answer with details and information from the article.

_____

_____

_____

_____

_____

_____

_____

_____

_____

_____

_____

_____

_____

7 Which of the following is a solution suggested in the article?

    A. educate the public

    B. remove laws that do not work

    C. adopt European privacy practices

    D. ban the exchange of personal information

8 How does the information about life in an Irish village help achieve the author's purpose? Support your answer with details and information from the article.

_____

_____

_____

_____

_____

_____

_____

_____

_____

_____

_____

_____

Chapter five

Gathering, Analyzing, and Evaluating Information

Benchmark L.A.A. 2.4.4

Locates, gathers, analyzes and evaluates written information for a variety of purposes, including research projects, real-world tasks, and self-improvement. (Includes **LA.A. 2.4.6.** Selects and uses appropriate study and research skills and tools according to the type of information being gathered or organized, including almanacs, government publications, microfiche, news sources, and information services.)

When we think about doing *research,* we usually think about writing a research paper. But there are reasons other than making a good grade to gather information, analyze it, and even present it.

Suppose you wanted to find out what your mother was like when she was in high school. How would you get that information? You might ask her, and then maybe follow-up by asking your grandparents for a different viewpoint.

If you wanted to know how far away your pen pal lived, you could look up her hometown in an atlas. And to find out what time a certain movie is showing, you would look at the movie section of your newspaper or call the theater. Finding any amount of information, no matter how big or small, involves research.

What about a more complex research task, such as gathering information about a college or technical school you would like to attend? You could start by asking your school counselor for materials, or looking up the school on the Internet. You might write the school's admissions office for information or even visit the campus. Maybe you could talk to friends or family members who attended the school.

However you choose to *gather* the information, once you have what you are looking for you need to break it down into smaller parts or *analyze* it. It is important to look closely at the school's good and bad points, and *evaluate* the prospect of attending it. All of this would help you decide whether or not this school is a good place for you to continue your education.

Understanding the Benchmark

Try using some of the suggestions below to practice gathering and locating information. The more you practice researching, the more you will understand how it applies to the FCAT and other aspects of life.

- Pick your favorite band, actor, sports star or other celebrity. What can you find out about their experiences and how they shaped their lives? Where can you find the most accurate and current information?
- Compile a list of places in your area that offer activities for teenagers to take part in. Be sure to get pertinent information such as location, hours, and fees. Ask your friends to sample the activities and rate or review them.
- Find an issue that interests you in your local area and gather information on the views of politicians, neighbors, or friends regarding the issue.

Making the FCAT Connection

On the FCAT, this benchmark will test you by using text as well as graphs, charts, and diagrams. It will ask you to synthesize information from various graphical representations of information and the text that accompanies it in order to draw conclusions. You may also be asked to evaluate a piece of information, analyze the meaning of specific text, or determine details that can support a particular point of view.

Multiple-choice, short-response, and extended-response items from both informational and literary texts will be used to evaluate your understanding of this benchmark.

Taking a Closer Look

Doing a research project in high school requires you to use all the skills included in the benchmark described in this chapter. You first have to decide on and narrow a topic. Then you have to search a variety of sources for the information. You need to ask yourself if the information you find is reliable and up-to-date, providing relevant information for your topic. Finally, you have to organize the information into the final product—your research paper.

The chart below will provide you with the information you need to begin critically evaluating sources you use. Once you have done research, the next step involves thinking about how reliable your sources are. Always keep in mind where a reading selection is from. This information will help you evaluate how current (up-to-date), biased (pushing one side of an argument or opinion), or complete a source is or is not.

SOURCES	QUESTIONS TO ASK ABOUT SOURCES
Library Reference Materials **Textbooks** **Internet Sources** **Magazines** **Newspapers**	Is it up-to-date? Is it objective—that is, factual rather than an author's opinion? Is it complete or only a brief excerpt on a topic? Is it credible, from a reliable source? Is it first-hand information?

Did the questions listed in the chart help you to see how a source can affect the information it contains? For example, a reference book published in 1980 might provide accurate information, and be objective in its viewpoint. But, how likely would it be to contain *current information*?

While some research might not require current facts, if you were trying to write about a subject like technology, you would need to find the most up-to-date sources possible.

When you are conducting research, it is essential that you use this kind of critical thinking to evaluate the appropriateness of your sources. Because this is an important skill for school, daily life, the workplace, and beyond, the FCAT assesses ability to locate, gather, and evaluate sources as they relate to a specific task or subject.

FCAT EXTRA!

Many of the extended- and short-response questions will ask for information that is located in different parts of the text. After you have read the questions, go back and underline any part of a passage that you think will help you write your answer. Always look for important details that can be used to support your answers.

The following is a passage from an Internet source containing information on fossil fuels.

Fossil Fuels—Heat From Prehistory

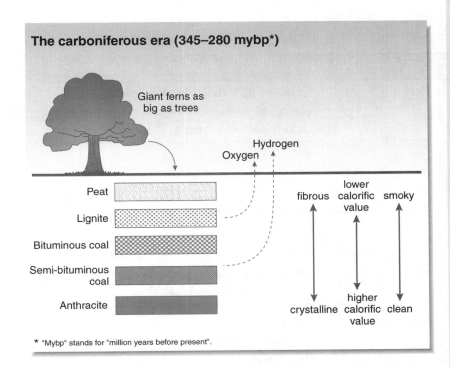

In the carboniferous era, most of Britain was tropical and swampy. Enormous primitive fern forests covered large parts of the land. As the ferns died and new ones grew, the dead ones formed layers of slowly rotting vegetable matter. New layers fell and compressed the old ones. As the millennia went by, thick deposits built up. Although five distinct layers are shown in the diagram, in reality it is a continuous spectrum as one merges into the other.

Plant material is made from carbon dioxide and water. Water itself is made up from hydrogen and oxygen. So the main three elements in newly dead plants are carbon, hydrogen, and oxygen, which can be combined into carbohydrates. Peat contains carbohydrates. As time goes by, oxygen leeches out and the material left becomes hydrocarbons. Lignite, bituminous coal and semi-bituminous coal consist of varying amounts of hydrocarbons. Eventually, the hydrogen leeches out and leaves behind carbon. Anthracite is almost pure carbon.

Predict:
Look at the graph, chart, and titles for ideas about what the selection will be about.

Evaluate:
What is the source of this article?

Analyze:
How is this information organized?

Most of the coal in Britain is bituminous and semi-bituminous. Wales has a good supply of anthracite. There is very little lignite in Britain, but it is found extensively in Eastern Europe.

The chart below shows three qualities of the fossil fuel types. Generally speaking, anthracite contains more heat per weight, and smokes less, than coal, lignite, or peat.

NATURAL FOSSIL FUELS		
SMOKY	Peat	Contains 80% moisture. Removal causes ecological damage to wildlife environments. Usually sold in blocks.
	Lignite (brown coal)	Rare in UK, common in Eastern Europe.
	Bituminous coal	Widely sold in Britain. OK for open or enclosed fires.
SMOKELESS	Semi-bituminous coal.	Known as "low volatile" or "dry steam" coal Some grades are smokeless. OK for open or enclosed fires.
	Anthracite	Almost pure carbon. Best in a stove—very few open fires can provide enough draught. Dense and slow burning.

Now answer the questions that follow.

1. How did the foliage in Great Britain contribute to fossil fuels present there today?

_____

_____

_____

_____

_____

_____

_____

Restate:
How can I put this in my own words?

Compare/Contrast:
This graph compares various fuels.

2. Which fossil fuel produces the most heat?

    A. peat

    B. lignite

    C. anthracite

    D. bituminous coal

See how you did by checking your answers below.

A top-scoring response for question one would begin with a sentence directly responding to the question. At least two details from the text, supporting your answer, should follow. Below is an example of a top-scoring response:

The foilage in Great Britain contributed greatly to the fossil fuels found there today. In prehistoric time, Britain was tropical and covered with huge fern forests. As the ferns died and rotted, they formed layers of compressed earth. The elements of the decaying plants are carbon, hydrogen, and oxygen. These elements escape gradually and leave behind different types of fuel.

For the second question, C is the correct answer. By analyzing the diagram we can see that anthracite has the highest calorific (heat) value. The text provides additional information, stating that anthracite contains more heat per weight than the other fuels discussed.

When reading fiction, you will need to use the same active reading strategies you have used with non-fiction selections. Look for main ideas and organizational patterns, and evaluate the information presented in those selections. Keep an eye out for photos, captions, or other graphical representations of information that are important when answering questions.

The following section includes reading selections that are similar to passages on the FCAT. Remember to stay actively involved while you read, using the reading strategies from this and previous chapters of the book.

Read the articles "Sea Turtles" and "Conservation—Threats to Sea Turtle Survival" before answering Numbers 1 through 6.

Sea Turtles

From *Marine Reptiles and Birds*

Of all the marine reptiles, the sea turtle is the most widely distributed. Sea turtles inhabit tropical and warm temperate oceans around the world. Along with freshwater turtles and land-dwelling tortoises, sea turtles belong to the order Chelonia. There are six species of marine turtles, and all are endangered: the hawksbill, leatherback, loggerhead, green sea turtle, and Pacific, or olive, ridley. The different sea turtle species can be distinguished from one another by their size and by the pattern of scales on their top shell, or carapace. All marine turtles have a hard carapace, except for the leatherback, whose top shell, as its name implies, is leathery in texture. In addition, the leatherback is the only sea turtle whose carapace is not fused to its backbone.

Sea turtles are born on land but spend their lives at sea. The mature sea turtles return every few years to the beaches on which they were born to mate and lay their eggs. Mating occurs in shallow off-shore water. (It is thought that the female stores the sperm from these matings to fertilize the eggs she will lay two or three years later.) After mating, the female turtle swims to the shore and during the night, emerges onto the beach. The flippers, which are adapted for swimming, cannot support the turtle's weight. So, using her hind limbs and forelimbs, the sea turtle drags herself up the slope of the sandy beach to find a nesting site above the high tide mark.

At the nesting site, the turtle first uses all four limbs to dig a depression in the sand; then she uses her hind limbs to scoop out a hole about 39 to 60 centimeters deep. Into this hole the sea turtle lays about 100 fertilized leathery eggs that look like ping-pong balls. The female fills in the hole with sand and then heads back down the beach to the water, where she mates again. Over the next few weeks, the female will come ashore four or five more times to lay several hundred more eggs.

While buried in the sand the eggs are kept warm and moist and protected from such predators as raccoons, gulls, and rats. The embryos develop inside the leathery eggs for about two months. Interestingly, the sex of a sea turtle is determined by the position, and resulting temperature, of its eggs within the nest. Sea turtle eggs that develop at about 28°C and below become males; those that develop at 30°C and above become females. After their development is completed, the baby turtles, called hatchlings, break through their shells and dig their way to the surface. Hatchlings usually emerge before dawn and are unprotected; they must quickly wiggle down to the sea. At this stage, they are vulnerable to predation by gulls and large fish.

Where do the hatchlings go after they enter the ocean? Marine biologists have been studying the

Ranger holds olive ridley sea turtle hatchlings.

migrations of sea turtles for a number of years. The green sea turtle, which lives in both the Atlantic and Pacific oceans, breeds every two to three years. One of the breeding grounds is Ascension Island. This tiny island, just 8 kilometers long, is located in the middle of the Atlantic Ocean, midway between South America and Africa. In one turtle study, young hatchlings were tagged on Ascension Island and then recaptured in the coastal waters of Brazil. Apparently, the young turtles were able to make this long journey by hitching a ride on clumps of seaweed that float on the South Equatorial Current, a large ocean current that moves across the Atlantic Ocean from east to west. In addition, it is thought that sea turtles may be sensitive to magnetic fields and rely on them during their migrations.

The green sea turtles had migrated to Brazil to feed on the turtle and eel grasses that grow abundantly in the shallow water. Mature turtles were also tagged in Brazil, and some of these turtles were later recovered on Ascension Island, where they nest. Marine biologists are not sure of the exact

route taken by these turtles on their return to Ascension Island. More accurate methods are now being used to track these animals. Radio transmitters, mounted on the backs of some turtles, emit signals that can pinpoint their exact location.

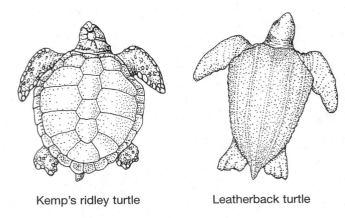

Kemp's ridley turtle   Leatherback turtle

Figure 1   Two types of sea turtles

Conservation—Threats to Sea Turtle Survival

Mature sea turtles have few natural enemies. The hard carapace (or, in the case of the leatherback, its huge size) affords most marine turtles sufficient protection. The tiger shark is probably the most dangerous predator on sea turtles. However, sea turtles do face other threats to their survival—most of them caused by people.

Sea turtles sometimes choke on garbage such as plastic bags, which they mistake for jellyfish. They also die when they are caught in the nets of shrimp trawlers; special devices have been installed on some boats to prevent such accidents. Sea turtle eggs are eaten by other animals and people, and the nesting female turtles are sometimes killed by people to make steaks, soup, and other products. Turtle shells are used to make jewelry and other items for tourists in the Caribbean. And important nesting sites have been lost to development as valuable beachfront property.

Now that people are more aware of these threats, nesting sites are being protected and the collection of eggs is either outlawed or regulated to ensure the survival of sea turtles. In an innovative approach to sea turtle conservation, the residents of the town of Ostional, Costa Rica, work together with scientists and government officials to protect the future of the olive ridley turtles that nest on their shores. The local people legally harvest a limited number of turtle eggs (about 10% of the eggs laid), while they protect the nesting adult turtles and their hatchlings. As a result, the survival rate for hatchlings at Ostional's beach is several times greater than that of turtles at other nesting sites. The sale of the turtle eggs brings money that helps the locals improve their standard of living, while it decreases potential sales for poachers who illegally harvest turtle eggs on other Costa Rican beaches.

Answer questions 1 through 6. Base your answers on the articles "Sea Turtles" and "Conservation—Threats to Sea Turtle Survival."

1 According to the information in both articles, what poses the greatest threat to sea turtles?

   A. humans
   B. low tides
   C. crowded beaches
   D. natural predators

2 What determines the sex of the sea turtle?

   F. the nesting site
   G. the location of the eggs
   H. the temperature of the sand
   I. the number of eggs in a nest

3 READ THINK EXPLAIN   How does the leatherback differ from other sea turtles? Use details and information from the first article to support your answer.

_____

_____

_____

_____

_____

_____

_____

4 The turtles' flippers have what two important functions?

   A. mating and swimming
   B. digging and swimming
   C. swimming and migrating
   D. trapping prey and digging

5 READ THINK EXPLAIN   Explain how people have contributed to the sea turtles endangered status. Support your answer with details and information from the articles.

_____

_____

_____

_____

_____

_____

_____

_____

6 READ THINK EXPLAIN   If you were an environmentalist, how would you use the information about Ostional to set up successful programs to save sea turtles? Use details and information from the articles to support your answer.

_____

_____

_____

_____

_____

_____

_____

_____

_____

_____

_____

_____

Read the article "Pushing the Envelope" before answering Numbers 1 through 7.

Pushing the Envelope

By Michael Kernan

At the National Postal Museum, envelopes are as critical a part of history as the letters inside

A painting by Dutch still-life painter Cornelius Norbertus Gysbrechts (1610–1675) depicting letters and envelopes from the sixteenth century.

In reading the various newsletters and calendars published by the Smithsonian, I have decided that the Institution is rather like Cairo: you can find just about anything there.

I see that one Maynard Benjamin gave a slide lecture on the history of envelopes at the National Postal Museum recently. He has also written a book on the subject, and he signed copies after the lecture, held in conjunction with two Postal Museum shows, "Undercover: The Evolution of the American Envelope" and "The Graceful Envelope," featuring beautifully handcrafted works by designers and calligraphers from around the world. The Postal Museum is one of my favorites, if only for the architecture—it's in the magnificent 1914 Washington City Post Office Building, right next to the equally grand 1908 Union Station.

Benjamin is a stamp collector with a special interest in the Civil War, which is why he belongs to the Confederate Stamp Alliance. He lives in Alexandria, Virginia, and he happens to be the president of the Envelope Manufacturers Association.

According to Benjamin, it was the Babylonians who first thought of enclosing clay tablets in clay "envelopes" baked hard around their contents.

I'm going to have to slip off the track here, already. It seems to me that the envelope must have been invented by that mythic emperor who wrote a message on the shaved pate of a slave, let the hair regrow, and sent the man to his destination to be shaved anew and read. The only drawback with this ingenious plan is that the message had better not be terribly urgent.

"No one knows when envelopes came to China," Benjamin announced, "but we do know that by 1200 B.C. the Chinese had developed a crude form of paper made from reeds and rice." Presumably, they would protect the letter with a paper casing. The ancient Egyptians protected missives by rolling up the papyrus scrolls. Because paper was so expensive, for many centuries letters were usually just folded, sealed and sent that way. But by the 17th century separate envelopes appeared in Spain and France.

And what a relief that must have been. We have some English friends who still insist on using those tissue-paper aerograms dating from the 1930s. You write the letter, fold it, lick some gummed flaps, and suddenly your letter has turned itself into an envelope.

The trouble is, our friends keep having afterthoughts, and they write all over the margins. No matter how carefully we cut open the flaps, we lose vital information. As in, "Yes we'd love to have you visit, but we'll be out of town after the first of..."

The early envelopes were often sealed to prevent the wrong people from reading them. For a really important letter a gallows mark could be put on the cover, meaning that it had to be delivered under pain of death.

That seems to me an empty threat. If you didn't receive it, how would you know? And since letters sometimes took months to deliver, the derelict postman would have absconded long since, anyway. Benjamin explains that you might actually have been able to trace it, as each wayside kept a record of passage.

It was Louis XIV of France, that master of the dramatic flourish, who popularized the use of a cover to ensure the privacy of letters, according to Benjamin. Louis had his secretary cut out forms with a template and fold and paste them to make envelopes for his communications to his court.

In America, Benjamin Franklin is known as the father of our postal service, hiring on in 1737 under the postmaster general for the Colonies. Franklin organized distribution, designed pigeonholes for collecting letters that were bound for the same place, and set milestones along the post roads, for in those days postmen were paid by the mile. It cost Samuel Adams, for instance, 11 pence in 1775 to send a letter from Boston to Philadelphia.

It is all too easy to veer off into a discussion of stamps here, or of the letters themselves, but I am determined to concentrate on the subject at hand. It just occurred to me: letter writing is coming back these days via e-mail and faxes, but what about the envelopes? In the virtual world, free of floods, fire, and puppies, there is no need to protect your letter from damage. Benjamin notes, however, that most people still prefer the esthetic advantages of paper for personal letters and resumes.

Of course, in the days of the Pony Express, letters needed

special protection. Already enveloped, they were then wrapped in oil silk and stuck into the four pockets of the mochila, a leather sling that fit over the saddle.

At that, the letters were still in for a rough ride. In 1860, "Pony Bob" Haslam, galloping up to an outpost on his exhausted horse, found it a smoldering ruin, the stationmaster killed and the spare horses stolen. Bob had to ride on, covering 120 miles in eight hours and ten minutes. When he reached safety he said he was a little tired.

As an ad for riders put it, "Wanted: Young, skinny, wiry fellows not over 18, must be expert riders, willing to risk death daily. Orphans preferred."

By the early years of Queen Victoria's reign the Mulready envelope had appeared in England, "the first prepaid postal wrapper and the grandfather of the modern envelope," Benjamin says. Soon, volume increased at a tremendous rate, and machines to make envelopes were invented. Mail service in Britain was a wonder of the world.

Even in the 1960s, living in London, I could mail a note in the morning from Earl's Court to a friend in Highgate and get a reply in the afternoon delivery on the same day. Benjamin explains that London has an automated subway system just for mail—trains zip letters around the city.

The French also developed a foot-powered envelope-making machine, the Rabbate, turning out more than 100 pieces an hour. The development of envelope-making machinery led to mass production; that and postal reform made postage affordable to everyone. Manufacturers still did not turn out enough envelopes, though, and many people persisted in just folding up their letters and sending them uncovered. One reason for the holdup was that the gum was still being applied by hand. Eventually, drying machines, like the Arnold Drying Chain, solved that problem. Later, geniuses even invented ways to vary the sizes of the envelopes in production.

A Nineteenth century letter with wax seal.

During the Civil War the Confederates had trouble getting paper for envelopes, which they had always imported from the North from England. When the blockade tightened they had to use wallpaper and book pages and other papers, all of which today are valued by collectors. Sometimes envelopes would be turned inside out for reuse. Handmade or not, some covers were used by both sides in the war for incidental propaganda, with patriotic slogans and drawings covering much of the face. Even before the war, merchants had begun putting their ads on envelopes.

Envelope decoration had a history of excess. In 1840, the British government offered a prize for the best designed prepaid envelope. William Mulready's winning design showed Britannia, the British lion and figures representing the farthest corners of the empire. With a massive Maltese-cross cancellation mark, it made an impressive collector's item, but the small blank space left for the name and address must have been a pest for the mailman to read.

Speaking of collector's items, there are many in the "Graceful Envelope" show, a result of the Postal Museum's third annual envelope-design contest. Usually the graphics and calligraphy are coordinated with certain commemorative stamps. On one envelope with a Paul Bunyan stamp, the artist has drawn a full figure of the giant to match, and attached a smaller crumpled envelope next to him. Hands out and leaning into the job, Paul is, of course, pushing the envelope.

Benjamin's book about envelopes chronicles the work of men like Ferdinand Ludwig Smithe, the Henry Ford of envelopes, and recounts the development of the Keating Adjustable Bed, the Arnold Drying Chain and the Smithe Plunger. I had no idea envelopes took so much manufacturing. But since this is the postindustrial age, there is now available on the market a kit with which you can make your own envelopes.

I've said it before and I'll say it again: this country is moving backward, and I don't like it one bit.

Answer questions 1 through 7. Base your answers on the article "Pushing the Envelope."

1 What is the author's purpose in writing this article?

    A. to relate the history of envelopes

    B. to tell the history of the postal service

    C. to explain the popularity of envelope collecting

    D. to compare postal delivery methods of different countries

2 Who is Maynard Benjamin?

    F. the inventor of the envelope

    G. the father of the U.S. postal service

    H. the author of a book about envelopes

    I. the manufacturer of prepaid envelopes

3 What is the most likely reason the "mythic emperor" wrote a message on a slave's shaved head?

    A. to keep the slave from reading the message

    B. so that the emperor would not have to pay postage

    C. so that the message could not be lost along the way

    D. to keep the message hidden until it reached its destination

4 Who were the first people to come up with the idea of using envelopes?

　F. the French
　G. the Spanish
　H. the Chinese
　I. the Babylonians

5 Which of the following were used by Southerners to make envelopes during the Civil War?

　A. tree bark
　B. wallpaper
　C. paper money
　D. magazine pages

6 READ THINK EXPLAIN　What is the main reason people use envelopes when they send letters? For what other purposes have people used envelopes? Support your answer with details and information from the article.

7 READ THINK EXPLAIN — What are some of the ways people made sure their letters were kept private and delivered? Support your answer with details and information from the article.

_____

_____

_____

_____

_____

_____

_____

_____

_____

_____

_____

Read the article "China" before answering Numbers 1 through 6.

China

From *Global History*

During the 1990s, China's economy moved toward a type of free-market system. But its central government continued to rule repressively. It blocked the inflow of new ideas by censorship and effective propaganda. It also kept opposition quiet with the threat of prison labor camps.

Continued Repression. The 1989 massacre in Tiananmen Square had provoked international outrage. Nevertheless, Deng Xiaoping, China's senior leader, tightened control over cultural and media activities. The Communist Party officials wanted to discourage further demands for democracy. Deng also allowed the torture of political suspects until they confessed and informed on their associates. Deng's policies reflected his belief that the people would continue to accept Communist rule as long as their standard of living kept rising and the country's economic growth persisted.

MFN Status. In May 1993, President Bill Clinton signed an executive order stating the improvements that he wanted China to make in the area of human rights before he would renew its trade benefits. Since the 1970s, China has enjoyed "most favored nation" (MFN) status. This has allowed China to send its products to the United States at the lowest available tariff. MFN status must be renewed annually.

Clinton's order called for China to stop using prison labor to make goods exported to the United States. It also required China to allow certain dissidents (opposition leaders) and their families to leave the country.

The presidential order touched off a debate within the administration and in Congress. Some leaders wanted the

president to stand by his executive order. Others argued that withdrawal of China's trade benefits would cost thousands of American jobs and billions of dollars in contracts. They claimed that trade had become an important instrument for opening up Chinese society and for promoting the rule of law and freedom of movement in that country. Trade was also viewed as a means of encouraging the Chinese government to allow its citizens to acquire a wide variety of products, including satellite dishes and foreign newspapers.

In May 1994, President Clinton decided unconditionally to renew China's MFN status. U.S.-Chinese relations remained uneasy, especially after the fall of 1996, when the Chinese sentenced a young dissident to long-term imprisonment for his democratic views.

Jiang's Visit to the United States. By 1997, relations between China and the United States had improved somewhat. Deng died in February. A new president, Jiang Zemin, continued Deng's economic policies and curbs on human rights. But he wanted to have good relations with the United States for economic reasons. Jiang visited the United States in

Soldiers walk along the Great Wall in China.

October. It was the first official visit by a Chinese leader since 1985.

Jiang and Clinton pledged to discuss differences on human rights. He claimed that China had already begun to control the export of nuclear and nuclear-related materials and would strengthen these controls in upcoming years. He also objected to U.S. interference in the internal affairs of China.

While Jiang was in the United States, U.S. officials told him that President Clinton would be unable to return the visit in 1998 if leading political dissidents were still in prison. In November 1997, the Chinese released Wei Jingsheng, one of China's most influential dissidents. Clinton did visit China in June 1998. In televised speeches, he urged more liberal human rights policies. He also renewed China's MFN status before the visit. Many in the United States had urged him not to do so.

Military. China's military policies disturbed U.S. leaders. Determined to be the dominant military power in East Asia, China used some of its new

wealth to build up its naval and air forces. U.S. strategists saw the Chinese buildup as a challenge to U.S. and Japanese interests in the region. The United States was one of many nations that protested Chinese underground nuclear tests in the mid-1990s.

Population Curbs. China's population-control policies also drew U.S. protests. With about 1.2 billion people, China has the largest population of any country in the world. The government strongly encourages only one child per couple, hoping to bring about a population decline in the 21st Century. The United States denounced China's use of harsh methods to enforce birth control, including compulsory sterilization, forced abortions, and fines for unauthorized pregnancies.

Under a so-called responsibility system, local officials were held accountable for meeting family planning targets in their districts. As a result, the birthrate dropped drastically. Government planners achieved goals they had not expected to reach until the year 2010.

China's Foreign Trade in the 1990s

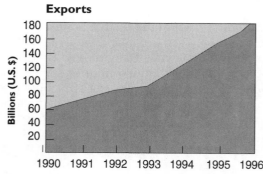

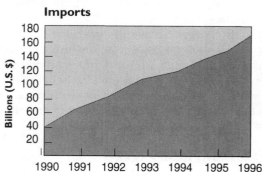

Answer questions 1 through 6. Base your answers on the article "China."

1 Which statement best describes the treatment of Chinese people by the government in China in 1989?

A. The government asked people to analyze Communist ideals.

B. The government encouraged business owners to compete openly.

C. The government offered the people the right to personal freedoms.

D. The government restricted voice in government and personal choice.

2 What is China's policy regarding population control?

F. They no longer have a position on family planning.

G. The government asks that couples have only one child.

H. The government urges its people to have large families.

I. Citizens are free to decide how many children they will have.

3 Why did Chinese leaders believe that people would accept Communist rule?

A. They believed people had no desire to oppose the government.

B. They believed people were interested in becoming a strong military force in Asia.

C. They believed people were satisfied because their standard of living kept improving.

D. They believed people were committed to zero-population growth in the 21st century.

4 Which statement best describes China's foreign trade in the 1990s?

F. China's imports exceeded their exports in billions of dollars.

G. In 1990, China's imports and exports totaled over $100 billion.

H. The U.S. permanently canceled China's MFN status in trading in 1993.

I. China's imports declined while exports continued to rise from 1990–1996.

5 READ THINK EXPLAIN How did the relations of the United States and China change during the late 1990s? Use details and information from the article to support your answer.

6 If you were a reporter who attended the meeting between Jiang Zemin and President Clinton in 1997, how would you report what the leaders discussed? Use details and information from the article to support your answer.

C h a p t e r   s i x

Analyzing Primary Source Information

Benchmark LA.A. 2.4.7

Analyzes the validity and reliability of primary source information and uses the information appropriately

Have you ever read a survey that gives you frightening statistics about a topic? Certainly you have seen information on the harmful effects smoking has on your health. You are probably well aware that excessive building in areas that were once part of the Everglades endangers the environment. Where does that information come from and how do people use the information? As a critical reader, you will need to determine if the information you read is accurate and dependable. Often the source of the information can help you determine how believable it is.

Throughout most of your high school career, you will be asked to use *primary source information* in your research. Do you know what that means? Primary source information is firsthand information that comes from a reliable or trusted source. Information from different sources may appear to be the same but most often are not. If you are going to use information you gather to write a report or present an argument, you must be sure the information you use is correct, current, and reliable.

Understanding the Benchmark

Try using some of the suggestions below to help you identify primary sources of information. If you keep an eye out for primary sources everyday, you'll be a whiz at spotting them on the FCAT.

- Look at magazine articles and analyze the information. How much of it is purely informational and how much is opinion?
- Read newspaper articles in the front section of the newspaper and compare them to the articles and letters in the editorial section. What makes them different?
- Check the bibliographies in the back of biographies. If possible, find the materials and compare them to the relevant section of the biography.

Making the FCAT Connection

You will be tested over this benchmark through the use of informational texts. You will probably see two or more passages on related topics that contain statistics, graphs, maps or charts. It is important that you are able to make connections between what you read and the graphs, maps or charts that accompany the article. Many times, you will be asked to use the information to suggest a change, explain an author's position, or present an argument.

In short, you will be expected to:

- look at primary source information
- decide if it is valid (correct) and reliable (dependable)
- use the information for a purpose

Multiple-choice, short-response, and extended-response items from informational texts will assess this benchmark. There will be no questions over literary texts testing this benchmark.

Taking a Closer Look

Here is a brief list of examples of primary sources:

- Original documents such as the US Constitution
- Letters written by people throughout history
- Survey results
- Interviews
- Your observation of an event

How can you know if information you encounter is really first hand? Becoming familiar with *secondary sources* will help you differentiate between a primary and secondary source. A secondary source is one containing information that has been gathered and interpreted. When you read a history textbook you are reading information that someone has derived from primary source information such as original documents or letters.

Look at the following list of sources. Which is likely to be a primary or secondary source? In the space provided, write what you think the source information is. The first ones have been filled in for you.

Interview with Alonso Morning	*Primary Source*
An article about professional basketball players	*Secondary Source*
Diary of a civil war soldier	_____
A review of a best-selling book	_____
A history of Ancient Egypt	_____
Classified ads from a newspaper	_____
Your notes from attending a lecture	_____
Video from the front lines of a war	_____
A biography of Madame Curie	_____
Network Broadcast of a Congressional Hearing	_____

Now come up with some primary and secondary source examples of your own.

Use the table below to chart some examples of primary and secondary sources of information.

Primary Source	Secondary Source

In the last chapter, you reviewed important information about deciding if a source is reliable or not. Revisit that chart to review the important key questions to ask yourself about any source you go to for information. Remember to be critical of not only the information you read, but the source that the information comes from.

If a question seems too difficult, skip it and move on to other questions for that reading. After you finish answering the remaining questions, return to the one you skipped. Sometimes later questions and answers give you the insight needed to answer more difficult questions you may have skipped.

Use the reading strategies from this and previous chapters to help you read the selection below.

Does Modern Society Make Us Fat?
by Tracy Boyd

All that great time-saving technology has created a more sedentary lifestyle.

Dr. Carl Karoub remembers with affection the winters of his childhood in Highland Park. "When we were kids, we'd spend Saturdays walking up and down Woodard, looking in stores, going in and out of the cold," recalls Karoub, an internist with William Beaumont Hospital. "That's walking about five miles in the cold. There were no electric defrosters, so we'd have to scrape the windshields. We shoveled snow. We huddled in the back seat of the car and froze, because there was no heat back there."

Today, he laments, technological wonders like the automobile, computer and video games, snow throwers, and riding lawn mowers mean less activity for everyone.

"We have become a mechanized society, and it's killing us," he says.

Inventions certainly offer us convenience and extra time. But these labor-saving devices have helped to push fitness out of our everyday lives—making us more sedentary and contributing to the fattest America in history. This combination of inactivity and obesity leaves us at extreme risk for conditions like diabetes, high blood pressure, heart disease, stroke, and joint problems.

Though some people blame our Western diet laden in fat and carbohydrates for the dramatic rise in obesity rates in this country, scientists say that our dreadful eating habits are really only a small part of the problem.

"Lots of folks believe that we're not really taking in all that many more calories over the last 20 years," says Dr. Jody Wilkinson, a research physician with Cooper Institute in Dallas who studies fitness and exercise. "Perhaps we're consuming an extra 100 calories a day, but we may be burning off 500 calories less per day."

The majority of those calories we don't burn off through exercise come from the big things we're not doing. Not mowing the lawn and raking the grass clippings for five or six hours every weekend means we don't burn those 600-800 calories. Hiring someone to clear the snow means we're missing out on 300-400 calories an hour.

Predict:
Examine the title and subtitle for hints about the content of the article.

Context Clues:
Use context and vocabulary strategies to decipher the meaning of words like *sedentary*.

Analyze:
What is the main idea of this article?

Vocabulary:
Simplify difficult words by finding a word or phrase that conveys the same idea.

"Today's woman goes to the local gym and jogs twice a week for 30 minutes and does weight training. Her grandmother scrubbed laundry by hand in a tub, rung it out with a ringer, carried it outside, put the heavy, soaking stuff on the line, then took it down again and folded it. If you asked today's so-called fit woman to do that she'd probably fall over," Karoub says. Such an afternoon of doing laundry that way probably burned between 600 and 800 calories, Karoub says. Assuming that laundry was done twice a week, our grandmothers burned more calories in one week than many of today's women do in one month.

So, what can you do?

Simple: Start doing things the old-fashioned way again. "Don't circle the mall 37 times looking for the closest spot," Karoub implores. Take a farther spot and walk. Spend time outside when it's cold out, forcing our body to stay at 98.6 degrees when it's zero degrees outside burns 50 percent more calories.

Stand up as much as possible, like our fathers did. That burns 20 percent more calories. It can even be as simple as walking. Walk outdoors instead of on a treadmill. Not only will you burn more calories as your body is forced to keep its temperature steady in hot or cold weather, but it's psychologically rewarding.

Taking care of household tasks, playing with the kids, and yard work can burn a considerable amount of calories. Here are the number of calories a 155-pound person can burn in an hour during various activities. If you weigh less, you'll burn fewer; if you weigh more, you'll burn more.

Activity	Calories burned
General carpentry	246
Dressing and/or feeding child while sitting	211
Dressing and/or feeding child while standing	246
Heavy cleaning with vigorous effort	317
General house cleaning	246
Light cleaning and moderate effort	176
Cooking or preparing food	176
Electrical or plumbing work	246
Milking by hand	211
General gardening	352
Golfing, carrying clubs	387
Miniature golf or driving range	211
Golfing, pulling clubs	352
Golfing, using power cart	246
Moving boxes/household items upstairs	633
Mowing lawn	387
Mowing lawn with riding mower	176
Painting, plastering, scraping, papering	317
Pushing child in stroller	176

Summarize:
The end of a large section is a good place to stop and summarize ideas.

Predict:
Try to guess what the end of the article will be about.

Research:
How does this chart help support the article?

After reading this selection, ask yourself: What parts of this article represent direct, primary information? What parts contain more opinion than fact?

Now answer the questions that follow.

1. Which factor contributes most to Americans' obesity?

    A. Americans eat more fattening food today than in the past.

    B. Adults today work and exercise indoors, thus burning fewer calories.

    C. Workouts on treadmills burn fewer calories than running outside.

    D. Technology has taken the place of most physical work in daily activities.

2. How would you support the argument that a person needs to exercise rather than diet to lose weight?

_____

_____

_____

_____

_____

_____

_____

_____

Check your answers below.

For the first question, D is the best answer. The main idea of the article is that modern technology causes people to burn fewer calories in every day activities. While the other answer choices were included in the article, they represented *supporting details* and not the main idea.

A top-scoring response to the second question would begin with an overall statement that answers the question. At least two supporting details taken from the text should follow. An example is found below:

People today have sedentary lifestyles and use very few calories in daily activity. Even though people are only consuming about 100 calories more per day, they are not burning as many calories through work as people did in the past. Therefore, scientists feel obesity is due in part to lack of exercise. For example, people may not burn off as many as 800 calories a week simply because they no longer cut their own lawns.

The following section includes reading selections that are similar to passages on the FCAT. Remember to stay actively involved while you read, using the reading strategies from this and previous chapters of the book.

Read the article "Nature's Classroom" and answer Numbers 1 through 8.

Nature's Classroom

By Gary Turbak

This year, take a learning vacation in Yellowstone National Park

Look. Quick. Red-Faced Baby Coots. Wow! This is better than seeing bears." This statement, uttered in the heart of Yellowstone National Park, bordered on sacrilege, but no one in John Martin's bird-watching class protested. Most of us were too busy focusing binoculars on the striking infant chicks swimming 150 yards away. In two days, we 13 amateur birders, under Martin's expert tutelage, matched more than 75 avian names and faces—many of us seeing peregrine falcons, ospreys, and sandhill cranes for the first time ever.

Birding is just one of many educational classes conducted by the Yellowstone Institute in this Rocky Mountain nature and wildlife mecca. You can learn about wolves, wildflowers, fly-fishing, grizzlies, bison, photography, the biology of fire, using map and compass, fossils, and much more. Most of the Institute's 125 classes run from two to five days. Some are designed for family participation. Many may be taken for college credit. "We try to cover the gamut of what Yellowstone has to offer," says Institute Manager Pam Gontz, "and having a lot of diversity allows most people to find a class or two that interest them." Naturally, one of the chief interests is wildlife—and the excitement the animals sometimes provide. While peering through binoculars at the distant slopes of Yellowstone's Antelope Valley for bears, one class turned around to find a female grizzly and her two cubs six feet behind them. After studying the startled humans for a moment, the bear family departed. They did not appear to be part of any organized people-watching class.

On another occasion, students watched in awe as a wolf pack battled a grizzly over an elk carcass. Initially, griz held the prize, but when the wolves nipped at the bear's rear, the bruin gave chase, and the canids took over the kill. Before long, the larger grizzly reclaimed the carcass—only to lose it again. The dispute raged for more than an hour until a stalemate ensued.

The Institute is one of several education endeavors of the 10,000-member Yellowstone Association, a private non-profit group. "The Institute picks up where the National Park Service's interpretive program leaves off," says Jeff Brown, the association's director of educational operations. "Our goal is to give people an in-depth look at Yellowstone's natural and cultural history." Long term, the association hopes to foster a permanent Yellowstone constituency. "Many people who take our courses become life-long supporters of the park," says Brown.

Some of the classes will take you to far-flung corners of the park, while others unfold near one of Yellowstone's lodges—for those who prefer amenities such as private rooms. About half of the courses are based at the rustic Lamar Buffalo Ranch

Grizzly bear mother and her cubs cool-off in a nearby river.

Entrance to Yellowstone National Park.

campus situated along the all-weather highway between Mammoth and Cooke City, Montana. In 1907, the National Park Service established this little outpost ranch to raise buffalo (bison) for replenishing North America's dwindling herds. Bison husbandry ceased here in the 1950's (Yellowstone's 2,500 bison now roam free), and in 1979 the Institute adopted the ranch as its campus.

The former bunkhouse is now the campus hub, where participants attend classes, cook their own meals, and shower after a long day afield. Nearby are 16 spartan but comfortable log cabins, where students stay overnight in groups of two or three. Cabin appointments include bunk beds, reading lights, a chair, and not much more. Electricity comes from a generator, and power-hungry appliances such as TV's and hair dryers are prohibited. The nearest plumbing is in the bunkhouse. Most classes are held during the summer, but the heated and insulated cabins make this a year-round program.

In the wilds of Yellowstone, amenities seem almost superfluous, and the let's-rough-it ambiance adds to the Institute's allure. The entire facility—from director to instructors to volunteers—is relaxed and friendly. Class size rarely exceeds ten to 15 participants, making it easy to learn names and make new friends. "It's fun meeting people who share your interests," says student Molly Baxter, "and the relaxed atmosphere is like a summer camp for adults." Many of the 1,200 or so people who take Institute classes each year are returns—often many times over.

The surrounding Lamar Valley, sometimes called the Serengeti of North America, abounds in wildlife and serves as a glorious backdrop for learning. Our birding class naturally concentrated on feathered fauna, but during our stay my wife and I also saw black bears, coyotes, elk, moose, and pronghorns. The nonavian highlight, though, was the two wolves that strutted through a meadow one evening as though they owned the place—which, in a sense, they do. Or perhaps it was the bull bison that spent most of one day snoozing among the Buffalo Ranch cabins.

The latest additions to the Institute's instruction lineup are winter classes designed for folks who may not relish the icy isolation of the Buffalo Ranch campus. Teaming up with Amfac Parks and Resorts, Yellowstone's hotel concessionaire, the Institute now offers winter packages that combine educational programs with hotel lodging and restaurant meals. Last year's inaugural course, called Winter Wonderland, featured five days of wildlife, geothermal, and skiing–snowshoeing tours led by a naturalist/guide—with cozy nights spent at Mammoth Hot Springs Hotel and Old Faithful Lodge. Added to the winter list this season will be Secret Snowscapes, a four-day ski and snowshoe adventure, and Winter Wolf Discovery, two days of looking for and studying the park's top predator.

Eventually, just about every American visits Yellowstone. But if you want to see this national park in an entirely new way, take a learning vacation.

Answer numbers 1 through 8. Base your answers on the article "Nature's Classroom."

1 Which of the following best supports the idea that people who have taken a class at Yellowstone are satisfied customers?

    A. People take classes in the wintertime.

    B. People make friends during their classes.

    C. People usually return to take another class.

    D. People enjoy "roughing it" in the primitive cabins.

2 What information could a college student find out from this article?

    F. whether teaching positions were available

    G. whether internship programs were available

    H. whether college credit courses were available

    I. whether scholarship programs were available

3 What can you infer from the passage about the animals at Yellowstone?

    A. They roam freely through the park.

    B. They are kept apart from each other.

    C. They can only be seen from a long distance.

    D. They can only be seen at certain times of the year.

4 What is the Yellowstone Institute's long-term goal?

    F. to increase the number of courses taught

    G. to increase the number of park supporters

    H. to increase the diversity of animals in the park

    I. to increase the number of students in each class

5 Which statement is best supported by the following excerpt?

> **You can learn about wolves, wildflowers, fly-fishing, grizzlies, bison, photograpy, the biology of fire, using map and compass, fossils, and much more.**

    A. People can take more than one course at a time.

    B. People can take courses on a variety of subjects.

    C. People can view many different species of birds.

    D. People can learn about the history of Yellowstone.

6 Read the sentence from the passage.

> **In the wilds of Yellowstone, amenities seem almost superfluous, and the let's-rough-it ambiance adds to the Institute's allure.**

What does *amenities* mean?

    F. destinations

    G. experiences

    H. hardships

    I. luxuries

7 READ THINK EXPLAIN How does the author support the idea that Yellowstone is also a winter destination? Support your answer with details and information from the article.

_____

_____

_____

_____

_____

_____

_____

_____

8 READ THINK EXPLAIN How useful would this article be in convincing parents to take their family to Yellowstone on vacation? Support your answer with details and information from the article.

_____

_____

_____

_____

_____

_____

_____

_____

_____

_____

_____

_____

_____

_____

Read the article "The Lifestyle Rx" and answer Numbers 1 through 8.

From *Consumer Reports*

The Lifestyle Rx

Can exercise or diet cure what ails you? Here's what the research and our reader survey say.

"Exercise is my new religion," says Diana Blumenthal, 66, still recovering from a fractured hip that occurred some years ago. "If I do it, I feel good. If I let it slide, I start walking lopsided." Blumenthal is among the growing number of people who take an active, independent approach to managing a chronic medical condition.

If wasn't too long ago that people with such conditions were usually told to take it easy—or stay in bed—and to rely exclusively on medication and possibly surgery. Physicians doubted the impact of lifestyle changes, including not only exercise but also specialized diet. As late as 1997, for example, Harvard researchers categorized nutritional strategies as "alternative" therapies in a major survey of treatments in America.

But today lifestyle changes are becoming standard treatments for an increasing number of ailments. Diet is the cornerstone of diabetes care, the usual first step in treating high cholesterol levels, and a supplemental treatment for hypertension and osteoporosis. And the role of exercise—alone or combined with diet—is even greater.

The American Heart Association now says physical activity can help "fix a broken heart," noting that a not-yet-published five-year study of some 5,300 heart-attack patients found a significantly lower death rate in those who exercise more. Today exercise is a major component of treatment after heart surgery and for many other cardiac problems as well. And the revolution in cardiac care has spread to other disorders such as arthritis, asthma, diabetes, gallbladder disease, anxiety, depression, and even the side effects of cancer treatment.

Exercise such as speed walking may help reduce the risk of developing disease.

WORTH THE EFFORT?

Are lifestyle treatments worth trying? The answer is clearly yes, according to a growing body of research (described in the box on the next page). And a recent survey of more than 46,000 Consumer Reports readers suggests that many individuals have found lifestyle changes effective for their most serious conditions. For this story we did a special analysis that focused on the ailments readers said they were more likely to treat with exercise (17 conditions) or diet (8 conditions). Three out of four readers who did try exercise or diet for any of those ailments called it at least somewhat helpful. About 40 percent said diet or exercise was very helpful. In fact, exercise was called at least as effective as prescription medications for a number of conditions: arthritis, back or neck pain, broken bones or torn ligaments, diabetes, irritable bowel syndrome, and menopausal symptoms.

Unfortunately the old passive approach to treatment still predominates: Despite the high marks lifestyle steps got from those who tried them, most readers stayed on the sidelines. In the entire survey, which included numerous medical conditions, exercise was used for a bit over a third (38 percent), while diet was used for only 18 percent. By contrast,

#1   The Lifestyle Benefits

This table shows the typical maximum benefit—either a reduction ▼ or an increase ▲—found in well-designed clinical trials of exercise or diet for six common disorders. We based the table on our review of the medical literature plus interviews with experts. Note that combining diet and exercise may yield even greater improvements. These lifestyle changes can also lead to weight loss, which eases many of these disorders.

Condition	Type of Exercise	Maximum Improvement with Exercise	Type of Diet	Maximum Improvement with Diet
High blood pressure	Aerobic	▼15% [1] ▼10% [2]	Low fat, high produce high dairy (low-fat) [3]	▼11% [1] ▼9% [2]
High LDL cholesterol	—	—	Low saturated fat	▼20%
Low HDL cholesterol	Aerobic	▲15%	—	—
High blood sugar	Aerobic	▼15%	High whole grain, high produce, limited calorie	▼30%
Arthritis pain	Strength training, flexibility, low-impact aerobic	▼40%	—	—
Low bone density	Weight bearing	▲3% [4]	High calcium (including supplements)	▲2% [4]

1 Systolic pressure (the upper number). 2 Diastolic pressure (the lower number). 3 Reductions may be greater if sodium intake is also decreased. 4 Improvements are greater than they seem, since bone density normally declines with age.

alternative treatments, such as supplements and hands-on therapies, were used for 34 percent of conditions, drugs for 70 percent.

MOVEMENT AS MEDICINE

For people with a chronic ailment, exercise used to be viewed as asking for trouble. And excessive or misguided exercise can precipitate problems in people with coronary disease, poorly controlled diabetes, asthma, arthritis, or osteoporosis. But evidence is accumulating that in both health and disease, the overall prognosis is better for the exerciser than for the sedentary. For example, a recent study showed that intensive workouts can not only slow the progress of coronary disease but actually restore lost coronary function when the disease is still stable. And it can help prevent a

snowballing effect in conditions like diabetes, which multiply the risk of other major ailments. In one study, for example, regular exercise, including walking, did indeed reduce the onset of coronary disease in women with diabetes.

"We've yet to find a disease state where exercise isn't helpful," says Miriam Nelson, Ph.D., a scientist at the Human Nutrition Research Center on Aging at Tufts University and an expert on women's exercise (author of "Strong Women Stay Young"). For example, clinical trials indicate that exercise can help reduce the pain and joint damage caused by arthritis, decrease attacks and the need for medication in asthma sufferers, and ease anxiety and depression. Other research indicates that regular workouts may cut the risk of symptomatic gallstones by one-third. And while lifestyle

measures may not slow the progress of cancer, recent research suggests that exercise can reduce the side effects of chemotherapy and improve adherence to such treatment.

For chronically ill individuals, the psychological as well as physical benefits of exercise can be profound. "They spend a lot of time in doctors' offices, where it's easy to feel hopeless and demoralized," says Bess Marcus, Ph. D., of Brown University's Division of Behavioral and Preventive Medicine. "Exercise is empowering [and] energizing, and [it] increases your sense of control over the situation. You're never too sick or too old to get started exercising," says Marcus.

EAT YOUR WAY TO HEALTH

Though there is strong evidence for the effectiveness of nutritional strategies for a number of diseases, dietary treatments can be difficult to deploy. They're recommended most often for those who are overweight, because research suggests that obesity may contribute to many disorders. It's not always clear whether the benefits of slimming down stem from the weight loss itself, the special diet and exercise that led to the loss, or some combination. Whatever the reason, shedding pounds can ease joint pain and reduce blood pressure as well as blood sugar and blood-cholesterol levels.

Our readers called diabetes and heart conditions the two ailments where diet helped most; about half of those who tried them called that strategy very helpful. (Our survey did not inquire about which special diets readers used. The table on the previous page briefly describes the diets generally used for various conditions.)

"It's easier to stick with a program if you see results right away or on a daily basis, as you do with blood-sugar levels," says Amy Peterson, R.D., diabetes and nutrition educator at Harvard's Joslin Clinic. For other conditions, results can take a lot longer—a few months of low-fat eating before you see a drop in cholesterol, for example.

However, most of the CR readers who reported that they tried diet to reduce cholesterol or blood pressure said they did stick with it for at least six months. So it's not clear why only about a third of them found a diet change very helpful. One theoretical explanation: Many readers may have tried only a low-salt diet to reduce blood pressure. Combining that with a newer approach—a low-fat diet high in produce and dairy—should yield better results.

Dietary treatments seem to be most successful when combined with exercise. Of the nearly 73,000 people trying to lose weight in one survey, about two-thirds reported using physical activity to do so. That's an important tactic. Aerobic exercise not only burns lots of calories during the workout itself but also revs up your metabolism, or basic calorie-burning rate, for hours afterwards. Strengthening workouts build muscles, which helps boost your basic metabolism. And regular exercise plus a nutritious diet can protect and improve your health whether or not you shed any pounds.

RECOMMENDATIONS

Studies show that most doctors still fail to counsel patients about lifestyle changes. Economic pressure for briefer doctor visits, lack of formal training in lifestyle medicine, and uncertainty about which exercise and dietary steps to recommend seem to underlie doctors' poor performance in this area.

People with medical problems should insist their health-care providers give them information on how life-style changes can affect the course of the disease. Stanford emeritus professor of epidemiology Ralph S. Paffenbarger, Jr., M.D., Dr. P.H., suggests you say to the doctor: "Either tell me how to change, or tell me who can tell me."

#2 Exercise vs. Diet

Survey Results: These graphs show how readers who tried them rated the efficacy of using exercise and diet for a specific condition they had in the past two years. (The survey did not ask exactly which exercise and diets were used.) Survey questions were included in the 1999 Annual Questionnaire sent to Consumer Reports subscribers in the U.S. and Canada,. We received 46,806 responses. (Note: Our readers' experiences may not be representative of the U.S. or Canadian population.)

Condition	Exercise % Used	Exercise Reader Score (%)	Diet % Used	Diet Reader Score (%)
Allergies	12			
Arthritis	53		7	
Asthma	29			
Back pain	66			
Broken bones/ torn ligaments	55			
Depression	44			
Diabetes	62		65	
Digestive problems	18		40	
Fibromyalgia	71			
Headaches	26		18	
Heart condition	58		33	
High blood pressure	46		23	
High cholesterol	55		52	
Irritable bowel syndrome	30		52	
Menopausal symptoms	44			
Neck pain	55			
Respiratory problems	12			

■ Helped me feel much better   ▢ Helped somewhat   ☐ Helped only a little or not at all

Answer numbers 1 through 8. Base your answers on the article "The Lifestyle Rx."

1 According to the readers' survey results, which statement best expresses the readers' opinion concerning diet and exercise?

    A. Most readers found diet to be the most efficient way to improve poor health.

    B. Most readers found that exercise or diet was helpful in treating their ailments.

    C. Most readers found that diet was faster than exercise in controlling health conditions.

    D. Most readers found no change in their condition as a result of changes in their exercise practices.

2 According to the information in the first chart, which type of condition would not benefit from aerobic exercise?

    F. arthritis

    G. high blood sugar

    H. low bone density

    I. high blood pressure

3 READ THINK EXPLAIN   If your parents were the victims of chronic medical conditions, how could you use the information in the article to suggest lifestyle changes? Support your answer with details and information from the article.

4 Which two conditions did readers say improved most because of diet changes?

    A. depression and asthma

    B. diabetes and heart disease

    C. broken bones and back pain

    D. respiratory problems and neck pain

5 What is the most valid argument for people with arthritis to exercise?

    F. Exercise reduces anxiety and depression in arthritis patients.

    G. Exercise enables arthritis sufferers to have fewer doctor visits.

    H. Exercise improves the respiratory condition of an arthritis patient.

    I. Exercise reduces pain and swelling in the joints of arthritis sufferers.

6 READ THINK EXPLAIN How does the writer present the argument that exercise is beneficial to people suffering from chronic medical conditions? Use information and details from the article to support your answer.

7 What does the article suggest is the best way to maintain health?

    A. People can have a sedentary lifestyle if their diet is healthy.

    B. People should combine a healthy diet with an active lifestyle.

    C. People should concentrate on exercise and not worry about their diet.

    D. People should have regular checkups and discussion with their doctors.

8 READ THINK EXPLAIN If you were researching the benefits of exercise, how could you use this article for a report on improving health? Use information and details from the article to support your answer.

Chapter seven

Synthesizing Information and Drawing Conclusions

Benchmark LA. A. 2.4.8

Synthesizes information from multiple sources to draw conclusions.

Every day, we make connections between different pieces of information in order to draw conclusions. If you are sitting in class and hear thunder, you would probably check the weather outside for rain. Likewise, when the sky is dark and cloudy with flashes of lightning, you presume a storm is on its way.

When you are choosing an elective to take in school, how do you decide which one is best for you? You might talk to a counselor to see what courses you need to fulfill your graduation requirements. Then, you might ask friends who have taken the class what they liked or didn't like about it. You probably would read the class description or visit the teacher who teaches that class for more information. After you have gathered information from several sources, you would combine what you have learned and then make a decision.

We take the information we gather from numerous sources to *draw conclusions*. When reading, you may have noticed that authors do not always state things directly. When this happens its important to ask yourself what the author suggests or implies in the writing. Based on that information, you are then able to draw a conclusion.

Understanding the Benchmark

Try one or both of the "synthesizing" suggestions listed below. If you practice synthesizing information in your everyday life, doing so on the FCAT will be a snap!

- Study a map of your community in order to choose the best route from your home to a movie theater on the other side of town. Check the times of the movie you would like to see. Then consider what you know about traffic patterns and traveling time. Based on the all the information you gather, tell your friends how to get to the theater and what time they will have to leave to make it in time for the movie.

- Look at the employment advertisements in a local newspaper. Choose a section that advertises jobs that interest you. Compare and contrast the benefits, salaries, and working hours mentioned in the ads. Use this information to help you decide where you would apply for a summer or dream job.

Making the FCAT Connection

On the FCAT, you will be asked to synthesize information from two or more sources. These sources might take the form of articles, textbook excerpts, graphs, charts, photographs, and so on. Your task will be to take the relevant information from each and answer the questions asked. Remember that you need to *make connections* among the different pieces of information and then draw conclusions.

Multiple-choice, short-response, and extended-response items from both informational and literary texts will assess this benchmark.

Taking a Closer Look

Authors don't always state every point they wish to make when they write about a topic. Sometimes they expect you to figure things out based on the evidence they provide and your own reasoning powers. That process of "reading between the lines" or "putting two and two together" is called drawing conclusions.

Drawing Conclusions and Generalizations in a Text

Drawing conclusions is such an automatic process that you may not even be aware of doing it. It happens all the time in everyday life. Suppose, for example, you were to see a manatee in one of Florida's coastal rivers or canals. On closer inspection, you notice that it has several deep scars on its back. From your own experience, you know that many motorboats cruise the waterways. So you draw a conclusion that a motorboat propeller caused the scars.

Drawing conclusions is just as natural when you are reading. By reading a passage carefully and asking yourself questions such as, "What is the author suggesting here?" or "What other ideas make sense based on this passage?" you can arrive at your own conclusions.

Read the following short news excerpt:

> In September of 1997, would-be thieves attempted to steal a Tyrannosaurus fossil that paleontologists had been excavating near Fort Peck, Montana, in the northeastern part of the state. Watchful neighbors notified the police, and the thieves were apprehended before any damage occurred to the fossil. News of the fossil discovery and the robbery attempt galvanized the local community. Anxious to keep the Tyrannosaurus rex in their community, residents of the Fort Peck area quickly raised $550,000 to build a museum to house the skeleton. According to a spokesman for the residents, the dinosaur, as part of their natural heritage, belongs to them all.

After reading this excerpt, you might conclude that dinosaur fossils are valuable. You might assume that thieves would not attempt a difficult robbery if there wasn't something valuable to be gained. You might also conclude that dinosaurs are very popular these days. That conclusion would be passed on the fact that the people in Fort Peck immediately raised funds for their own dinosaur museum. Your own awareness of popular dinosaur movies might support this conclusion too. Finally, you might conclude that it is easy to damage dinosaur fossils, since the article mentions this possibility.

Notice that none of these conclusions is stated *directly* in the passage. Rather, they're based on details in the article as well as the knowledge and experiences that a reader brings to the passage. It is important to remember that you should only make conclusions that are based on information in a passage, along with what you know.

Use the chart below to show what information supports each of the three conclusions made about the dinosaur news story.

Conclusion	Details, Support, Reader Knowledge
Dinosaur fossils are very valuable.	
Dinosaurs are very popular in this country.	
Dinosaur fossils are easily damaged.	

Synthesizing

As you research a topic, you will generally look for information in two or more sources. Often, you will be able to use facts drawn from different sources as the basis for a conclusion. This process of drawing information from different sources and using it to reach a new conclusion is called synthesizing.

Practice synthesizing information whenever you read a textbook, magazine, or newspaper. Think about how the textual and visual materials work together. How do the visual materials add to the text? How does combining textual with visual information make ideas and information easier to understand?

When reading a selection, remember to go back to any accompanying graphs or charts to synthesize the information it provides with what you have already read. Doing this before you respond to questions will assure that your answers are *complete* and based on *all information* with which you have been provided.

Use the reading strategies that have been discussed throughout the book to help you make sense of the sample reading below.

From Recycling and Reuse

By John Naar

The more trash we reuse, the less there is to get rid of. This saves money and energy as well as conserving natural resources. Recycling is not a new idea. In the 1920s and 30s it was a basic way of life in North America, especially in rural communities, where waste reuse and composting were commonplace. In World War II, recycling became a patriotic duty for all citizens, and industry recycled 25 percent of the solid waste stream. Since then, affluence, cheaper consumer products (especially plastics), and the appeal of "convenience" have worked against recycling. However, with an ever-mounting garbage crisis, more and more people are seeing the need to preserve natural resources and conserve energy.

The composition of our municipal solid waste, showed that many products and materials we usually throw away can be restored to a useful second life. The largest component (42 percent) is paper—corrugated cardboard, newspaper, magazines, books, paperboard, and office paper. Next are organic wastes (23 percent), composed of yard waste and food waste, glass containers, plastic, and other items including wood wastes, rubber, and textiles.

Estimates of how much solid waste can be recycled range from a low of 20 percent (National Solid Waste Management Association) to a high of 88 percent by weight (CBNS). In fact, many communities in Europe, Asia, and North America are already achieving overall recycling rates as high as 65 percent. Certain products—paper, glass, and aluminum—have high reuse rates. In Denmark, an incredible 99.6 percent of bottles and glass containers is recovered. Countries that are more energy-conscious than the U.S.—Japan, Germany, the Netherlands, and Italy, for instance—recover more than twice what we do.

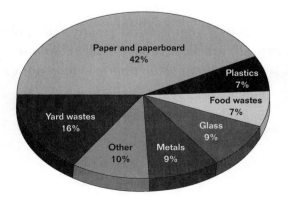

Predict:
What does the title tell you this article will be about?

Synthesize:
How do the chart and article support each other?

Now answer the questions that follow.

1. In the U.S. plastics and glass waste make up the same percent of total waste as

   A. paper waste.

   B. metal waste.

   C. food wastes.

   D. yard wastes.

2. How does the pie chart support the information about the composition of garbage in the United States?

   _____

   _____

   _____

   _____

   _____

   _____

   _____

   _____

Taking your time to analyze the reading selection and chart that accompanied it should have helped you to answer the questions listed above. Check your answers below.

The first question requires you to examine the chart closely. You are expected to take the information from the chart in order to come to a conclusion. In this instance, adding the percent of plastic and glass waste will give you a total of 16 percent. Only one slice of the pie chart totals 16 percent. This means that answer D, yard wastes, is the correct choice.

The second question requires you to synthesize information from both the chart and the article. A top-scoring response would begin with a topic sentence that directly responds to the question. At least two supporting details from the text should also be included. An example of a top-scoring response follows.

The information in the pie chart supports the information in the text visually. The chart represents solid waste consumption in the country as a whole. Each piece of the pie is a different size, representing different kinds and amounts of waste we consume. Also, the sections of the pie correspond directly to the information provided in the article. For example, the article states that paper and paperboard make up 42 percent, or the majority, of all waste consumed in the United States. Consequently, this section of the pie chart represents 42 percent and the largest piece.

The following section includes reading selections that are similar to passages on the FCAT. Remember to stay actively involved while you read, using the reading strategies from this and previous chapters of the book.

 **Read "What Makes a Safe Driver?" and answer Numbers 1 through 8.**

What Makes a Safe Driver?

From *TRANSPORTATION—AMERICA'S LIFELINE*

According to the National Highway Transportation Safety Agency, approximately three-quarters of the more than 6 million motor vehicle collisions which occur on the U.S. highways annually are caused by drivers' attention being diverted in the moments before collision. Despite every device that auto manufacturers can provide to ensure car safety, it is primarily the driver of a vehicle who ultimately determines whether or not a car or truck will be involved in an accident. Many factors play a part in traffic fatalities, including the amount of alcohol consumed before getting behind the wheel, the age of the driver, and the speed of the vehicle. The U.S. General Accounting Office study, *Factors Affecting Involvement in Vehicle Crashes*, Washington, DC, 1994, revealed that, when other factors are controlled, driver characteristics far outweigh vehicle factors in predicting a crash.

Alcohol Impairment

The use of alcohol as a contributing factor in fatal traffic accidents has been steadily decreasing since 1982, most likely because of tougher enforcement of liquor and DWI laws in most states and the raising of the drinking age to 21. In 1982, about 57 percent of all traffic fatalities involved an intoxicated driver (this includes motorcyclists). NHTSA reported that 41 percent of all traffic deaths in 1995 involved a person who was legally intoxicated (blood alcohol concentration of 0.10 or higher)—more than 17,270 alcohol-related fatalities.

The highest rates of intoxication were for drivers in their early 20s. About 35 percent of all drivers ages 21 through 24 involved in a fatal accident were legally drunk. The rate of intoxication decreased steadily with age, and only about 6.8 percent of drivers on the road over age 65 involved in fatal accidents were drunk.

In its 1996 survey, *Prevention® Magazine* found that 17 percent of drivers said they sometimes drive after drinking. Men were about twice as likely as women (23 percent vs. 12 percent) to say that they sometimes drive after drinking. Unfortunately, heavy drinkers were the most likely to drive after drinking.

Young Drivers and Accidents

The youngest drivers, those under age 20, are the most accident-prone. Accident rates decrease between ages 25 and 34 and then gradually increase between ages 35 and 74. After the driver reaches 74, the accident rate increases sharply.

Young drivers between the ages of 16 and 24 are disproportionately high contributors to traffic accidents and highway deaths. Young drivers also pose the greatest loss for insurers. According to the AAA Foundation for Traffic Safety, about 75 percent of young driver citations are issued for speeding. Young males consistently have more costly claims, and in addition to speeding, principal factors involved in young driver accidents are losing control of the vehicle and rear-ending the car in front. The AAA also reports that insurance companies are reducing the number of young policy holders covered under traditional coverage by sending them to more costly risk insurers.

Many young people object to being penalized with high insurance rates and are proposing "age-free" insurance policy programs. Under such policies, young beginning drivers would be required to pass rigorous driver education courses and sign contracts agreeing to abide by safety belt laws, drinking-and-driving laws, and other safety behaviors. In return, they would pay higher premiums for a specified time and then be eligible for refunds if they lived up to the contract terms.

Citing inadequate driver training as contributing toward teenage driving error, several organizations such as the National Highway Traffic Safety Administration, the Insurance Institute for Highway Safety, and the National Association of Independent Insurers, support "graduated licensing" for the future. Under such a program, teens would not go directly from learner's permit to adult license. Rather there would be an intermediate stage involving driving years from 16 to 18. The aim is to control and monitor their progress toward full driving privileges, as restrictions are lifted when drivers gain added experience and maturity.

Older Drivers and Accidents

As the U.S. population matures, an increasing number of older drivers will be on the road. The U.S. General Accounting Office (Factors Affecting Involvement in Vehicle Crashes, Washington, DC, 1994) reported that when the miles they drive are considered, elderly persons are disproportionately involved in collisions, particularly two-vehicle collisions. The National Safety Council has found that there are definite crash patterns among older drivers. They often fail to yield the right-of-way and

Figure I

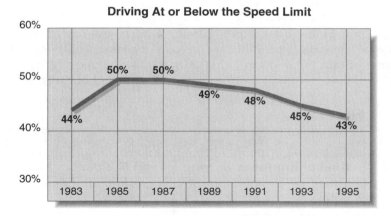

Source: *Auto Safety in America, PREVENTION® Magazine, Emmaus, PA*

sometimes do not pay attention to, or do not see, signs and signals.

Senior citizens' driving skills may diminish in other ways, including functional losses in vision, reaction time, and the speed of information processing. They often have more difficulty with backing and parking maneuvers. Older drivers have the most accidents making left turns across traffic. The American Automobile Association's Foundation for Traffic Safety notes, however, that it is not chronological age but the driver's overall functional ability which predicts driving difficulties. This means that one cannot assume that a driver who is age 60 is necessarily more able to drive than one who is 75.

Older people enjoy the freedom and independence of driving their own cars as much as anyone else. In looking toward the future, when many more senior citizens will be on the road, the AAA has sponsored a study which is developing guidelines for a "grade" licensing program—a license that carries some restrictions. Several states are already experimenting with these licenses which attempt to balance the risks and safety needs of older drivers and others. The goal of the

program is to help elderly drivers maintain their mobility for as long as they can safely do so.

Obeying the Speed Limit

The *Prevention® Magazine* 1996 annual study on American behavior revealed that less than half (43 percent) of Americans who drive claim they always stay within the speed limit. A majority (55 percent) say they sometimes or never adhere to speed laws. (See Figure 1.) Careful observance of speed laws is more prevalent among older drivers. Along with age, income and education are determining factors in compliance with speed laws. As income and education levels increase, compliance with speed laws declines. Men are more likely than women to break speed laws.

Accidents and Driver Error

Most accidents on the road result from the interaction of three factors—the driver, the vehicle, and the road conditions. While motorists have little or no control over highway conditions and usually cannot predict whether their vehicles will perform correctly, they can control the way they drive. Cellular telephone use in a moving vehicle increased the risk of having an accident four-fold—the same risk as when a person's blood alcohol level is at the legal limit. Figure 2 lists types of improper driving that resulted in injuries or fatal accidents in 1995.

Right-of-way mistakes and speeding cause the most accidents and fatal injuries. The National Safety Council estimates that 76 percent of all accidents were caused by some type of driver error. Of collisions between motor vehicles, angle-collisions (collisions which are not head-on, rear-end, rear-to-rear, or sideswipe) cause most deaths, while rear-end collisions generate the most nonfatal injuries and injury accidents.

Figure 2

IMPROPER DRIVING REPORTED IN ACCIDENTS, 1995			
Kind of Improper Driving	**Fatal Accidents**	**Injury Accidents**	**All Accidents**
Total	100.0%	100.0%	100.0%
Improper Driving	68.1	73.5	75.5
Speed too fast or unsafe	19.8	13.9	14.0
Right of way	15.2	25.5	22.9
Failed to yield	*10.2*	*18.1*	*17.0*
Disregarded signal	*3.0*	*5.0*	*4.0*
Passed stop sign	*2.2*	*2.4*	*1.9*
Drove left of center	9.1	2.4	2.2
Made improper turn	2.3	2.8	4.2
Improper overtaking	1.5	1.3	1.5
Followed too closely	0.5	7.0	7.2
Other improper driving	19.7	20.7	23.6
No improper driving stated	**31.9**	**26.5**	**24.5**
Source: Based on reports from 20 state traffic authorities			
Source: Accident Facts, 1996 Edition, National Safety Council, Itasca, IL, 1996			

Answer questions 1 through 8. Base your answers on the article "What Makes a Safe Driver?"

1 Which of the following would an investigator of a car collision be least likely to suspect as the cause of the accident?

A. drinking

B. speeding

C. brake failure

D. driver distraction

2 What can you conclude from the passage about laws controlling drinking?

F. They are targeted at teenage drivers.

G. They are enforced equally in every state.

H. They are enforced strictly in some states.

I. They are helping to reduce traffic deaths.

3 What conclusion can you draw about the young people in the passage who object to paying high insurance rates?

   A. They could benefit from driver education.

   B. They are safer drivers than senior citizens.

   C. They need help finding better insurance rates.

   D. They drive safely and shouldn't be punished by high rates.

4 Which conclusion about older drivers is best supported by the passage?

   F. Everyone should lose their driving privileges at age 70.

   G. Everyone should be evaluated for driving on a case-by-case basis.

   H. No one should be allowed to drive past age 65 without restrictions.

   I. No one should be denied the freedom and independence of driving.

5 READ THINK EXPLAIN Are men or women safer drivers, in general? Support your answer with details and information from the article.

6 Which detail from the passage does Figure 1 support?

   A. Men are more likely than women to drive too fast.

   B. Older drivers are more likely to drive the speed limit.

   C. Less than half of American drivers drive the speed limit.

   D. People who are better educated are more likely to speed.

7 Which detail from the passage does Figure 2 best support?

    F. Drivers have no control over highway conditions.

    G. Drivers are capable of controlling their own behavior.

    H. Improper driving causes more accidents than other factors.

    I. Cellular telephone use increases the risk of having an accident.

8 How could a driver's education teacher use the information in the passage? Support your answer using information and details from the article.

Read the article "The Motion Picture Industry" and answer Numbers 1 through 9.

The Motion Picture Industry

From *California Then and Now*

Oil was one source of new wealth for southern California; movies were another. Today, the name Hollywood is practically synonymous with motion picture production. But California cannot claim that moviemaking began in the state. Many of the earliest movies of the 1890s were produced in Thomas Edison's laboratory and studio in New Jersey. Other early moviemaking companies were based in New York City (Brooklyn in particular). California, however, soon demonstrated that it had advantages lacking in East Coast film production. For one thing, it had a sunny climate. Consistent weather and sunlight allowed movies to be made on outdoor sets at greatly reduced costs.

Between 1908 and 1914, more than 70 companies made movies in southern California. In 1911, Thomas Ince built a major facility, Inceville, on 18,000 acres by the beach at Pacific Palisades. The greatest moviemaker of his time, David W. Griffith, chose to shoot his Biograph films in the open spaces of the San Fernando Valley.

The early films were short (a one-reeler lasted about ten minutes) and without much plot. But they provided a training ground for actors, actresses, directors, and technicians. Noticing that audiences enjoyed seeing certain performers on screen over and over again, producers launched the star system—with its astronomical salaries. For example, the salary of comedian Charlie Chaplin zoomed from $150 a week in 1914 to $10,000 a week in 1916.

The motion picture industry really took off in the 1920s. Movies were better technically, and imaginative moviemakers spun celluloid tales of adventure, drama, and comedy. Although these were "silent" films, they would be accompanied in the theater by music that enhanced scenes of excitement, fear, or romance. Hollywood movies were so successful in the 1920s that they accounted for at least one-fifth of the income of products made in California.

Hollywood and the American Dream

The effect of Hollywood movies on American life and values was nothing short of colossal. Going to the movies became a weekly habit for millions. By the late 1920s, an average of 50 million Americans entered the nation's movie houses every week to enjoy some romantic adventure or zany comedy concocted in Hollywood. Admission was often as low as a nickel, but the nickels added up to fabulous sums for the fortunate few— Hollywood's producers, directors, scriptwriters, and stars.

The glamour of a movie star both on-screen and off soon began to define for Americans what it meant to be successful. Men and women alike began to imitate the flashy dress and rich lifestyle of their cinematic idols. They went on diets to slim their bodies and bought fashionable sportswear made in Los Angeles. From one end of the country to the other, Americans talked of Hollywood as a dazzling world of irresistible make-believe. Newspapers and magazines poured out an endless stream of reports about the Hollywood way of life. This account by the *New York World* in 1923 was typical: "But Beauty, ye gods, the place is choked, blocked, heaped to the gunwales with female beauty. One has to elbow beauties out of the way to make a passage down Hollywood Boulevard."

Movies and Morality

Many Americans were shocked by reports of the extravagant lifestyle of rich and famous Hollywood movie stars. Within the period of 1921–1922 alone, actor Wallace Reid died of a drug overdose, director William Desmond Taylor was murdered, and comedian

Fatty Arbuckle was implicated in the death of a starlet. In an age when divorce was considered shameful, far too many film stars seemed to be casually shedding their marriage partners.

Many communities demanded that government regulate motion pictures and stop them from showing *sexy* scenes and scandalous behavior. Recognizing the threat of censorship, Hollywood studios set up an office in 1922 to uphold standards of morality both on and off the screen. For the next decade, strict rules governed the making of Hollywood movies. There was no nudity and no "indecent" language. Characters who did bad things always met a bad end.

In 1928, Warner Brothers released *The Jazz Singer,* a mostly silent film that included several scenes in which actor-singer Al Jolson could be heard talking and singing. Audiences were thrilled.

Within two years all major studios made the switch to sound production. Warner Brothers, MGM, Paramount, Columbia, and 20th Century-Fox survived a succession of corporate mergers and went on to dominate movie production for the next 40 years.

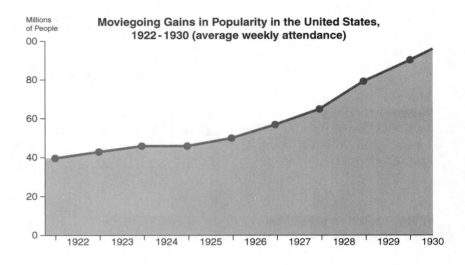

Answer questions 1 through 9. Base your answers on the article "The Motion Picture Industry."

1 What can you conclude from the passage about the purpose of movies made in the 1920s?

  A. They were meant to entertain audiences.

  B. They were meant to influence the audience's lifestyle.

  C. They were meant to train actors, directors, and technicians.

  D. They were meant to inform audiences about current events.

2 Which of the following details from the article leads you to believe that audiences were influenced by the lifestyles of their favorite movie stars?

  F. The motion picture industry experienced growth in the 1920s.

  G. The salaries of the most popular actors and actresses skyrocketed.

  H. Many communities asked for government regulation of the industry.

  I. Men and women began to dress like their favorite actors and actresses.

3 What can be concluded about some of the movie stars in the 1920s?

  A. They felt a need to set a moral example for audiences.

  B. They wanted to change their audiences' sense of morality.

  C. They had a less strict sense of morality than their audiences.

  D. They felt that morality in Hollywood needed to be regulated.

4 What can you conclude about the news media's reports of Hollywood from the following excerpt from the article?

> **This account by the *New York World* in 1923 was typical: "But Beauty, ye gods, the place is choked, blocked, heaped to the gunwales with female beauty. One has to elbow beauties out of the way to make a passage down Hollywood Boulevard."**

F. Newspapers exaggerated the truth about Hollywood.

G. Newspapers stuck strictly to the truth about Hollywood.

H. Newspapers made up totally false stories about Hollywood.

I. Newspapers cleared up misguided notions about Hollywood.

5 What is suggested by the fact that David W. Griffith shot his films in the San Fernando Valley?

A. Southern California was the most expensive movie-making location.

B. Southern California was the place where movie-making was invented.

C. Southern California was the preferred movie-making location of the time.

D. .Southern California was the place where lesser-known directors made their films.

6 | READ THINK EXPLAIN | What information from the article does the chart support? Support your answer with details and information from the article.

_____

_____

_____

_____

_____

_____

_____

_____

7 What conclusion can be drawn from the fact that within a two year period, all major studios switched to sound production?

    F. Sound movies featured the audience's favorite stars.

    G. Silent movies were not very popular with audiences.

    H. Audiences preferred sound movies over silent movies.

    I. Sound movies told tales of adventure, drama, and comedy.

8 What best explains the sharp increase in movie-going shown in the chart, beginning with the year 1928?

    A. In that year stars began to be paid higher salaries.

    B. In that year Hollywood began to enforce morality rules.

    C. That was the year that admission was as low as a nickel.

    D. That was the year that sound movies began to be shown.

9 READ THINK EXPLAIN   How did the motion picture industry and its audience influence each other? Support your answer with details and information from the article.

Read the article "Teens and Sleep" and answer Numbers 1 through 8.

TEENS & SLEEP

from KidsHealth.com

You're busy with school, sports, after-school activities, homework, **and** a job. So be honest—how high on your priority list is a good night's sleep? For many teens, not very. Perhaps you don't think you need much sleep ("I can get by on 6 hours") or maybe you figure you can make up for it on the weekend ("I always sleep until noon on Saturday").

Although you may think getting the right amount of ZZZs isn't all-important, it is. In the same way that you make sure to get enough to eat, good sleep habits are a big part of staying healthy. And it's not just about making your parents and teachers happy. If you want to do well on tests, play sports without falling on your face, and hang out with your friends without turning into a zombie, you'll want to take a hard look at your sleep routine. Read on for some sleepy surprises—you'll be amazed what a few ZZZs can do for you!

The Skinny on Sleep

Sleep isn't simply the opposite of being awake. In fact, while you're in sweet slumber, your brain is still active. As you sleep, your brain passes through stages that are necessary for you to stay healthy. Sleep is actually food for your brain! And like food, sleep is not an option—it's a need.

Many people—both teens and adults—believe that if they don't get enough sleep during the week, they can catch up on that lost sleep over the weekend and it will all even out. Although this seems like a simple trade-off, trying to pay back your sleep "debt" on weekends doesn't always work.

One of the most important stages of sleep is **REM** (**r**apid **e**ye **m**ovement) sleep, or the dream stage. REM is necessary because this is when your mind processes your experiences and helps you adjust to the world around you. REM sleep usually happens after you've already been asleep for about 4 hours. So if you only sleep for 6 hours a night and you use naps or weekends to make it up, you may not get the same quality of sleep that you would have if you had tacked on an extra 2 hours at the end of the 6 hours.

Some teens experience sleep problems that go beyond the occasional late night out. If you experience any of the following symptoms (see chart) that make you think that you may have a problem, talk to your doctor.

How Many ZZZs Do I Need?

Do you think that as a teen you need less sleep than your younger sister or brother? Actually, research shows that for teens to feel tops, on average they need a whopping 9.2 hours of sleep each night! But this number can be hard to reach—you don't need to be a math whiz to figure out that if you wake up for school at 6 AM, you'd have to go to bed at 9 PM to reach the 9-hour mark. Recent studies have shown that many teens have trouble going to sleep so early - not because teens want to rebel against bedtime, but because their brains naturally work on later schedules and aren't ready for bed.

What happens if you don't get enough sleep? Plenty. You'll probably feel very sleepy during the day and you may have trouble staying awake in class. This can affect your ability to concentrate, make good judgments, and get good grades. Most importantly, you run the risk of falling asleep while driving your car, which could lead to a serious accident. Some teens experience emotional problems such as depression if they don't get enough sleep. You might also feel irritable, cranky, or more emotional than usual. Not getting enough sleep can also contribute to skin problems, such as acne.

Tips for Getting the Right Amount of ZZZs

If you want to make good sleep a habit, take a look at your everyday schedule. Are you working so many hours at your after-school job that you end up staying up late to finish homework? Does football practice take up so much time that you never get to bed before 11 PM? If so, think about ways to make your schedule more manageable. Can you work fewer hours if your job isn't essential? If football is especially important, can you drop another activity to make time for sleep?

If you are getting enough rest at night and you are still falling asleep during the day, it's a good idea to visit your doctor. He or she will look at your overall health and sleep habits and may do a test to find out whether anything is happening during the night to disturb your sleep, like sleep apnea.

There are ways that may make it easier for you to fall asleep when you hit the sack. Here are some tips for good sleep "hygiene":

- Have a regular bedtime and try to arrange your schedule so that you can stick to it.

- Don't nap a lot during the day. If you do take naps, limit them to 20 to 30 minutes.

- Leave some time to unwind before bed. This may mean saving a little time for the

SLEEP PROBLEMS

Sleepwalking is when you walk or move around during sleep. Because most sleepwalkers don't sleepwalk very often, it usually doesn't become a serious problem. But some sleepwalkers move around almost every night, and they are at risk of getting hurt if they go into the kitchen where there are sharp items, for example, or if they go outside.

Sleep apnea is a disorder that causes a person to stop breathing temporarily during sleep. Causes of apnea include enlarged adenoids (tissues located in the passage that connects the nose and throat) and tonsils and obesity. A person with sleep apnea may experience snoring, difficulty breathing, choking, and heavy sweating during sleep. Other symptoms include feeling extremely sleepy or irritable during the day.

Insomnia is what happens when you have a lot of trouble falling asleep, especially when it happens often. The most common cause for insomnia is stress caused by a big change in routine, such as starting at a new school or moving. **Chronic insomnia** lasts more than a month and may be caused by problems such as depression.

Narcolepsy (pronounced: **nar**-kuh-lep-see) is a sleep disorder in which a person has sleep "attacks" during the day during which she can't stay awake no matter how much sleep she has gotten the night before. Narcolepsy can be dangerous because people with it can fall asleep in dangerous situations, such as while driving a car.

stress-reducing techniques such as meditation that work best for you.

- Don't exercise right before bed. It's important to get enough regular exercise, but plan to do it in the early afternoon if possible.

- Avoid beverages that contain caffeine, such as coffee or soft drinks, after late afternoon.

- Try to stay on schedule even if it's a weekend. Don't go to

sleep more than an hour later or wake up more than 2 to 3 hours later than usual.

- Get into bright light as soon as possible in the morning, but avoid it in the evening. Bright light signals the brain that it's time to wake up.

- Say no to cramming for exams with all-nighters. The best way to prepare for a test is to spread your studying out over time and to get plenty of sleep.

Answer questions 1 through 8. Base your answers on the article "Teens and Sleep."

1 What can you conclude from the article about today's teenagers?

    A. They lead very busy lives.

    B. They experience many sleep problems.

    C. They need more sleep than teens did in the past.

    D. They have more homework than teens did in the past.

2 If a person needed to stay awake to catch a late airplane flight, which of the following tips should he or she follow, based on the information in the passage?

    F. Don't take a long nap.

    G. Do stress-reducing techniques.

    H. Avoid beverages with caffeine.

    I. Stay in a room with bright lights.

3 Which of the following is believed by teens to be least important?

    A. doing well at sports

    B. doing well in school

    C. getting enough sleep

    D. getting enough to eat

4 What can you conclude from the article about the causes of insomnia?

    F. The causes are physical.

    G. The causes are unknown.

    H. The causes are unimportant.

    I. The causes are psychological.

5 READ THINK EXPLAIN   What can you conclude about how well teens understand the importance of sleep? Support your answer with details and information from the article.

6 Which two sleep disorders does the article lead you to believe are most dangerous?

    A. insomnia and sleep apnea

    B. sleepwalking and insomnia

    C. narcolepsy and sleep apnea

    D. sleepwalking and narcolepsy

7 Which tip for getting the right amount of sleep would be most useful to a person who suffers from insomnia?

    F. Have a regular bedtime.

    G. Don't nap a lot during the day.

    H. Avoid beverages that contain caffeine.

    I. Leave some time to unwind before bed.

8 READ THINK EXPLAIN How could you use the information in this article to help a friend who complains about being tired all the time? Support your answer with details and information from the article.

Recognizing Cause-and-Effect Relationships

Benchmark LA.E. 2.2.1

Recognizes cause-and-effect relationships in literary texts. (Applies to fiction, nonfiction, poetry, and drama.)

Why do things happen? When your favorite team loses an important game you might try to analyze why they lost and figure out what the loss means to their ranking. Can they still make the play-offs? You may use this same kind of thinking when you do poorly on a test. Why did you do badly? Can you still pass the class?

When you ask the questions "Why?" and "What are the results?" you are examining important aspects of living. If you seek to understand and explain things that happen, you are exploring *cause and effect*.

A *cause* is an event or action that makes something happen. It tells us why something happened.

An *effect* is a change that takes place as a result of a cause. It tells us what happened.

These two elements work together. The cause tells us why; the effect tells us what.

In addition to understanding causes and effects in our lives, it is important to remember that literature is filled with cause-and-effect relationships. An author creates a character with a personality trait (for example, jealousy) that motivates an action (a murder) forming the basis for a mystery. A story is often made up of a chain of related events. Often one event (a storm at sea) causes something to happen (shipwrecked passengers living on a deserted island), which leads to the development of an adventure story.

Understanding the Benchmark

Here are some suggestions for locating and identifying some common cause-and-effect relationships that exist in our daily lives. Practice recognizing causes and effects and you'll breeze through FCAT questions that assess this benchmark.

- Look at the comics in your local newspaper. A comic strip often shows a cause-and-effect sequence in a few frames.

- Read a sport reporter's analysis of a player's performance.

- Become familiar with the common key words that signal cause and effect.

- Read and consider news story headlines about important events. Read the articles that accompany the headlines to see if you can find out *what* and *why* events occurred.

Making the FCAT Connection

On the FCAT, this benchmark will be tested using both informational and literary texts, including poetry and drama. You will be asked to identify causes and/or effects. The passages will include a cause-and-effect relationship that may be directly stated or implied.

Multiple-choice and short-response items from both informational and literary texts will be used to evaluate your understanding of this benchmark.

Taking a Closer Look

Our daily lives are filled with cause-and-effect relationships. This is even reflected in the things we read. The fact is, much of what we read explains either the cause or reason for something happening, or the effect or result of what happened. When authors write about something that happens, they generally will explain *why* it happened.

The things that happen in life often have more than one cause, and it is also true that one cause can result in many effects. Being able to recognize cause-and-effect relationships can help you better understand life and its events as they unfold around us.

One of the best ways to identify cause-and-effect relationships in a writing passage is by looking for certain linking, or *signal words*. Some of these words are shown in the table below.

Cause:			
because	bring about	contributed to	due to
the reason for	give rise to	led to	since
on account of	created by		

Effect:			
as a result	consequently	hence	so
outcome	therefore	effect	thus
finally	for this reason	then	

Examine the sentences below. The causes and effects are labeled for you. Circle any signal words you recognize.

         cause   **effect**

Because my alarm didn't ring this morning, I was late for work.

         effect   **cause**

We lost the championship on account of our quarterback being injured.

Sometimes a passage will not contain any signal words. In these instances, the cause-and-effect relationship is not clearly stated, but instead is *implied*. To answer questions on implied cause and effect, use logic and reasoning. As you read the passage, ask yourself:

Why did something happen? (if you are looking for the cause)

What happened? (if you are looking for the effect)

See how well you are able to recognize causes and effects by labeling the italicized sections of the sentences below. Is the last part of the sentence a cause or an effect? Also, circle any signal words you find that help you determine which parts of the following sentences are a cause or an effect.

Because of three days of heavy rain, *the streets were flooded.*   _____

The general was forced to retreat since *his supplies were almost gone.*   _____

Maria was upset because *her appointment was cancelled.*   _____

Lowering the speed limit to 55 m.p.h. resulted in *fewer deaths on the nation's highways.*   _____

Shy children sometimes suffer in school due to *teasing by other students.*   _____

FCAT EXTRA!

Whenever you read a selection on the FCAT and recognize a signal word, *circle it*. Remember that writing on the test is allowed! Circling signal words will help you keep track of the "what" and the "why" of any selection you read. It will also save you time when you begin answering FCAT questions.

Use the reading strategies discussed in this and previous chapters to read the selection below and answer the questions that follow it.

Silent Spring

Rachel Carson (1907–1964) was a marine biologist and skillful writer who alerted the public to the dangers of DDT and other pesticides. Her book *Silent Spring*, published in 1962, detailed the damage pesticides had caused to the environment. It signaled the beginning of the environmental movement in the United States.

Carson's writing inspired scientists, nature lovers, and the news media to broadcast the message of the dangers to human health and the environment posed by pesticides. The book raised a storm of controversy regarding DDT and led to a search for alternative methods of pest control.

Silent Spring presented evidence that pesticides killed more than pests. Other organisms in the community were eating pesticide-contaminated insects and plants, thus concentrating the pesticides in their own bodies. This posed problems for all life, including people. Pesticides in agricultural runoff were reaching the waterways. It was found that the concentration of DDT in fish was so high that they were unfit for human consumption. High concentrations in the tissues of fish-eating birds, such as ospreys and brown pelicans, caused them to produce thin-shelled eggs and reduced their reproductive ability. The DDT residues found in milk were a concern because of potential effects on infants who drank the milk.

By 1971, the use of DDT was restricted by law in the United States. Safer, biodegradable pesticides were developed, and biological controls were exploited to eliminate insect pests. Rachel Carson's legacy to all of us is a lasting public awareness of the dangers of pesticides and deep interest in environmental conservation.

Predict:
What can you tell about the piece from its title?

Examine:
What problem is presented in the reading?

Analyze:
What are the *effects* of the problem?

Identify:
Circle words that signal cause and effect.

Now answer the questions that follow.

  1. How did Carson effect the start of the environmental movement?

   A. Her work helped the government begin an environmental movement.

   B. She talked to the media and they reported her concerns about pesticides.

C. Her writings informed the public about the environmental hazards of pesticides.

D. She helped create alternatives to dangerous pesticides, including biodegradable versions.

2. How did DDT affect animals and humans?

_____

_____

_____

_____

_____

_____

_____

If you paid attention to the *what* and the *why* of the selection as you read, then answering the questions that followed was probably easier for you.

For the first question, C is the correct answer. We know choice A is incorrect because the article does not state that the environmental movement was started by the government. Choice B is also incorrect because the article does not say that Carson spoke directly with the media. Choice C is a conclusion that a reader could make based on the facts of the article. Because we know Carson's book detailed the negatives of pesticides, it is a safe to conclude that it was informative and that the public learned from it. This makes C a valid choice. Answer D is false, because the article does not state that Carson was involved in the development of safer alternatives.

For the second question, a top-scoring response would begin by making a general statement in response to the question posed. At least two supporting details from the article would follow. A top-scoring response might read like the example provided below.

DDT had many adverse effects on animals and humans alike. High concentrations of the chemical affected fish, making them unfit for human consumption. The pesticide also affected fish-eating birds by causing them to produce thin-shelled eggs, jeopardizing their reproductive abilities. DDT used on grasses and ingested by cows led to an increase of hazardous chemicals found in milk. People were concerned that infants who drank the milk might also be affected.

The following section includes reading selections that are similar to passages on the FCAT. Remember to stay actively involved while you read, using the reading strategies from this and previous chapters of the book.

Read the article "Women Win the Right to Vote!" and answer Numbers 1 through 8.

★ ★ ★ ★ ★

Women Win the Right to Vote!

By Bridget E. Smith, *Historical Gazette*

After 72 years of concerted steady effort by women and their fair-minded men allies, the right to vote along side their brothers is finally granted! It is a tragedy that women such as Alice Paul had to be jailed and suffer untold indignities to gain the attention of the nation, but the fight to win the vote was becoming desperate and women were tiring of the long battle.

What began innocently at a tea party in Seneca Falls, N.Y. as a plan to gain political and societal rights afforded to even the poorest of men in 1848 has now found what then seemed to be the boldest of the women's demands made into a reality: the right to vote.

When Elizabeth Cady Stanton and Lucretia Mott first met in London while accompanying their husbands to the first World Anti-Slavery Convention, they were refused a place in the hall, instead they were seated behind a grille, and were refused, as was customary at the time, a chance to speak.

It would be eight years before they would meet again. That day in July 1848, Mott and Stanton hastily organized the first Woman's Rights Convention to be held on July 19 and 20 at the Wesleyan Chapel in Seneca Falls.

The first day, men would be refused entrance while the women discussed and amended a Declaration of Sentiments and 11 Resolutions which had been written up by the organizers. The next day the doors were opened to men, many of them well-known and respected.

Among the men, Fredrick Douglass, a freed slave and self-taught publisher, spoke in favor of the women's resolutions. A total of 100 persons signed the document: 68 women and 32 men. The 9th Resolution, written by Stanton, regarding the right to vote, was nearly voted down. But, with the help of Douglass and Stanton's own inspirational oratory, the Resolution passed!

> *United States of America, August 26, 1920*
>
> *It Started in Seneca Falls, New York*
>
> *Amendment Ratified*
>
> *Last state needed to pass finally acts*
>
> *Tennessee Legislature Passes by One Vote*
>
> *Blame it on Elizabeth Cady Stanton and Lucretia Mott*

Suffrage Parade in New York City, May 6, 1912

The stir that these women caused would not be known for a while, but their boldness was seen as revolutionary and "radical" according to *The Seneca County Courier* which carried a story in their paper the day following the convention and published the sentiments and resolutions in their number published on Aug. 4th.

"This convention was novel in its character, and the doctrines broached in it are startling to those who are wedded to the present usages and laws of society. The resolutions are of the kind called radical. Some of the speeches were very able, all the exercises were marked by great order and decorum. When the Declaration of Sentiments (fashioned after the American Declaration of Independence) and Resolutions shall be printed and circulated, they will provoke much remark. Some will regard them with respect, others with... contempt."

Many of the women attending were active in the anti-slave movement and born into the Quaker religion which allowed their women a little more voice than many mainstream religions of the day. One of the major factors that made these Resolutions so difficult to carry out was that women, as a rule, were not allowed to speak at a public forum.

Another movement that was gathering support at the time was the temperance movement. Out of this movement, another Quaker woman would soon join the ranks of the woman's movement, but only after great encouragement from E. Cady Stanton. This new strong ally would become one of the most famous of the movement even though she was not convinced at first that she should spend her time and energy on such a project. Susan B. Anthony would become a life-long friend and Stanton supporter. They published a newspaper *Revolution* for a while which called for equality of the sexes, temperance and fair divorce laws. Anthony was arrested and then put on trial for voting illegally in the 1872 election, although she lost the case, she won national support for women's rights.

Anthony traveled all over the United States, including trips to the Northwest where Abigail Scott Duniway accompanied her to many places, to lecture on the rights and plights of women. Her temperance ideas were opposite of Duniway's, but they agreed on the main topic—woman's suffrage, so Duniway stuck it out and carried many letters from Anthony in her newspaper, the *New Northwest*.

Since newspapers and lecture circuits were the only real way of getting one's message out, many different suffrage newspapers were needed. *No TV, Radio or Internet then.* But, it seemed that as soon as one would go out of business, usually bankrupted, (Anthony assumed a $10,000 debt from the *Revolution*) another would rise to take its place.

The main topic always included the topic of voting rights, but their other leanings might be totally opposite. While Anthony was true Temperance, Duniway was against trying to legislate morality. Another early publisher sought to simplify woman's clothing and free her body as well as mind:

Amelia Bloomer, publisher

Promotes Sensible Fashion, Temperance in her newspaper

*A monthly Journal **The Lily** is Devoted to the Emancipation of Woman from Intemperance, Injustice, Prejudice and Bigotry*

Between 1851 and 1854, Lucy Stone, Elizabeth Cady Stanton, Susan B. Anthony and others of the women's rights movement followed Bloomer's fashion ideas about women's clothing and adopted The Bloomers as their attire, only to be treated with contempt wherever they went: jeered at in the streets and criticized from the pulpit. They continued as long as they could bear the public condemnation. It essentially made them ineffectual because their lectures would be continuously interrupted with snide remarks.

The August 1852 number of *The Lily*, carried an address from the Woman's Rights Convention that had been held that year in Worchester, Pa., given by Miss Ann Preston. Here is a small quote:

"We place not the interests of woman in antagonism to that of her brother, for 'The woman's cause is man's; They rise or sink together; Dwarfed or God-like, bond or free'. ...We ask for her, as for man, equality before the law, and freedom to exercise all her powers and faculties under the direction of her own judgment and volition."

The struggle to raise people's awareness to the plight of women became more intense. The suffragists pointed out many injustices: taxation without representation (women paid taxes, but could not vote); the disgrace that widows experienced after their husbands died was not ever experienced by the man (children could be taken by the state with no regard for the mother's wishes and the state could seize property since women could not legally own property in many states); and, divorces were difficult, if not impossible to obtain, when requested by women. It became apparent that men needed to speak up for their own daughters' future, if not for their own wife.

The question that became resounding, *How long must we wait for freedom?* was repeated by speakers at every opportunity. The length of time one had to wait depended upon in which state you lived.

Wyoming Gives Women Suffrage When Becoming A Territory—1869

The Westward movement that had already begun when Mott and Stanton organized the first Women's Rights Convention in 1848 was to change the scene of politics forever. Women were in great demand in the West and even the lowliest women were treated with respect to encourage them to stay on the frontier.

In Wyoming, Esther Morris, a milliner from New York who followed Anthony's philosophy, managed to convince the territorial legislature that women could help establish law and order if they had the vote. This one woman, at a tea party in her frontier home, convinced these men that it would benefit them to enfranchise women. The battle there was won without a fight.

In 1890, when Wyoming entered the Union as a state, it became the first woman's suffrage state. Colorado soon followed in 1893. Utah became the third state to join the suffragist states in 1896. Idaho gave women the vote the same year Utah entered the Union. The victory in Colorado and Idaho was won primarily by the efforts of Carrie Chapman Catt (founder of League of Women Voters) who taught women how to lobby and organize.

Answer questions 1 through 8. Base your answers on the article "Women Win the Right to Vote!"

1 How did Elizabeth Cady Stanton and Lucretia Mott react to the ban on women speaking at public meetings?

A. They wrote a Declaration of Sentiments.

B. They organized a convention for women.

C. They published the first suffrage newspaper.

D. They traveled to London to give their lectures.

2 What is the most likely reason that Frederick Douglass was a women's rights supporter?

F. As a self-taught man, he understood the importance of education.

G. As a former slave, he knew what it was like to be denied basic rights.

H. As a well-known speaker, he realized how much his speeches could help.

I. As a publisher, he understood the importance of publicity to the movement.

3 What was the result of Susan B. Anthony getting arrested for voting illegally?

A. She discouraged other women from voting.

B. She damaged the women's rights movement.

C. She encouraged other women to break the law.

D. She gained support for the women's rights movement.

4 What caused Stone, Stanton, and Anthony to join forces?

    F. Each was a radical feminist and a supporter of the temperance movement.

    G. Each was oppressed in her religion and joined together to fight persecution.

    H. They believed in the importance of fighting for every individual's right to vote.

    I. They each wanted to work for the paper, *Revolution,* to voice their political views.

5 Why were women treated with more respect in Western states?

    A. There was a shortage of women in the West.

    B. There were more fair-minded men in the West.

    C. There was more interest in women's rights in the West.

    D. There were more Quaker men and women in the West.

6 How did Carrie Chapman Catt help the women's rights movement in Colorado and Idaho?

    F. She lectured at women's rights conventions.

    G. She taught women how to lobby and organize.

    H. She brought attention to women's rights by voting illegally.

    I. She convinced men that women could make the West more lawful.

7 READ THINK EXPLAIN   Besides not being able to vote, what were some of the other injustices that made women fight to gain more rights? Support your answer with details and information from the article.

What key actions did the activists in the women's rights movements take to win the right to vote for women? Support your answer with details and information from the article.

_____

_____

_____

_____

_____

_____

_____

Read the excerpt from the story "Leiningen Versus the Ants" and answer Numbers 1 through 6.

Leiningen Versus the Ants

by Carl Stephenson

. . . . Moreover, during his three years as planter, Leiningen had met and defeated drought, flood, plague, and all other "acts of God" which had come against him—unlike his fellow settlers in the district, who had made little or no resistance. This unbroken success he attributed solely to the observance of his lifelong motto: The human brain needs only to become fully aware of its powers to conquer even the elements. Dullards reeled senselessly and aimlessly into the abyss; cranks, however brilliant, lost their heads when circumstances suddenly altered or accelerated and ran into stone walls; sluggards drifted with the current until they were caught in whirlpools and dragged under. But such disasters, Leiningen contented, merely strengthened his argument that intelligence, directed aright, invariably makes man the master of his fate.

Yes, Leiningen had always known how to grapple with life. Even here, in this Brazilian wilderness, his brain had triumphed over every difficulty and danger it had so far encountered. First he had vanquished primal forces by cunning and organization, then he had enlisted the resources of modern science to increase miraculously the yield of his plantation. And now he was sure he would prove more than a match for the "irresistible" ants.

That same evening, however, Leiningen assembled his workers. He had no intention of waiting till the news reached their ears from other sources. Most of them had been born in the district; the cry "The ants are coming!" was to them an imperative signal for instant, panic-stricken flight, a spring for life itself. But so great was the Indians' trust in Leiningen, in Leiningen's word, and in Leiningen's wisdom, that they received his curt tidings, and his orders for the imminent struggle, with the calmness with which they were given. They waited, unafraid, alert, as if for the beginning of a new game or hunt which he had just described to them. The ants were indeed mighty, but not so mighty as the boss. Let them come!

They came at noon the second day. Their approach was announced by the wild unrest of the horses, scarcely controllable now either in stall or under rider, scenting from afar a vapor instinct with horror.

It was announced by a stampede of animals, timid and savage, hurtling past each other; jaguars and pumas flashing by nimble stags of the pampas; bulky tapirs, no longer hunters, themselves hunted, outpacing fleet kinkajous; maddened herd of cattle, heads lowered, nostrils snorting, rushing through tribes of loping monkeys, chattering in a dementia of terror; then followed the creeping and springing denizens of bush and steppe, big and little rodents, snakes and lizards.

Pell-mell the rabble swarmed down the hill to the plantation, scattered right and left before the barrier of the water-filled ditch, then sped onwards to the river, where, again hindered they fled along its banks out of sight.

This water-filled ditch was one of the defense measures which Leiningen had long since prepared against the advent of the ants. It encompassed three sides of the plantation like a huge horseshoe. Twelve feet across, but not very deep, when dry it could hardly be described as an obstacle to either man or beast. But the ends of the "horseshoe" ran into the river which formed the northern boundary, and fourth side, of the plantation. And at the end nearer the house and outbuildings in the middle of the plantation, Leiningen had constructed a dam by means of which water from the river could be diverted into the ditch. So now, by opening the dam, he was able to fling an imposing girdle of water, a huge quadrilateral with the river as its base, completely around the plantation, like the moat encircling a medieval city. Unless the ants were clever enough to build rafts, they had no hope or reaching the plantation, Leiningen concluded.

The twelve-foot water ditch seemed to afford in itself all the security needed. But while awaiting the arrival of the ants, Leiningen made a further improvement. The western section of the ditch ran along the edge of a tamarind wood, and the branches of some great trees reached over the water. Leiningen now had them lopped off that ants could not descend from them within the "moat."

The women and children, then the herds of cattle, were escorted by peons on rafts over the river, to remain on the other side in absolute safety until the plunderers had departed. Leiningen gave this instruction, not because he believed the noncombatants were in any danger, but in order to avoid hampering the efficiency of the defenders. Finally, he made a careful inspection of the "inner moat"—a smaller ditch lined with concrete, which extended around the hill on which stood the ranch house, barns, stables, and other buildings. Into this concrete ditch emptied the inflow pipes from their great petrol tanks. If by some miracle the ants managed to cross the water and reach the plantation, their rampart of petrol would be an absolutely impassable protection for the besieged and their dwellings and stock. Such, at least, was Leiningen's opinion.

Answer questions 1 through 6. Base your answers on the excerpt from "Leiningen Versus the Ants."

1 How did the news of the ants affect Leiningen's workers?

    A. Workers constructed boats in order to escape the stampede.

    B. The workers wanted to flee because they were panic stricken.

    C. The workers believed that Leiningen would protect them from the ants.

    D. They were worried about the safety of their families and asked for Leiningen's help.

2 Why were the various animals in the story stampeding?

    F. They knew ants could be destroyed by a stampede.

    G. The animals were fleeing the coming invasion of ants.

    H. The workers were driving herds of animals toward the moat.

    I. The various animals were running toward the safety of the water.

3 Why would the gasoline pipes be an important part of the defense against the ants?

A. The gasoline would kill the tamarind wood.

B. The gasoline would provide fuel for the trucks.

C. It would be diverted into the ditch through a dam.

D. It would serve as a backup in case the ants crossed the ditch.

4 READ
THINK
EXPLAIN
How does the author show that the ants are dangerous? Use details and information from the story to support your answer.

_____

_____

_____

_____

_____

_____

_____

_____

5 Read the following sentences from the story.

> Most of them had been born in the district; the cry "The ants are coming!" was to them an imperative signal for instant, panic-stricken flight, a spring for life itself.

What does *imperative* mean?

A. instinct

B. irresistible

C. native

D. urgent

6 READ THINK EXPLAIN According to Leiningen, why would his lines of defense cause the ants to be defeated? Use details and information from the story to support your answer.

_____

_____

_____

_____

_____

_____

_____

Read the article "The Paper Chase" and answer Numbers 1 through 8.

The Paper Chase
by Fenella Saunders

Focused blasts of sound may be the key to saving trees and reducing the flow of garbage.

The computer revolution has brought many improvements to the workplace, but the long-promised "paperless office" is not one of them. In theory, people can read information on the Web, communicate via email, and shuttle files by disk or network, performing all of their tasks electronically. In practice, the paper that once went into legal pads and typewriter sheets has just been replaced by even larger stacks of paper that spew out of laser printers and copying machines. All that paper translates into a lot of landfill garbage and a lot of lost trees.

Paper recycling can reduce that waste, but photocopier and printer inks contain water-repelling compounds like styrene, making them difficult to dissolve. The harsh chemicals required to remove these kinds of ink for bulk recycling are themselves environmentally unfriendly. One solution is to develop a gentler chemical process. Sushil Bhatia of Imagex Technologies in Framingham, Mass., is developing a "decopier" that uses nontoxic compounds to strip the ink from paper right in the office. His invention was a finalist in the 1998 Discover Technology Awards.

Sameer Madanshetty, a mechanical engineer at Kansas State University, has come up with another way. He has devised a recycling procedure that dispenses with chemicals entirely; it also does so little damage to the paper fibers that pages can be reused multiple times. And all he needs to do it is some water and precisely controlled pulses of sound.

As a sound wave travels, it creates a ripple of expansion and compression: a low-pressure pulse followed by a high pressure pulse, and so on. Tiny bubbles that can sometimes form in water and other liquids react to this change in pressure. The low pressure pulse expands the bubbles and the high pressure pulse makes them contract.

With certain sound waves, the contraction caused by the high pressure part of the sound wave can be strong and fast enough to make the bubble collapse in on itself, creating a surprisingly large concentration of energy. Called cavitation, this process is powerful enough that it can damage things like ship propellers and water pipes, eventually eroding them away. Engineers therefore usually try to create cavitation-proof designs, but this goal is hampered by the unpredictable nature of cavitation.

Madanshetty does not see cavitation as a bad thing. "It's such a fascinating energy manifestation, but we are removing it because we don't understand it and we can't control it," he says. "If you think of fire, any fire is devastating, but if you contain it you can do some good cooking." Indeed, Madanshetty has found a way to control when and where cavitation will occur.

With the cavitation process, recycling newspapers could be endless.

Along with a strong sound pulse that causes the bubbles to expand and contract, he uses a weaker background sound wave that destabilizes the bubbles so that they collapse at a lower pressure; the result is that they release less energy and their effect is more localized. When a piece of paper is placed in water, tiny bubbles are most likely to form around the inked parts of the page, because the ink repels water.

Madanshetty's sound system blasts these microbubbles; when they collapse, they literally explode the ink off the page. "It's like micro-jackhammers," he explains. "It chisels away the ink and throws it up." The process can strip the ink from a page in a few seconds, and the ink particles can then be filtered out of the water.

Although the bubbles have enough energy to destroy the ink, Madanshetty's control process keeps them weak enough that they do not seriously damage the paper fibers below. In most cases, the paper need not be mashed up to be recycled—the microbubbles erase the ink effectively enough that the original paper is as good as new, Madanshetty says.

"Present practice mechanically pulps the paper, and in the churning process they damage the paper fibers, so it limits the recycleability to three times," he notes. "In this case, you are not touching the paper fibers at all, so the number of times you can recycle the paper would be endless."

Answer questions 1 through 7. Base your answers on the article "The Paper Chase."

1 What was supposed to happen as a result of the computer revolution?

A. Offices would no longer need to use paper.

B. Offices would no longer need to recycle paper.

C. Offices would need to recycle paper more efficiently.

D. Offices would need to recycle computers instead of paper.

2 Which statement best describes the reason offices use more paper than ever before?

F. People are not recycling paper products.

G. Office workers today write more memos.

H. Printer and copy machine use has increased.

I. "Decopiers" waste more paper than ever before.

3 In the cavitation process, what causes water bubbles to expand?

A. background sound pulses

B. low pressure sound pulses

C. high pressure sound pulses

D. alternating low and high pulses

4 What effect does styrene have on the environment?

F. It makes recycling easier.

G. It contributes to pollution.

H. It has no effect on the environment.

I. It helps develop cleaner paper resources.

5 Why do bubbles form around the inked part of paper placed in water?

A. The ink repels the water.

B. The ink absorbs the water.

C. The ink damages the paper.

D. The ink destabilizes the paper.

6 What effect do collapsing microbubbles have on paper being recycled?

F. They protect the paper fibers.

G. They filter ink from the water.

H. They damage the paper fibers.

I. They explode the ink off the paper.

7 READ THINK EXPLAIN How did Sameer Madanshetty overcome the problems caused by cavitation? Support your answer with details and information from the article.

Why is Sameer Madanshetty's sound wave process a better way to recycle paper than the methods used today? Support your answer with details and information from the article.

_____

_____

_____

_____

_____

_____

_____

_____

Appreciating Narrative Writing

Benchmark LA.E. 2.4.1

Analyzes the effectiveness of complex elements of plot, such as setting, major events problems, conflicts, and resolutions.

When choosing a book to read for pleasure, what do you look for? Some students go right to the science-fiction section of their school library, while others search for the newest titles by their favorite authors. Books about historical figures, sports personalities, or the other famous people are also favorite reading choices for people.

Have you noticed that when you are interested in what you are reading, the material seems easier to understand? Unfortunately, there are times that reading selections are made for you. In school you are assigned readings, and in tests you are expected to read whatever has been included in the exam. In these instances, it might seem like the reading choices are less interesting, and more difficult to understand.

One way to help you cope with these "more difficult and less interesting" reading selections, is to become more familiar with the basics of literature. The more you understand about the elements of plot mentioned in this chapter, the easier it will be for you to understand—and even enjoy—literature you are required to read.

This is also a good reason why it's important to practice learning and reviewing these fundamental elements *outside* of the classroom. If you take the time to do this, you'll soon find that applying what you learn to readings on the FCAT or in school will not be difficult.

Understanding the Benchmark

There are plenty of opportunities to observe plot elements. Even while you are reading your favorite books, or watching a film, you can be learning the elements of plot. The more aware you are of how writers use these elements, the more you will enjoy reading and the better you will do on questions that assess this benchmark on the FCAT.

- Look at your literature book. You will find selections of different types that include poetry, drama, short stories, myths, essays, personal letters, and perhaps even a full-length novel. What makes each type of literature unique? Are there particular aspects and conventions within each group that set them apart from each other? What are they?

- Remember that nonfiction works of special importance are considered as literary texts. When you are reading nonfiction, note instances when an author uses the elements of plot (including setting, characterization, mood, or conflict) to make her writing more entertaining.

- Watch your favorite television show and see if you can identify some of the elements of the plot. Ask yourself: What is the problem in tonight's episode? How do the characters interact with each other? Where do events take place?

- Watch a movie and then talk to a friend or family member about it. Discuss the film, trying to answer questions like: Whose story is being told? How was the story developed? Which events in the film were pivotal to advancing the story and developing relationships between characters? How was the location of the movie important to the events that took place?

Making the FCAT Connection

On the FCAT, this benchmark will be tested by informational or literary selections, including poetry and drama. You may be asked to read texts linked by a common theme or a single passage consisting of two or more related sections. You will be asked to identify and analyze elements of plot, such as sequence of events, and conflict and resolution. You may be asked to discuss the importance of setting or the author's purpose for characters' actions.

Multiple-choice, short-response, and extended-response items from literature and informational texts, will be used to evaluate your understanding of this benchmark.

Taking a Closer Look

To begin recognizing the elements of plot, we should start with a few definitions. Understanding the meaning of key literary terms, plot, setting, character, and theme, will help you understand questions that assess this benchmark. Keep in mind that these definitions are introduced in this chapter in simplistic terms. Not all stories you read are developed in exactly this format. In order to keep storytelling interesting and different, authors take liberty with this basic format, playing with the sequence of events and complexity of story lines.

Plot

The *plot* is the sequence of events in a work of literature. We usually think of the plot as what happens in a story with a clear beginning, middle, and end. The major components of plot are the next important terms to be defined.

The beginning, or *exposition*, introduces the characters, setting, and the key circumstances of the story. Within a story, an incident will occur that usually introduces a central *conflict* or problem to the characters. This problem then helps develop the story through *rising action*. The action will then reach a *climax* or high point. Next comes the turning point. This is where an important decision made by a character leads to the story's end—or *resolution*, of the conflict.

The diagram below is a common illustration you may be famililar with that helps us to map the plot of a story. This example maps the plot of a familiar tale:

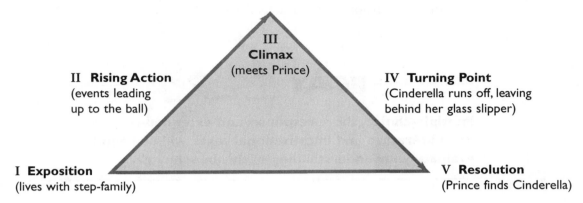

At the beginning of the story, Cinderella lives with her two wicked stepsisters, and her stepmother. A sequence of events, or rising action (including several obstacles—the conflict), lead up to Cinderella's attending the ball. At the ball, the high point of the story occurs when she meets the handsome prince and falls in love. This is when the turning point of the story takes place: Cinderella has to hurriedly rush home to meet her curfew, leaving the baffled prince to wonder about her identity. The resolution of the story comes when the prince scours the kingdom and finally finds Cinderella, his new love.

Using a plot to map a story's events can help present complex stories in a more straightforward fashion. Have you tried mapping a story's plot before? Take this opportunity to practice by mapping the plot of another familiar story or literature selection you have recently read in class. Use the graph above to guide your efforts.

I Exposition

_____

_____

II Rising Action (including the Conflict)

_____

_____

III Climax

_____

_____

IV Turning Point

_____

_____

V Resolution

_____

_____

You can practice using this method with any type of story, whether it is published in a book, sung as lyrics, or told in a film or an episode of your favorite show.

Setting

The *setting* of a story is the time and the place in which the action takes place. The time may be a period in history, a particular time of year, or even a specific time of day. The place might be a country or region, city or town, or even a specific room in a house. In some narratives, the information describing the setting is provided in great detail, and in other selections it is left for readers to piece together. In these instances, a reader must pay attention to details like clothing descriptions, mentions of historical figures, and references to customs of the time in order to determine the setting.

Can you determine the setting of the following paragraph?

> His wide-brimmed Stetson pulled down to cast his face in a shadow, the sheriff rode slowly down the dusty main street. Sunlight sparkled on his silver spurs and on the handle of his rarely used revolver which hung casually by his right side. Stretching his long frame, he dismounted outside the telegraph office.

Where is this paragraph set? Take a few moments to determine what you can about the setting based on what you just read. Write your ideas down below.

_____

_____

_____

_____

_____

_____

_____

_____

Did the author give a detailed description of the setting? Unfortunately, this author left much of that for us to determine based on the details she provided. If you notice, the sheriff was riding down a "dusty" street, most likely on a horse. We also know this story was set in a time when the telegraph was an important form of communication. Based on this information we can assume the story is set in a western town about 100 years ago.

The setting of a narrative is important because it provides a background, where and when the story takes place, and can also be essential to the plot. Sometimes it may have an effect on the events of the plot, or it may reveal information about a character.

Sometimes the setting of a story will help set the mood and provide clues as to what type of story will unfold. When we read about an abandoned house at the top of the hill, and learn that people have disappeared upon entering it, we know that this setting is likely a place where scary events will transpire.

Character

The *characters* are the people or animals (or sometimes objects given human qualities) who participate in the story's action. Each character has certain qualities, or character traits, that the reader discovers as the narrative unfolds. Sometimes a character's traits are indirectly described through the character's actions, thoughts, or the ways in which a character interacts with others.

When considering "character" ask yourself the following questions:

- How is this character physically described? Does this character's appearance say anything about him/her?
- What does this person say or do? What do the actions and speech of this character say about him/her?
- Is there any significance to this character's name?

- What other attributes does the author describe this character as having?
- How do other characters view him/her?

Take a few moments to think of a character you know from a book, play, film, or television show. Use the questions listed on the previous page and above to help you evaluate this character.

_____

_____

_____

_____

_____

_____

_____

Theme

The main idea of a literary work is called the *theme*. It is the primary message or insight about life that is uncovered in a work. All other elements of a story—plot, character, and setting—work together to develop the theme. In fables, stories that teach lessons about human characteristics and behavior, the theme (called the moral) is directly stated. However, the theme in most narratives is usually not directly stated. To help you discover the theme it is a good idea to ask yourself some questions as you read:

- What is the story *really* about?
- How does the author describe the characters and events?
- What was the author's purpose in writing this story?
- What inferences can I draw from what the author is saying?
- What is the lesson I can draw from this story?

Read the following excerpt and complete the questions that follow. Use the reading strategies in this and earlier lessons to help you as you read.

A Celebration of Grandfathers
by Rudolfo Anaya

I grew up speaking Spanish, and oh! how difficult it was to learn English. Sometimes I would give up and cry out that I couldn't learn. Then he would say, *"Ten paciencia."* Have patience. *Paciencia,* a word with the strength of centuries, a word that said that someday we would overcome... . "You have to learn the language of the *Americanos,*" he said. "Me, I will live my last days in my valley. You will live in a new time."

A new time did come; a new time is here. How will we form it so it is fruitful? We need to know where we stand. We need to speak softly and respect others, and to share what we have. We need to pray not for material gain, but for rain for the fields, for the sun to nurture growth, for nights in which we can sleep in peace, and for a harvest in which everyone can share. Simple lessons from a simple man. These lessons he learned from his past, which was as deep and strong as the currents of the river of life.

Predict:
Use the title to identify the theme of this selection.

Vocabulary:
Foreign words are often italicized. Use context clues to help you understand their meaning.

Analyze:
What do the Spanish words tell you about the grandfather's character?

Analyze:
What details help to create setting?

Now answer the questions that follow.

1. Which statement best describes the theme of this passage?

   A. Change is important for old men.

   B. Grandfathers teach from experience.

   C. English is a difficult language to learn.

   D. Old ways are always better than new ones.

2. How does the author describe his grandfather?

_____

_____

_____

_____

_____

_____

_____

_____

Did you choose to use a graphic organizer? Focusing on the elements of theme, character, and setting should have helped you to answer the questions. Check your answers below.

For the first question, you might have found it helpful to ask yourself, "What is the lesson I can draw from this passage?" We immediately know that answer-choice A is not well supported by the text. Although the passage does speak of change, it does not focus on its importance. Choice B states that grandfathers teach from experience. This statement is supported by the end of the selection, making B a likely answer. While the article does speak of learning English, it does not comment on the degree of difficulty involved in doing so. This makes choice C incorrect. Choice D is not likely the answer as it makes a general statement that is an opinion not supported by the text. Therefore, B best describes the theme of the selection.

A top-scoring response to question two would begin with a general statement that directly responds to the question. It would then be followed by at least two supporting details drawn from the text. An example of a top-scoring response follows:

The author describes his grandfather as being a simple and wise Spanish-speaking man from whom he learned much. He describes instances when his grandfather counseled him to be patient in his efforts to learn English. He also credits his grandfather with teaching him important lessons about how to live his life. The author also implies that the grandfather is a spiritual and modest man who has learned from his experiences.

The following section includes reading selections that are similar to passages on the FCAT. Remember to stay actively involved while you read, using the reading strategies from this and previous chapters of the book.

Read the poem "Lost Sister" and answer Numbers 1 through 8.

And the daughters were grateful:
They never left home.
To move freely was a luxury
stolen from them at birth.
Instead, they gathered patience,
learning to walk in shoes
the size of teacups,
without breaking—
the arc of their movements
as dormant as the rooted willow,
as redundant as the farmyard hens.
But they traveled far
in surviving,
learning to stretch the family rice,
to quiet the demons,
the noisy stomachs.

2

There is a sister
across the ocean,
who relinquished her name,
diluting jade green
with the blue of the Pacific.
Rising with a tide of locusts
she swarmed with others
to inundate another shore.
In America,
there are many roads
and women can stride along with men.

But in another wilderness,
the possibilities,
the loneliness,
can strangulate like jungle vines.
The meager provisions and sentiments
of once belonging—
fermented roots, Mah-Jong tiles and firecrackers—
set but
a flimsy household
in a forest of nightless cities.
A giant snake rattles above,
spewing black clouds into your kitchen.
Dough-faced landlords

1

In China,
even the peasants
named their first daughters
Jade—
the stone that in the far fields
could moisten the dry season,
could make men move mountains
for the healing green of the inner hills
glistening like slices of winter melon.

slip in and out of your keyholes,
making claims you don't understand,
tapping into your communication systems
of laundry lines and restaurant chains.

You find you need China:
your one fragile identification,
a jade link
handcuffed to your wrist.

You remember your mother
who walked for centuries,
footless—
and like her,
you have left no footprints,
but only because
there is an ocean in between,
the unremitting space of your rebellion.

Answer questions 1 through 8. Base your answers on the poem "Lost Sister."

1 "Lost Sister" is a poem about

  A. a Chinese child's visit to the United States.
  B. a Chinese child born in the United States.
  C. a Chinese woman with memories of life in China.
  D. a Chinese woman who has never before left China.

2 What is the author's most likely purpose in this poem?

  F. To describe the lives of peasants in China.
  G. To express regrets about the lives of Chinese women.
  H. To bring to light different struggles faced by Chinese women.
  I. To express feelings and concerns about ancient Chinese traditions.

3 READ
THINK
EXPLAIN How does the author describe a Chinese woman's challenges in the first stanza? Use information and details from the poem to support your answer.

_____

_____

_____

_____

_____

_____

_____

4 What is the demon referred to in the first stanza?

    A. fear

    B. hunger

    C. isolation

    D. pain

5 Which statement best describes the author's attitude toward Chinese women?

    F. The women in China were grateful to do the will of men to survive.

    G. Chinese women in the past were not as strong as the Chinese women today.

    H. The Chinese women who came to America were more content than those in China.

    I. The women both in China and America have deep-seated values rooted in the past.

6 What does jade symbolize in this poem?

    A. envy and regret

    B. fear and loneliness

    C. gratefulness and joy

    D. hope and determination

7 READ THINK EXPLAIN   What tone does the author create when describing the setting in America for the life of a Chinese woman? Use details and information from the poem to support your answer.

_____

_____

_____

_____

_____

_____

_____

8 READ THINK EXPLAIN How do the worlds of China and America, as presented by the author, differ? Use details and information from the poem to support your answer.

Read the excerpt from "With All Flags Flying" and answer Numbers 1 through 7 that follow.

Excerpt from

With All Flags Flying

By Anne Tyler

Weakness was what got him in the end. He had been expecting something more definite—chest pains, a stroke, arthritis—but it was only weakness that put a finish to his living alone. A numbness in his head, an airy feeling when he walked. A wateriness in his bones that made it an effort to pick up his coffee cup in the morning. He waited some days for it to go away, but it never did. And meanwhile the dust piled up in corners; the refrigerator wheezed and creaked for want of defrosting. Weeds grew around his rosebushes.

He was awake and dressed at six o'clock on a Saturday morning, with the patchwork quilt pulled up neatly over the mattress. From the kitchen cabinet he took a hunk of bread and two Fig Newtons, which he dropped into a paper bag. He was wearing a brown suit that he had bought on sale in 1944, a white T-shirt and copper-toed work boots. These and his other set of underwear, which he put in the paper bag along with a razor, were all the clothes he took with him. Then he rolled down the top of the bag and stuck it under his arm, and stood in the middle of the kitchen staring around him for a moment.

The house had only two rooms, but he owned it—the last scrap of the farm that he had sold off years ago. It stood in a hollow of dying trees beside a superhighway in Baltimore County. All it held was a few sticks of furniture, a change of clothes, a skillet and a set of dishes. Also odds and ends, which disturbed him. If his inventory were complete, he would have to include six clothespins, a salt and a pepper shaker, a broken-toothed comb, a cheap ballpoint pen—oh, on and on, past logical numbers. Why should he be so cluttered? He was eighty-two years old. He had grown from an infant owning nothing to a family man with a wife, five children, everyday and Sunday china and a thousand appurtenances, down at last to solitary old age and the bare essentials again, but not bare enough to suit him. Only what he needed surrounded him. Was it possible he needed so much?

Now he had the brown paper bag; that was all. It was the one satisfaction in a day he had been dreading for years.

He left the house without another glance, heading up the steep bank toward the superhighway. The bank was covered with small, crawling weeds planted especially by young men with scientific training in how to prevent soil erosion. Twice his knees buckled. He had to sit and rest, bracing himself against the slope of the bank. The scientific weeds, seen from close up, looked straggly and gnarled. He sifted dry earth through his fingers without thinking, concentrating only on steadying his breath and calming the twitching muscles in his legs.

Once on the superhighway, which was fairly level, he could walk for longer stretches of time. He kept his head down and his fingers clenched tight upon the paper bag, which was growing limp and damp now. Sweat

rolled down the back of his neck, fell in drops from his temples. When he had been walking maybe half an hour he had to sit down again for a rest. A black motorcycle buzzed up from behind and stopped a few feet away from him. The driver was young and shabby, with hair so long that it drizzled out beneath the back of his helmet.

"Give you a lift, if you like," he said. "You going somewhere?"

"Just into Baltimore."

"Hop on."

He shifted the paper bag to the space beneath his arm, put on the white helmet he was handed and climbed on behind the driver. For safety he took a clutch of the boy's shirt, tightly at first and then more loosely when he saw there was no danger. Except for the helmet, he was perfectly comfortable. He felt his face cooling and stiffening in the wind, his body learning to lean gracefully with the tilt of the motorcycle as it swooped from lane to lane. It was a fine way to spend his last free day.

Half an hour later they were on the outskirts of Baltimore, stopped at the first traffic light. The boy turned his head and shouted, "Whereabouts did you plan on going?'

"I'm visiting my daughter, on Belvedere near Charles Street."

"I'll drop you off, then," the boy said. "I'm passing right by there."

The light changed, the motor roared. Now that they were in traffic, he felt more conspicuous, but not in a bad way. People in their automobiles seemed sealed in, overprotected: men in large trucks must envy the way the motorcycle looped in and out, hornetlike, stripped to the bare essentials of a motor and two wheels. By tugs at the boy's shirt and single words shouted into the wind he directed him to his daughter's house, but he was sorry to have the ride over so quickly.

His daughter had married a salesman and lived in a plain square stone house that the old man approved of. There were sneakers and a football in the front yard, signs of a large, happy family. A bicycle lay in the driveway. The motorcycle stopped just inches from it. "Here we are," the boy said.

"Well, I surely do thank you."

He climbed off, fearing for one second that his legs would give way beneath him and spoil everything that had gone before. But no, they held steady. He took off the helmet and handed it to the boy, who waved and roared off. It was a really magnificent roar, ear-dazzling. He turned toward the house, beaming in spite of himself, with his head feeling cool and light now that the helmet was gone. And there was his daughter on the front porch, laughing.

Answer questions 1 through 7. Base your answers on the excerpt from "With All Flags Flying."

1 Which statement probably best expresses the character's attitude about material possessions?

  A. He has a strong attachment to all of the material things from his life.

  B. They are not very important to him since he leaves most things at home.

  C. He is proud of the possessions he has accumulated throughout the years.

  D. He inventories all of his possessions so he will always remember what he has.

2 What is the primary reason the old man must leave his home?

  F. He has suffered a stroke.

  G. He misses his daughter and her family.

  H. He is too feeble to continue to live alone.

  I. He is no longer able to take care of his property.

3 According to the story, in what kind of atmosphere does his daughter live?

    A. She lives alone since her husband travels.

    B. She lives with her family which seems happy and active.

    C. She lives in a very elegant home with a beautiful front porch.

    D. She lives very near a busy highway thus creating a noisy setting.

4 Why is the old man sorry to end the motorcycle ride?

    A. He wants to continue to enjoy the outdoors.

    B. He was enjoying the exhiliration of the ride.

    C. He has enjoyed the company of the young driver.

    D. He is unsure about arriving at his daughter's house without an invitation.

5 READ THINK EXPLAIN   How does the character change from the time he leaves his home until the time he arrives at his daughter's house? Use details and information from the story to support your answer.

6 Read the sentence from the passage.

> **He left the house without another glance, heading up the steepbank toward the superhighway.**

What can we conclude about the old man?

A. He is happy to leave his home.

B. He made a final decision about leaving.

C. The old man is unsure about his choice to leave.

D. The old man has already taken inventory of his house.

7 READ THINK EXPLAIN   What details in the story help to create a sense of loneliness? Use details and information from the story to answer the question.

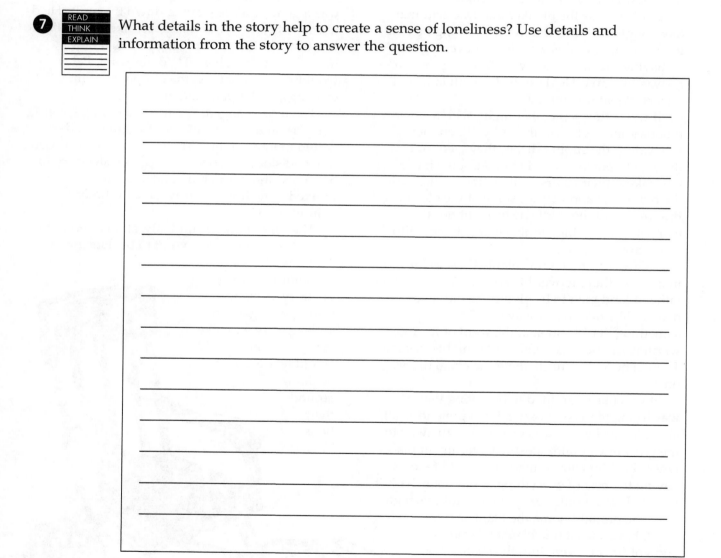

Read the story "The Blanket" and answer Numbers 1 through 8.

The Blanket

by Floyd Dell

Petey hadn't really believed that Dad would be doing it—sending Granddad away. "Away" was what they were calling it. Not until now could he believe it of Dad.

But here was the blanket that Dad had that day bought for him, and in the morning he'd be going away. And this was the last evening they'd be having together. Dad was off seeing that girl he was to marry. He'd not be back till late, and they could sit up and talk.

It was a fine September night, with a silver moon riding high over the gully. When they'd washed up the supper dishes they went out on the shanty porch, the old man and the bit of a boy, taking their chairs. "I'll get me fiddle," said the old man, "and play ye some of the old tunes." But instead of the fiddle he brought out the blanket. It was a big, double blanket, red, with black cross stripes.

"Now, isn't that a fine blanket?" said the old man, smoothing it over his knees. "And isn't your father a kind man to be giving the old fellow a blanket like that to go away with? It cost something, it did—look at the wool of it! And warm it will be these cold winter nights to come. There'll be few blankets there the equal of this one!"

It was like Granddad to be saying that. He was trying to make it easier. He'd pretended all along it was he that was wanting to go away to the great brick building—the government place, where he'd be with so many other old fellows having the best of everything.... But Petey hadn't believed Dad would really do it, until this night when he brought home the blanket.

"Oh, yes, it's a fine blanket," said Petey, and got up and went into the shanty. He wasn't the kind to cry, and, besides, he was too old for that, being eleven. He'd just come in to fetch Granddad's fiddle.

The blanket slid to the floor as the old man took the fiddle and stood up. It was the last night they'd be having together. There wasn't

any need to say, "Play all the old tunes." Granddad tuned up for a minute, and then said, "This is one you'll like to remember."

The silver moon was high overhead, and there was a gentle breeze playing down the gully. He'd never be hearing Granddad play like this again. It was as well Dad was moving into that new house, away from here. He'd not want, Petey wouldn't, to sit here on the old porch of fine evenings, with Granddad gone.

The tune changed. "Here's something gayer." Petey sat and stared out over the gully. Dad would marry that girl. Yes, that girl who'd kissed him and slobbered over him, saying she'd try to be a good mother to him, and all... His chair creaked as he involuntarily gave his body a painful twist.

The tune stopped suddenly, and Granddad said: "It's a poor tune, except to be dancing to." And then: "It's a fine girl your father's going to marry. He'll be feeling young again, with a pretty wife like that. And what would an old fellow like me be doing around their house,

getting in the way, an old nuisance, what with my talk of aches and pains! And then there'll be babies coming, and I'd not want to be there to hear them crying at all hours. It's best that I take myself off, like I'm doing. One more tune or two, and then we'll be going to bed to get some sleep against the morning, when I'll pack up my fine blanket and take my leave. Listen to this, will you? It's a bit sad, but a fine tune for a night like this."

They didn't hear the two people coming down the gully path, Dad and the pretty girl with the hard, bright face like a china doll's. But they heard her laugh, right by the porch, and the tune stopped on a wrong, high, startled note. Dad didn't say anything, but the girl came forward and spoke to Granddad prettily: "I'll not be seeing you leave in the morning, so I came over to say good-bye."

"It's kind of you," said Granddad, with his eyes cast down: and then, seeing the blanket at his feet, he stooped to pick it up. "And will you look at this," he said in embarrassment, "the fine blanket my son has given me to go away with!"

"Yes," she said, "it's a fine blanket." She felt of the wool, and repeated in surprise, "A fine blanket—I'll say it is!" She turned to Dad, and said to him coldly, "It cost something, that."

He cleared his throat, and said defensively. "I wanted him to have the best... ." The girl stood there, still intent on the blanket. "It's double too," she said reproachfully to Dad.

"Yes," said Granddad, "it's double—a fine blanket for an old fellow to be going away with."

The boy went abruptly into the shanty. He was looking for something. He could hear that girl reproaching Dad, and Dad becoming angry in his slow way. And now she was suddenly going away in a huff... As Petey came out, she turned and called back, "All the same, he doesn't need a double blanket!" And she ran up the gully path.

Dad was looking after her uncertainly. "Oh, she's right," said the boy coldly. "Here, Dad" —and he held out a pair of scissors. "Cut the blanket in two." Both of them stared at the boy, startled. "Cut it in two, I tell you, Dad!" he cried out. "And keep the other half!" "That's not a bad idea," said Granddad gently. "I don't need so much of a blanket." "Yes," said the boy harshly, "a single blanket's enough for an old man when he's sent away. We'll save the other half, Dad; it will come in handy later." "Now, what do you mean by that?" asked Dad. "I mean," said the boy slowly, "that I'll give it to you, Dad when you're old and I'm sending you—away."

There was a silence, and then Dad went over to Granddad and stood before him, not speaking. But Granddad understood, for he put out a hand and laid it on Dad's shoulder. Petey was watching them. And he heard Granddad whisper, "It's all right, son—I knew you didn't mean it..." And then Petey cried. But it didn't matter— because they were all three crying together.

Answer questions 1 through 8. Base your answers on the story "The Blanket."

1 What is the main conflict in the story?

   A. Petey is angry at the woman his father is about to marry.

   B. Petey is angry at his granddad for deciding to move away.

   C. Petey is mad because his father gave his granddad a blanket.

   D. Petey is upset because his father is sending his granddad away.

2 Which words best describe Granddad?

   F. sad and frightened

   G. scared and uncertain

   H. kind and considerate

   I. angry and uncooperative

3 Why was Petey glad that he and his father would be moving to a different house?

    A. He knew they would need a bigger house once his father married.

    B. He knew they needed a bigger house so that Granddad could stay.

    C. He knew their old house wouldn't be the same without Granddad.

    D. He knew their old house wouldn't be good enough for his father's wife.

4 What can you infer about Granddad's leaving the blanket on the floor?

    F. He doesn't think the blanket is very expensive.

    G. He doesn't need the blanket on such a hot night.

    H. He doesn't like the blanket as much as he said he did.

    I. He doesn't want the blanket to get in the way of his fiddle playing.

5 When does Petey's dad realize that sending Granddad away is a terrible idea?

    A. when Granddad starts to cry

    B. when he hears Granddad playing the fiddle

    C. when Petey tells him to cut the blanket in two

    D. when the girl complains that the blanket is too expensive

6 READ THINK EXPLAIN — Why did Petey not allow himself to cry at the beginning of the story, but let himself cry at the end of the story? Support your answer with details and information from the story.

7 Which statement best expresses the theme of the story?

    A. Gifts should be chosen with care.

    B. Family members should be cherished.

    C. Children should always respect their parents.

    D. Difficult decisions are made easier with love.

8 READ THINK EXPLAIN   How well does the writer illustrate the character of the girl? Support your answer with details and information from the story.

FCAT Practice Test 1

PART 1

Read the article "Jackie Robinson," the excerpt from "I Never Had it Made" and the poem "jackie robinson" and answer Numbers 1 through 13.

Jackie Robinson

From *Enjoying American History*

In the years after World War II, the United States took a new look at laws and customs that kept Black Americans apart from other Americans.

For years blacks had complained that they were second-class citizens. In many parts of the United States, blacks were required to attend separate, racially segregated schools. They were barred from "white" hotels, restaurants, and places of worship. They were confined mainly to low-paying jobs, often the hard and dirty jobs that no one else wanted to take. In both North and South, blacks lived mostly in "black" neighborhoods because "white" neighborhoods were often closed to them. In parts of the South, blacks were not allowed to vote or even to register to vote. In the army, blacks were placed in separate units apart from whites.

During World War II, some Americans, black and white, had spoken out against such practices. How could the United States claim to be fighting for basic freedoms abroad, they asked, when it denied full rights to black Americans at home? In 1946 President Truman appointed a committee on civil rights to look into the question of race relations. What problems existed? How could they be resolved?

About this time, a white baseball executive was making a move that would have lasting effects. The executive's name was Branch Rickey, and he was head of the Brooklyn Dodgers. Rickey hired a baseball player named Jackie Robinson—the first black American to be hired for a major league team.

Once Jackie Robinson had broken the color line, other black players entered the major leagues. Within a few years, blacks were the leading players on many of the teams.

Meanwhile, new efforts were made to end discrimination against blacks. In 1948, President Truman asked Congress to pass a variety of civil rights laws. He wanted laws to protect blacks' rights to vote, travel, and get good jobs. He also wanted a law against lynching and a law to end discrimination in the armed forces.

When Congress failed to act, Truman went ahead on his own. He ordered equality in the armed services and in federal hiring. He also set up a committee to make sure that companies doing work for the government did not discriminate against blacks.

Robinson retired from baseball in 1957 to become a business executive. He also devoted more time to the civil-rights movement. In 1972 he died of a heart attack at the age of 53.

Jackie Robinson in his Brooklyn Dodgers uniform, 1950s. Robinson was the first African-American to play major-league baseball.

excerpt from

I Never Had it Made

By Jackie Robinson

That same spring the Benjamin Franklin Hotel in Philadelphia, where my teammates were quartered, refused to accommodate me. The Phillies heckled me a second time, mixing up race baiting with childish remarks and gestures that coincided with the threats that had been made. Some of those grown men sat in the dugout and pointed bats at me and made machine-gunlike noises. It was an incredibly childish display of bad will.

I was helped over these crises by the courage and decency of a teammate who could easily have been my enemy rather than my friend. Pee Wee Reese, the successful Dodger shortstop, was one of the most highly respected players in the major leagues. When I first joined the club, I was aware that there might well be a real reluctance on Reese's part to accept me as a teammate. He was from Ekron, Kentucky. Furthermore, it had been rumored that I might take over Reese's position on the team. Mischief-makers seeking to create trouble between us had tried to agitate Reese into regarding me as a threat—a black one at that. But Reese, from the time I joined Brooklyn, had demonstrated a totally fair attitude.

Reese told a sportswriter, some months after I became a Dodger, "When I first met Robinson in spring training, I figured, well, let me give this guy a chance. It may be he's just as good as I am. Frankly, I don't think I'd stand up under the kind of thing he's been subjected to as well as he has."

Reese's tolerant attitude of withholding judgment to see if I would make it was translated into positive support soon after we became teammates. In Boston during a period when the heckling pressure seemed unbearable, some of the Boston players began to heckle Reese. They were riding him about being a Southerner and playing with a black man. Pee Wee Reese didn't answer them. Without a

Baseball infielder Jackie Robinson points to #42 on the Dodgers scoreboard at his retirement, Ebbets Field, Brooklyn, NYC, January 1957.

glance in their direction, he left his position and walked over to me. He put his hand on my shoulder and began talking to me. His words weren't important. I don't even remember what he said. It was the gesture of comradeship and support that counted. As he stood talking with me with a friendly arm around my shoulder, he was saying loud and clear, "Yell. Heckle. Do anything you want. We came here to play baseball."

The jeering stopped, and a close and lasting friendship began between Reese and me.

jackie robinson

Lucille Clifton

ran against walls
without breaking.
in night games
was not foul
but, brave as a hit
over whitestone fences,
entered the conquering dark.

Go On ▶

Answer questions 1 through 13. Base your answers on the article, excerpt, and poem about Jackie Robinson.

1 To what does Lucille Clifton compare Jackie Robinson in the poem?

    A. a rocket

    B. a missile

    C. a baseball

    D. a baseball bat

2 What is the author's purpose in the first article?

    F. to explain the racial climate of the 1940s

    G. to persuade readers to fight discrimination

    H. to persuade readers to fight for their rights

    I. to describe the feelings of a Black American

3 Choose the statement that best expresses the author's point of view in "I Never Had it Made."

    A. Accepting one's role in life can make things easier to bear.

    B. Overcoming obstacles can be easier with the help of a friend.

    C. Feeling sorry for oneself often helps a person accomplish goals.

    D. Understanding the hatred of others can help you ignore prejudices.

4 Pee Wee Reese could best be described as

    F. a courageous man who accepted Robinson as a person.

    G. a crafty ballplayer who recognized an opportunity for publicity.

    H. a bigoted Southerner who made Robinson's work more difficult.

    I. a fair man who thought Robinson would eventually leave baseball.

5 What conclusion can you draw from the three passages about Jackie Robinson?

    A. He was a brave man who fought tirelessly for civil rights.

    B. He was an athlete who tried to remain neutral on race issues.

    C. He was a fighter who overcame obstacles by confronting his hecklers.

    D. He was an athlete who understood his role as the first black player in the major league.

Go On ▶

6 Read the following lines from the poem.

> *ran against walls*
> *without breaking.*

What may be one of the "walls" to which the poet is referring?

F. prejudices of the other players

G. the hatred of the team's owner

H. an inability to play baseball well

I. walls surrounding baseball fields

7 What would be another good title for the article "Jackie Robinson"?

A. Breaking Barriers

B. A Black Man's Story

C. Discrimination in Baseball

D. A Struggle On and Off the Field

8 How does the author develop the story in the excerpt from "I Never Had it Made"?

F. He uses the testimony of other people to tell his story.

G. He discusses the history of the times and how it influenced baseball.

H. He uses some examples from his early career to illustrate his struggles.

I. He mostly discusses the relationships he had with other baseball players.

9 Read the sentence below.

> **In Boston, during a period when the heckling pressure seemed**
> **unbearable, some of the Boston players began to heckle Reese.**

What does *heckle* mean?

A. cheer on

B. curse at

C. make fun of

D. feel sorry for

10 What was the reason a friendship developed between Reese and Robinson?

F. Reese was afraid of being identified as prejudiced.

G. Robinson cherished the support Reese gave him early in his career.

H. Both men were discriminated against and sought out each other's friendship.

I. Reese knew Robinson was a better player and sought his advice about baseball.

Go On ▶

11 Read the following sentence from the article.

> **Once Jackie Robinson had broken the color line, other black players entered the major leagues.**

In this sentence, the term *color line* refers to the

A. mark that separated blacks from whites in society

B. indicator that blacks were still discriminated against

C. line formed around stadiums keeping black Americans out.

D. barrier that kept black Americans from playing professional baseball.

12 What action of President Truman best illustrated his commitment to end discrimination?

F. He appointed a committee on civil rights to examine race relations.

G. He allowed Jackie Robinson to be drafted into major league baseball.

H. He ordered that armed service and federal hiring be guided by policies that did not discriminate.

I. He supported citizens in World War II who voiced opposition to racial inequities in the United States.

13 READ THINK EXPLAIN How does the author of the article "Jackie Robinson" support the fact that blacks were treated unfairly during the 1940s? Use information and details from the passage to support your answer.

Go On ▶

Read the article "Galactic Gateway" and answer Numbers 14 through 24.

Galactic Gateway

By Bob Sillery

High-tech computers and projectors make the new Hayden Planetarium our best portal to explore Earth's place in the universe.

What's the difference between flying a spacecraft through the Milky Way and pretending to do so? Plenty-until now, that is. New technology at the recently reopened Hayden Planetarium in New York City is putting the reality in virtual reality like never before. To wit: "When we sweep past the rings of Saturn," says Neil de Grasse Tyson, the planetarium's director, "I duck." So do I. Every time.

Looking august and otherworldly—shown at left bathed in blue light at midnight—the 4-million-pound, 87-foot-diameter planetarium rises on spindly legs above the American Museum of Natural History's recently unveiled Cullman Hall of the Universe. That hall and its centerpiece planetarium, together with the adjacent Gottesman Hall of Planet Earth, make up the new Rose Center for Earth and Space, which opened in February. Museum officials are calling the $210 million center the most ambitious endeavor in the organization's 131-year history. The planetarium, they say, is the most advanced, powerful, and highest-resolution virtual reality simulator in the world.

Dramatic and architecturally stunning as the outer sphere is, the planetarium's cutting edges lie within. The first component is, to aficionados of the now-demolished original planetarium at least, an old friend. That's the Zeiss Star Projector, now version Mark IX. Zeiss and the planetarium were in negotiations for a top-of-the line Mark VIII, but Tyson and his colleagues asked for so many extra tweaks that Zeiss declared the new projector a one of-a-kind Mark IX.

As the audience settles into the planetarium's 429 seats for its *Passport to the Universe* show, narrated by Tom Hanks, the Zeiss rises from the floor. It uses 9,100 optic fibers to illuminate the same number of stars on the 38-foot-high dome. The projector sends high-intensity white light through "star masks"—plates just behind the lenses with tiny pin-holes representing stars—and then onto the dome. Because fiber optics transmit the light directly to the star masks, the stars are small and sharp, 10 times as bright as the stars from the earlier projector. In the old projector, the light source was a foot from the lens, so the stars looked like small disks rather than pinpoints.

Another 400 fibers represent more diffused, deep-sky objects. If you brought binoculars into the planetarium, you would see the objects exactly as you would in the night sky. And for even more reality, a special structure rotating in front of each bundle of fibers in the Zeiss projector creates a natural flickering effect, so the stars twinkle.

The new Zeiss projector is seen at the Rose Center for Earth and Space of American Museum of Natural History in New York.

UNVEILING THE ROSE CENTER

The Rose Center for Earth and Space at the American Museum of Natural History comprises the Hall of the Universe—with its crown jewel, the new spherical Hayden Planetarium—and the Hall of Planet Earth, which opened in 1999.

Hayden Planetarium

At the planetarium's Space Theater, scientists and artists have modeled the latest astronomical data into a 3-D, high-definition 20-minutie trip through the universe that's projected onto the planetarium's dome. The Zeiss Star Projector (on the previous page) captures the majesty of the night sky. Then, controlled by Silicon Graphics supercomputer, seven high-powered projectors simulate flight through the stars.

Big Bang Theater

The bottom half of the sphere houses the Big Bang Theater. Visitors look down into a large bowl on the inverted dome for a simulation of the birth of the universe. Rumbling effects accompany rushing, swirling sensations as pent-up forces explode.

Cosmic Pathway

This 350-foot ramp, with 220 images, represents 1.3 billion years of cosmic evolution. The period of human history is the width of a strand of hair.

Scales of the Universe

This walkway uses the size of the Hayden sphere itself as a reference to create proportions for everything from the size of the universe to that of the atom.

After the dome display has brought an awed hush, Hanks announces that the "virtual starship" is ready to blast off into the far reaches of the galaxy. What the museum calls its Digital Dome System will take us for the ride. Speakers wired to each seat deliver low rumbles as we depart Earth, with clusters of stars streaming past us on the curved screen. Our interplanetary voyage takes us past Jupiter and then to the rings of Saturn.

Shifting into interstellar flight, we head toward the Orion nebula, about a dozen light-years across and 1,500 light-years away. The 2 minutes during which the film escorts us through the nebula—an immense cloud of dust and gas in which stars are formed—represent the most accurate rendering possible of this much-studied place. The team on the project, including manager Dennis Davidson, visualization director Carter Emmart, and programmer Erik Wesslak, worked closely with Rice University's Robert O'Dell, an expert on nebulae.

From a flat photo taken by the Hubble Space Telescope, Wesslak used 3-D software to convert the nebula images into something shaped more like, say, an omelet. After corrections from O'Dell, the team placed stars, planets, and other realistic objects into the nebula. These included something that O'Dell first called proplyds, material encapsulating planetary disks—"stellar placentas," says Emmart. In other words planetary systems in the making.

The next challenge: how to render such a huge, amorphous mass. The team turned to the San Diego Supercomputer Center, which has at its disposal an IBM RS/6000 SP supercomputer known as "Blue Horizon," the 10th most powerful computer in the world. The scientists at San Diego are proponents of a powerful form of graphics rendering known as volumetrics, or volume rendering, which uses mathematical expressions to create three-dimensional forms. "Can you render smoke?" Emmart asked them. The answer: Sure. The result

is a voyage into the midst of what has been a smoky abstraction in the night sky until now.

Passport to the Universe is not without its fanciful moments. As we reach the edge of the observable universe, Hanks tells us we're taking a shortcut home, through a black hole. "No one knows what it may look like inside," he says, "so we're free to imagine it." The journey through the swirling vortex of the hole, with flashing lights and thunderous roars, is pure theater.

A muscular array of hardware and software, the Digital Dome System delivers these and other 3-D celestial images after taking over the show from the Zeiss. The system uses a Silicon Graphics Onyx2 computer with 28 300 MHz processors, seven "pipes"—racks full of custom hardware to process graphics—and seven projectors to display the universe at 7.3 million pixels of resolution.

As compelling as *Passport to the Universe* is, it is merely a script that plays multiple times daily. Other pre-choreographed flight experiences will eventually be offered. But the most amazing thing about the system is that it will allow a pilot to guide the imaginary spacecraft, by joystick, anywhere in the universe in real time. "If someone asks, 'What's it like on the far side of the moon?' we could take them right there," is how senior engineer Aram Friedman describes a presentation possibility.

Well, it's not quite that simple. Until you get a flight or two under your belt, operating the joystick can be tricky. "The simulation is moving at incredible speeds, so it's not easy to turn. You tend to overshoot things," says Friedman. "But if we really did have a rocket ship that could fly faster than the speed of light, this would be a great training device for it."

Answer questions 14 through 24. Base your answers on the article "Galactic Gateway."

14 The Rose Center for Earth and Space can best be described as

A. an entertaining museum offering the latest in virtual reality shows.

B. a huge planetarium that has been criticized as being too expensive to operate.

C. a place for space enthusiasts to explore a virtual starship and simulation flights.

D. a new ultra-modern section of a museum containing an impressive planetarium.

15 Which of the following centers would make viewers feel as though they were present at the beginning of time?

F. Cosmic Pathway

G. Big Bang Theater

H. Hayden Planetarium

I. Scales of the Universe

16 The author's purpose in this article is

A. to convince the reader to visit the new planetarium.

B. to explain methods used in creating virtual reality star shows.

C. to describe the newest additions to the Museum of Natural History.

D. to provide readers with a preview the new *Passport to the Universe* show.

17 Which of the following areas would help viewers better understand their proportional relationship to the rest of the universe?

F. Cosmic Pathway

G. Big Bang Theater

H. Hayden Planetarium

I. Scales of the Universe

18 Based on the article, the most popular attraction of the future at the Rose Center will most likely be

A. the Digital Dome System

B. the Cosmic Pathway exhibit

C. 3-D celestial images created by mega computers

D. a virtual reality spacecraft that the visitor can operate

19 Which aspect of technology has had the most impact on the *Passport to the Universe* show?

    F. The Blue Horizon

    G. Zeiss Star Projector

    H. Digital Dome System

    I. The Hubble Space Telescope

20 What would an additional paragraph at the end of the article probably discuss?

    A. Scientists who contributed to the Rose Center

    B. More flight experiences that will be offered in the future

    C. Computers that will improve exhibits at the planetarium

    D. The history of the center from it beginning to the present

21 What causes the stars to twinkle in the *Passport to the Universe* show?

    F. optic fibers that illuminate the dome

    G. diffused light bouncing off the dome

    H. plates that have tiny pin holes poked in them

    I. a rotating structure that passes in front of fibers

22 READ THINK EXPLAIN   Some friends are planning a trip to Rose Center for Earth and Space. What would you suggest they do at the museum and why? Use details and information from the article to support your answer.

Go On

Read the following sentence from the article.

> **The next challenge; how to render such a huge, amorphous mass.**

What does *amorphous* mean?

A. firm

B. dense

C. star-filled

D. shapeless

  How would you promote the *Passport to the Universe* show? Support your answer using details and information from the article.

PART 2

Read the story excerpt "Ta-Na-E-Ka" and the articles "Kay County" and "History of Kaw Mission State Historic Site" and answer Numbers 25 through 33.

"Ta-Na-E-Ka"

by Mary Whitebird

As my birthday drew closer, I had awful nightmares about it. I was reaching the age at which all Kaw Indians participate in Ta-Na-E-Ka. Well, not all Kaws. Many of the younger families on the reservation were beginning to give up the old customs. By my grandfather, Amos Deer Leg, was devoted to tradition. He still wore handmade beaded moccasins instead of shoes, and kept his iron gray hair in tight braids. He could speak English, but he spoke it only with white men. With his family he used a Sioux dialect.

Grandfather was one of the last living Indians (he died in 1953 when he was eighty-one) who actually fought against the U.S. Cavalry. Not only did he fight, he was wounded in a skirmish at Rose Creek—a famous encounter in which the celebrated Kaw chief Flat Nose lost his life. At the time, my grandfather was only eleven years old.

Eleven was a magic word among the Kaws. It was the time of Ta-Na-E-Ka, the "flowering of adulthood." It was the age, my grandfather informed us hundreds of times, "when a boy could prove himself to be a warrior and a girl took the first steps to womanhood."

"I don't want to be a warrior," my cousin, Roger Deer Leg, confided to me. "I'm going to become an accountant."

"None of the other tribes made girls go through the endurance ritual," I complained to my mother.

"It won't be as bad as you think, Mary," my mother said, ignoring my protests. "Once you've gone through it, you'll certainly never forget it. You'll be proud."

I even complained to my teacher, Mrs. Richardson, feeling that, as a white woman, she would side with me.

She didn't. "All of us have rituals of one kind or another," Mrs. Richardson said. "And look at it this way; how many girls have the opportunity to compete on equal terms with the boys? Don't look down on your heritage."

Heritage, indeed! I had no intention of living on a reservation for the rest of my life. I was a good student. I loved school. My fantasies were about knights in armor and fair ladies in flowing gowns being saved from dragons. It never once occurred to me that being Indian was exciting.

Go On ▶

Kay County

The lands in the area of Kay County and surrounding the present Kaw Lake were once claimed by the Osage Indian Nation. Controversies about this claim let to the ratification of a treaty in 1870 forced the Osage east into what is now Osage County. In 1871, a Congressional Commission and a delegation of Kaw Indians selected the northeast portion of the former Osage holdings as a future home for the Kaw Indians. Chief Washungah, or Washunga, both spellings are correct, led 516 Kaw Indians from Council Grove, Kansas to the 100,000 acres set aside for the Kaw Reservation.

The old settlement of Washungah is located within the Federal Corps of Engineers project lands of Kaw Reservoir. It was the site for the Kaw Agency, Kaw Cemetery, and a trading post. Included among its buildings were a boarding school dormitory, infirmary, the superintendent's home and the school which later became the Kaw Council House. The council house has been moved to higher ground and reconstructed, stone by stone, and is now listed on the National Register of Historic Places. The Kaw Cemetery was also relocated to a higher elevation and is now located near the city of Newkirk, Oklahoma.

Another historical site located on the corps lands is the Deer Creek archeological site located in the vicinity of Traders Bend Park area. This site, which is also listed in the national Register of Historic Places, is believed to represent an early French trading post and Indian village. The French first entered the area in 1719, and shortly thereafter, trade with the Indians was established.

Other points of historical interest located in the county are the famed "Pioneer Woman" statue and museum and the Marland Mansion, both of which are located in Ponca City. Also located seven miles southwest of Ponca City is the site of the once sprawling famous 101 Ranch "White House." This was once one of the world's largest ranches and was often visited by Presidents and Kings and the rich and famous from all points of the world.

In 1902 "Old Kaw City," now inundated by the waters of Kaw Lake, was founded as a farming community in the fertile oxbow bend of the Arkansas River. It later became a booming oil town when oil was discovered nearby. Today, a new Kaw City is located on higher ground near the lake.

—http://www.lasr.net

"Pioneer Woman" statue, Ponca City, Oklahoma

Go On ▶

History *of* Kaw Mission State Historic Site

Kansas State Historical Society

When the Santa Fe Trail was the great highway between the Missouri border, then the western limit of American settlement, and the Spanish town of Santa Fe, Council Grove was an important way point on the route. Situated on the Neosho River, it was a natural stopping place, well watered with abundant grass and timber.

At this grove in 1825, the U.S. commissioners negotiated with the Osages for a passage across their lands. This right-of-way, surveyed by the government in 1825-1827, became the Santa Fe Trail as it is known today, and from this council with the Osages the town took its name.

In 1846 a treaty with the Kansa or Kaw Indians gave them a diminished reservation twenty miles square that included the site of present-day Council Grove. Traders and government agents soon followed the tribe to the new location. Seth M. Hays, the first white settler at Council Grove, established his home and trading post in 1847 just west of the Neosho River on the north side of the Santa Fe Trail.

The treaty of 1846 had provided that the government would make an annual payment of one thousand dollars to advance the education of the Kaw Indians in their own country. In 1850 the Methodist Episcopal Church South, which had ministered to the tribe since 1830, entered into a contract with the government, and construction of the mission and school building was completed by February 1851.

The building was of native stone, two stories high, with eight rooms, and was designed to accommodate fifty students as regular boarders, in addition to teachers, missionaries, and farmers. School began in May 1851 under the direction of Thomas Sears Huffaker, a twenty-four year old teacher who had served in the same capacity at the Shawnee Manual Labor School near present-day Kansas City. Classes for Indian children were held until 1854, when the school was closed because of the excessive cost—fifty dollars a year—of maintaining each student. The Kaw Indians never responded well to the efforts of

the missionaries and sent to the school only boys who were orphans or dependents of the tribe. Girls were not allowed to attend. Members of the tribe considered the ways of the white man degrading to the Indian character.

During this period the school averaged about thirty pupils a year. Instruction was given in spelling, reading, writing, and arithmetic. The Indian boys showed facility in learning the principles of agriculture, but they received no instruction in the trades.

A treaty with the Kaw Indians in 1859 provided that the reservation be further diminished to an area nine by fourteen miles. These lands were relinquished in the 1870s, and the tribe moved to a reservation in present-day Oklahoma.

The mission building and grounds were sold to Thomas Huffaker in 1865, and he continued in possession for fourteen years. Thereafter, the property was owned by several individuals until 1926 when Carl I. Huffaker, a son of Thomas, bought the part on which the mission building stands.

In 1951 the Kansas legislature authorized the purchase of the mission property from Mr. Huffaker, and the Kansas State Historical Society, as trustee for the state, now operates it as a museum.

Answer questions 25 through 33. Base your answers on the story excerpt "Ta-Na-E-Ka" and the articles "Kay County" and "History of Kaw Mission State Historic Site."

25 The main purpose of the article "Kay County" is to

   A. persuade readers to visit the Kaw Reservation.
   B. inform readers of the history of Kaw County land.
   C. show the importance of Indian Nations in Kay County.
   D. inform readers of the National Register of Historic Places.

26 According to the two articles, what effect did government treaties have on land belonging to the Kaw Indians?

   F. Treaties increased the amount of land on the reservations
   G. Treaties protected the land for the Kaw Indians for hundreds of years.
   H. Kaw's were forced to move to smaller parcels of land because of the treaties.
   I. The treaties helped to maintain the Kaw land and helped protect their society.

27 READ THINK EXPLAIN What conflict does the narrator face in "Ta-Na-E-Ka"? Support your answer with details and information from the story.

28 Based on all three reading selections, what statements can be made about the Kaw Indians?

    A. They were a tribe who fought for their land and refused government help.

    B. They used treaties to their advantage to get more assistance for their people.

    C. They were determined and were not defeated by other tribes or the US Calvary.

    D. They were a tribe who held on to traditions and made concessions when they had to.

29 According to the article "History of Kaw Mission" what role did the U. S. government play in the Kaw children's education?

    F. The government paid for the school and later closed it.

    G. The government supported but didn't pay for education.

    H. The government gave the tribe money to educate the children.

    I. The government paid for the education of Kaw children through college.

30 Which statement best describes the significance of the age of eleven in the story?

    A. At eleven, male children participated in a battle.

    B. At eleven, female children were expected to marry.

    C. At eleven, children were supposed to become adults.

    D. At eleven, children were made members of the Kaw tribe.

31 How is the article "Kay County" developed?

    F. by tracing the Kaw Indians' lives

    G. through telling the history of the area

    H. by tracing various tribes who lived there

    I. with stories about what happened in the county

32 What is the author's purpose in writing "Ta-Na-E-Ka"?

    A. to describe the childhood of a Kaw Indian

    B. to explain the early history of the grandfather

    C. to illustrate the narrator's conflict with her culture

    D. to show the narrator's relationship with the grandfather

Go On ▶

In the story "Ta-Na-E-Ka," how was Mary's opinion of Indian tradition different from the opinions held by her grandfather, her mother, and her teacher? Use details and information from the story to support your answer.

Go On

Read the poems "That Day" and "Abuelito Who" and answer Numbers 34 through 41.

That Day

By David Kherdian

Just once
my father stopped on the way
into the house from work
and joined in the softball game
we were having in the street,
and attempted to play in *our*
game that *his* country had never known.

Just once
and the day stands out forever
in my memory
as a father's living gesture
to his son
that in playing even the fool
or clown, he would reveal
that the lines of their lives
were sewn from a tougher fabric
than the son had previously known.

❧ Abuelito Who ❧

By Sandra Cisneros

Abuelito who throws coins like rain
And asks who loves him
Who is dough and feathers
Who is a watch and glass of water
Whose hair is made of fur
Is too sad to come downstairs today
Who tells me in Spanish you are my diamond
Who tells me in English you are my sky
Whose little eyes are string
Can't come out to play
Sleeps in his little room night and day
Who used to laugh like the letter k
is sick

is a doorknob tied to a sour stick
is tired shut the door
doesn't live here anymore
is hiding underneath the bed
who talks to me inside my head
is blankets and spoons and big brown shoes
who snores up and down up and down up and
down
again
is the rain on the roof that falls like coins
asking who loves him
who loves him who?

Answer questions 34 through 41. Base your answers on the poems "That Day" and "Abuelito Who."

34 How does Abuelito change throughout the poem?

   A. He is initially full of life, then becomes sick when he is older.
   B. First, he speaks only Spanish and later learns to speak English.
   C. He is fat and soft at first and later becomes thin and hardened.
   D. He throws money away and later is more frugal, protecting his coins.

35 What do the main characters of both poems have in common?

   F. They are both men from foreign cultures.
   G. They are old men who love their grandchildren.
   H. They both act silly to make their children laugh.
   I. They both have problems with speaking English.

36 How does the father in "That Day" cause his son to look at him differently?

   A. The father makes gestures of affection towards his son.
   B. The father includes his son in the stories from the father's past.
   C. The father reminds the son of the heritage of their home country.
   D. The father chances looking foolish when he plays softball with his son.

37 How does the speaker in "Abuelito Who" create an image of her grandfather?

   F. She compares him to familiar things.
   G. She descibes her feelings about his illness.
   H. She gives a detailed physical description of him.
   I. She discusses details that illustrate his love of life.

38 Which statement expresses the speaker's feelings for his father in "That Day"?

   A. He is ashamed of his father's inability to play softball.
   B. He sees his father's attempt to play ball as a sign of love.
   C. He can't image how difficult his father's life must have been.
   D. He thinks of his father as a strange man from a different world.

Go On ▶

39 Why did the author emphasize the words our and his in the first stanza of "That Day"?

    F. to indicate the resentment the son had for his father

    G. to help explain why the son was ashamed of his father

    H. to illustrate the level of the father's commitment to his son

    I. to show the difference between the father's and son's experiences

40 READ THINK EXPLAIN How does the narrator of "Abuelito Who" tell the reader she knows her grandfather very well? Support your answer with details and information from the poem.

41 Which statement best expresses how the speakers in both poems related to an older family member.

    A. Each has been embarrassed by the family member.

    B. Each feels love and understanding for a family member.

    C. Each understands the family member better in adulthood.

    D. Each misses the closeness once felt to the family member.

Go On

Read the article "Gridiron Girls" and answer Numbers 42 through 50.

GRIDIRON GIRLS

By Kelley King

Women's pro football can't touch the NFL in fan base or high finance. But in term of passion, players in the new leagues are second to none. For them it's not about winning, losing or even how they play the game. It's all about playing.

On an unseasonably chilly day in October, gusty winds weren't doing anyone any favors, especially the women of the New York Sharks football team. As they warmed up for their home opener against New England Storm at Mitchell Stadium in Uniondale, N.Y., players cringed as kicks and passes were blown in embarrassing directions. It was so bad that the four members of the Brentwood High color guard shivered in the press box until it was time to march out onto the field for the opening ceremony, and a good portion of the 700 spectators huddled under quilts. "NFL players would have trouble in this wind," said J.T. Turner, the former Minnesota Viking who is commissioner of the two-year-old Women's Professional Football League.

Well-inulated with long underwear and protective padding underneath their baby blue uniforms, the Sharks were sweaty with excitement when they jogged into the locker room for a pregame pep talk. "Nobody comes to *your* house and embarrasses you," bellowed Al Rose, a longtime Long Island-area high school football coach. He's been responsible for guiding these 50 women, more than half of whom had never played in an organized football game before team tryouts in August, through two months of twice-weekly practices. Most of the Sharks whooped and hollered and banged their helmets on the lockers, while a

few bit their lips and stared at their cleats. Almost all had played college sports (mostly softball, basketball and rugby), but what they were here for today—smashmouth tackle football—was different.

Like the Sharks, who range from 20 to 50 years old and hail mainly from Long Island and Brooklyn, a growing number of females around the country are eschewing powder puff and flag versions of football for the real deal. The WPFL, which featured two teams in 1999, expanded to 11 teams in four divisions for 2000. If that's not enough, the National Women's Football League takes to the field in March with at least eight teams.

Turner knows what you're thinking—*two* women's football leagues?—and it's his hope that the two will join forces, so they don't compete for fans and sponsorship. As of yet, high finance and merger strategy have not been the focus of either league. For now, the WPFL and NWFL rely primarily on the enthusiasm and generosity of team owners, each of whom bought in for about $35,000. "I purchased the Sharks when it appeared that no one was going to step up to the plate," says Andra Douglas, a 41-year-old promotion designer for MONEY (a sister Time Inc. publication) who is the Sharks' owner and starting quarterback. "So many corporations have been on the verge of providing sponsorships. (Donna Karan and Tommy Hilfiger have both shown interest.) At present we rely on private donations." The NFL has no immediate plans to provide a financial umbrella for a women's league. "Right now, we're focused on our grassroots organization for girls and young women," says NFL spokesman Brian McCarthy.

Neither women's league has had a problem fielding teams, however. Once the Sharks–Storm game got rolling, it was clear these women had been champing at the bit to release their inner aggression. Everyone from 5' 11", 300 pounds offensive lineman Anna "Tonka" Tate to 5-foot, 110-pound running back Jacqueline Colon hit and took hits with a sort of gleeful abandon. "Many of these girls learned to

tackle from older brothers in the living room," says Douglas, who petitioned unsuccessfully to join her Zephyrhills (Fla.) High School football team in the late 1970s. Defensive back Val Halesworth was luckier. The 34-year-old three-sport coach at Oyster Bay (N.Y.) High was voted MVP four times while playing on all-boys youth teams form age eight to 14.

"I think it's great that these girls are living out their dreams," says David Keiper, who spent the afternoon snapping photographs of his girlfriend, Fay Pohl, a defensive back, in action: Pohl throwing a block; Pohl leaping for an interception; Pohl getting mauled by a Storm offensive lineman. Other loved ones were not content to watch from a distance. A friend of offensive lineman Nikki Cerrato kept defensive stats. The mother of running back Shelly Cinque sold Sharks sweatshirts. Four-year-old Cobi Rose, distraught at having lost a favorite toy, sat on a corner of the bench and cried—not for his father, Coach Al, but for his mother, Carol, who was busy playing tight end.

"It can be hard on us, time wise," admits Carol, an athletic director at Wyandanch Memorial High in Suffolk County on Long Island, and co-owner, with Al, of a fitness center, *and mother* of sons Cobi and Cameron. It was she who suggested him for the head coaching job when Douglas was having trouble finding volunteers. The WPFL doesn't mandate the job of coach be unpaid, but since the Sharks must draw an estimated 1,000 fans per game to turn a profit and were averaging 500 through Nov. 30, neither coach nor players expects to be compensated much. (Most WPFL players earn between $50 and $100 per game.) "Maybe that will happen down the road," says Carol. "I just love hanging out with the girls and not being a mom for a moment."

While only one of the Sharks is a mom, many have moms who cringe at the sight of bruises on their daughters' arms. "I've always been proud of my children," said Angela Leary, whose twin daughters, Jen and Marion, are both free safeties for the Sharks. "But I'm afraid when one of them goes down."

Members of a women's professional football team gather before an exhibition game, December 2, 2000 in Hempstead, New York. Women's professional tackle football, still in its infancy, is gaining steam across the country.

Team doctor Phil Santiago, who has donated his services for the Sharks, paces the sideline to make sure the team's medical needs are met. Along with having breasts and ovaries to protect, women also are more susceptible to injuries of the anterior cruciate ligament. "We keep a watch on knee problems," says Santiago, who's working with other WPFL team doctors to develop protective pads for the chest and lower abdomen. "Women are prevention minded," said Santiago. "They're more into chiropractic treatment and herbal supplements." An empty vial of liquid ginseng, left on the locker room floor after the halftime huddle, illustrates his point, while three cigarette butts, left in a bathroom stall, provide evidence to the contrary.

But if these women played by all the rules, they wouldn't have been at Mitchell Stadium that Saturday. Certainly 50-year-old Carol Sullivan, the only Shark with a full head of silver hair, wouldn't have been there. Sullivan, whose high school, Middletown (N.J.) Township didn't offer varsity sports for girls in the 1960s, has always loved football. "I watch myself out there," says Sullivan. "But this is tons of fun."

Go On ▶

Which, for these athletes, is truly the reason they're here. After a 17-yard field goal with no time left on the clock gave the Storm a 3-0 victory, the Sharks hung their heads for just moment before grinning again. "We all win together, we all lose together," piped up a voice amid the mixed group of Sharks and Storm players slapping hands at the 20-yard line. These women, after all, had jobs to go to on Monday, loved ones to meet in the parking lot and no one but themselves to answer to for a kick that had been lost in the wind.

WPFL Playoffs

New England	**29**
Daytona Beach	26
National Conference Championship Game	
Houston	**35**
Minnesota	14
American Conference Championship Game	
NY Sharks	7
New England	**10**
National Con. Wildcard Game	
Colorado	0
Houston	13
American Con. Wildcard Game	

National

South	W-L-T	PF	PA
Daytona Beach	6-0-0	206	45
Miami	3-4-0	134	135
Tampa	1-6-0	54	253
East	**W-L-T**	**PF**	**PA**
New England	4-2-0	123	35
NY Sharks	4-2-0	114	77
NY Galaxy	4-2-0	6	164
Exhibition Teams			
Carolina Cougars	1-1-0	28	8
Sacramento Sirens	0-1-0	0	53

Go On ▶

Answer questions 42 through 50. Base your answers on the article "Gridiron Girls."

42 What evidence does the author present to indicate that women's football is becoming more popular?

A. Fans are willing to pay higher prices for their tickets.

B. Corporations are providing sponsorships to fund team expenses.

C. The salaries of coaches and players are rising at astonishing rates.

D. The number to teams has increased significantly over the last few years.

43 According to information in the charts, how did the New York Sharks compare to the New England Storm at the end of the season?

F. Neither team had a winning record, but the Sharks won the playoff game.

G. The Sharks had more wins than the Storm and went on to win the playoff game.

H. The Storm had more wins than the Sharks but the Sharks' won the playoff game.

I. Both teams had the same number of wins and losses but the Storm won the playoff game.

44 Read the following sentence from the article.

> Like the Sharks, who range from 20 to 50 years old and hail mainly from Long Island and Brooklyn, a growing number of females around the country are *eschewing* powder puff and flag versions of versions of football for the real deal.

What does *eschewing* mean?

A. embracing

B. giving up

C. participating in

D. recruiting

45 What effect did the loss have on the players on the Sharks team?

F. They were upset since they always play to win.

G. They were sad about the loss yet hopeful about their next meeting.

H. They were excited because even though they lost, it was a close game.

I. They were satisfied because they are having fun playing a game they love.

Go On ▶

46 Which statement best expresses the main idea of the article?

    A. Coaches and players of the WPFL are more dedicated than those in the NFL.

    B. Players in the WPFL are involved in the coaching and managing of their team.

    C. The WPFL anticipates support from owners and corporations to help the league expand.

    D. People involved in the WPFL are passionate about the sport and look forward to its growth.

47 How does the author establish the setting in the article "Gridiron Girls"? Support your answer with details and information from the article.

---

48 Which statement describes an important difference between the NFL and the WPFL?

    A. The NFL has plans to sponsor the WPFL under their corporate sponsorship.

    B. The NFL has a huge following while the WPFL is suffers from lack of fan interest.

    C. The NFL operates on a large budget and has corporate sponsors while the WPFL is privately funded.

    D. The WPFL regularly cancels games because of low attendance while most NFL games are usually sold out.

Go On ▶

49 How does the author organize information in the article?

    F. by telling events in order of importance

    G. by telling the events in chronological order

    H. by stating her feelings and ignoring the events

    I. by giving play descriptions of the events of the game

50 READ THINK EXPLAIN   How would you convince a corporation to give money to support a WPFL team? Use information from the article to support your answer.

STOP

FCAT Practice Test 2

Part 1
Read the article "Wow! A Mile a Minute!" and answer Numbers 1 through 8.

Wow! A Mile a Minute!

But 60 MPH was a breeze Oldfield, better known as
the "Speed King" of the Horseless Carriage World

By Michael Kernan

"You have every sensation of being hurled through space. The machine is throbbing under you with its cylinders beating a drummer's tattoo, and the air tears past you in a gale. In its maddening dash through the swirling dust the machine takes on the attributes of a sentient thing ... I tell you, gentlemen: no man can drive faster and live!"

It is June 20, 1903. Barney Oldfield, billed as "America's Premier Driver," has just become the first man in America to drive a gas-powered automobile around a dirt track at—think of it—a mile a minute! Now his agent is telling a group of rube reporters about the thrilling rigors of unimaginable speed. "The chest of a driver is forced in," he says. "Average lungs can't overcome the outward force and the result is like strangulation. Blood rushes to the head, temporary but complete paralysis of mind over body occurs." The thrill of such speeds, and such hype, was not confined to flacks.

A month later Oldfield drove even faster at the Empire City Track in Yonkers, New York, and *The Automobile* magazine described him taking a curve: "The rear wheels slid sideways for a distance of 50 feet, throwing up a huge cloud of dirt. Men were white-faced and breathless, while women covered their eyes and

sank back, overcome by the recklessness of it all."

They named cars in those days; that day Oldfield was driving old *999*—named after the record-breaking locomotive on the New York Central line. The car had been designed and built by Henry Ford, an obscure Detroit automaker. Ford had driven *999* himself in a few races, but in 1902 he turned it over to this 24-year-old bike racer from Ohio. It was Barney Oldfield who made Ford a household word. "Race on Sunday, sell on Monday" was the watchword. Of course *999* was nothing like the regular cars Ford made, but they were pretty good, too.

It would be nice to report that the Smithsonian owns *999*, but it belongs to the Henry Ford Museum in Dearborn, Michigan,

where it has resided since 1919. But Oldfield, who dominated car racing for ten years, set records in the object at hand, namely a Winton Bullet, one of two owned by the Smithsonian and now on long-term loan to the Crawford Auto-Aviation Museum in Cleveland.

Just after the turn of the century the whole world was car-crazy. In the United States, there were scores of automakers, and most of them built for the rich. Ford made history—and a fortune—by building for the masses. In 1908 he came out with the great *Model T*, a simple machine ("the customer can have any color he wants so long as it's black," he said) that could be fixed with a hacksaw, a hammer and a pair of

Henry Ford (R), American auto maker, standing outside his race car, the "999", which set the world speed record in 1902 of over 90 miles, 1902. In the driver's seat is racer Barney Oldfield, who began his racing career in this car.

Go On ▶

Family driving in a Ford Model T on a rural road, 1910s.

pliers, and cost $825. His idea was to produce cars that his workers could afford to buy, a radical concept that, some historians say, helped ensure that America would never have a worker-led revolution.

The more you read about the early cars, the more you realize that some of the wind-whistling hype was true—at least driving them was often a very dangerous adventure. Before one early race, *999's* engine began to sputter for lack of fuel. Quick as a wink Oldfield cut a hole in the gas tank, stuck in a hose and kept blowing air in as his partner, seizing the tiller, drove all the way around the track. Thereafter, he liked to call himself a human gas pump.

Soon every small boy in the country was copying Oldfield's swagger and round goggles. "We love his grimy, goggled face / His matchless daring in a race," a bit of popular doggerel declared. He used to come to towns for races in his private railroad car. His agent would announce that he would take on all comers at the local horse track, a dirt oval found in

almost every village. Suspense built, and finally the great man emerged, cigar clamped in his mouth to cushion the place where he'd broken some molars in a crash. He usually grinned at the crowd, shouted "You know me, Barney Oldfield!" and took off around the track, steering with a tiller, fighting the bumps. Oil from the open crankshaft jetting up in his face, a hurricane of dirt thrown up on his skidding turns. He always won—he had the fastest car, after all, and each time his promoters would claim he'd set a new speed record. The crowd, feeling a part of history, went wild.

This was a time before garages: cars were still kept in carriage houses and stables. Only a fraction of the nation's roads were paved. By 1902, only 909 cars had been registered in all of New York. The first official gasoline-powered auto race in the country had been held in Chicago in 1895, when Frank Duryea's one-cylinder car beat all contenders after a grueling ten-hour, 52 mile trek—average speed

5.1 mph. The first official auto show was held in 1900 at Madison Square Garden, with 31 cars displayed, many of them still steam-powered.

The first *Winton Bullet,* built in 1902, had four cylinders and a leather clutch facing that wore out quickly. Pistons were cast irons. Tires blew out with frightening frequency. The second *Bullet* had eight cylinders: two in-line four-cylinder engines that were bolted together. In 1904 Oldfield drove it 84 mph at Ormond Beach, Florida. These machines were monsters. *Bullet No. 1* had cylinders as large in diameter as a coffee can. The *999* had a wooden clutch and a 230-pound flywheel that was two feet across a six inches thick.

August 1903 headline: "A Carnival of Speed at Yonkers' Track." Oldfield drove 64.52 mph. By the end of 1904, Barney Oldfield held most of the dirt track records from one to 50 miles. In a time when a skilled worker made $2 a day, Oldfield once won $650 in a single race; he eventually commanded thousands of dollars just to show up. He set records in a *Peerless Green Dragon,* a *Stutz,* a *Blitzen Benz,* and the *Miller Golden Sub*—the first enclosed racing car, gilded and shaped like an egg. In 1910 he nudged the *Blitzen Benz* to 131.25 mph, "fastest ever traveled by a human being," to become "Speed King of the World."

He raced against airplanes. He raced against trains, including once in a Mack Sennett movie where he arrived just in time to save Mabel Normand.

With his agent, the ingenious Will Pickens, Oldfield soon was making money hand over fist. He often sported thousands of dollars' worth of jewelry,

Go On ▶

including a four-carat diamond pinky ring, and he handed out $5 tips when a dime would do. Once in San Francisco, greeted at the station by a brass band, he invited all 65 musicians to dinner at the Palace Hotel and paid a tab of $845, two years' income for many Americans at the time. He spent thousands in bars, where he gained a scandalous reputation as a brawler. What money he didn't drink up or bet on horses seemed to go for fines posed by the American Automobile Association, which, from 1902, was the self-proclaimed arbiter of all speed records and which

insisted on a certain decorum around the tracks.

Officials at the AAA didn't like it either when Oldfield turned actor in 1906 and went onstage on Broadway, revving the *Green Dragon* on a treadmill. It started a fad; the next year 11 characters in various Broadway plays entered driving a car.

Oldfield finally retired from racing at 40, and with Harvey Firestone's help opened the Oldfield Tire and Rubber Company in Akron. The hangovers were lasting longer, and he kept losing the bar fights, but there was still a race or two in

him. In 1927 he averaged 76.4 mph in a 1,000-mile nonstop stock car event at Culver City in California. In 1931 he retreated to a celebrity's retirement in Beverly Hills and watched for years while others broke his records. He died in bed in 1946, at age 68.

There is a story that in old age he was stopped for speeding after a wild chase featuring three motorcycle cops. He watched calmly as the toughest of them strode up.

"Who do you think you are? The cop snarled at him. "Barney Oldfield?"

Go On ▶

Answer questions 1 through 8. Base your answers on the article "Wow! A Mile a Minute!"

1 What is the author's purpose for writing this article?

A. to pay tribute to one of the first race car drivers

B. to explain to readers the history of the automobile

C. to explain the importance of the horseless carriage

D. to advise readers about the pleasures of the early automobiles

2 According to the article, which of the following conditions made driving dangerous?

F. Engines were risky to fix, injuring many people.

G. Roads were not paved and engines weren't dependable.

H. Cars were difficult to steer and often went off the roads into fields.

I. Traveling at high speeds caused such force that drivers felt strangulated.

3 The expression "Race on Sunday, sell on Monday" can best be explained by which of the following statements?

A. Henry Ford offered his car at a discount on Mondays after races.

B. People watching Oldfield race on Sunday would then want to buy a car.

C. The car industry depended on advertisements at Sunday races to help sell cars.

D. Car dealers in New York, were closed on Sunday for the races with sales resuming on Monday.

4 Read the following sentences from the article.

> **The car had been designed and built by Henry Ford, an obscure Detroit automaker. It was Barney Oldfield who made Ford a household word.**

What does *obscure* mean?

F. ambitious

G. entrepreneurial

H. little-known

I. well-known

Go On ▶

5 Which statement best describes the contribution that Oldfield made to the Ford car company?

   A. He risked his life while helping to promote Ford cars.

   B. He contributed most of his time to improving Ford cars.

   C. He helped make the Ford name recognizable by racing their cars.

   D. He became wealthy racing Ford cars and contributed to the company.

6 According to the article, which statement describes a difference between Oldfield and the average American of the time?

   F. Oldfield spent more money in one day than most people earned in one year.

   G. Most Americans were fearful of new inventions and Oldfield was a brave man.

   H. Oldfield was more reckless, extravagant, and daring than the average American.

   I. Oldfield was never satisfied with his career and most Americans liked their jobs.

7 READ THINK EXPLAIN   What evidence does the author use to support the idea that people were "car-crazy" at the beginning of the twentieth century? Use details and information from the passage to support your answer.

_____

_____

_____

_____

_____

_____

_____

_____

Go On ▶

8 READ THINK EXPLAIN   How did Oldfield's character contribute to his popularity? Support your answer using details and information from the article.

_____

_____

_____

_____

_____

_____

_____

Go On ▶

Read the articles "New Studies Suggest Babies Have 'Feelings' Too" and "Development of Food Acceptance Patterns in Early Childhood" and answer Numbers 9 through 20.

New Studies Suggest Babies Have 'Feelings' too

By Patrick Ryan

DUBLIN—Though perhaps not noted for their progressive attitudes towards children, it seems our Victorian forebears knew more about infants than many today give them credit for.

New studies into infants' reactions by an Italian scientist could mean a rewrite by the editors of pediatric textbooks, and a re-think by human experts everywhere, in much the same way as his famous forebear changed the way we look at animals' actions.

Academics must now reconsider the possibility that by their fourth month, infants can become jealous by simply watching mom lavish her attention on another tiny tot.

Experimental Psychologist Riccardo Draghi Lorenz became intrigued by what seemed classic signs of jealousy ... in a four-month-old baby.

Currently based at the UK's Surrey University, Lorenz is involved in PhD research at Portsmouth University in development psychology, which involves studying the development of emotions, and the sense of self and sense of other, in the first year of life. He decided to investigate signs of

infant jealousy further, and analyzed the behavior of 24 babies, aged between four to six months: at least a year and a half younger than the age modern psychologists believe youngsters are capable of complex emotions.

Ironically, back in the early 1900s several leading authors reported instances of jealousy within the first 8 months of life.

"It just show how science progresses," Lorenz told the Earth Times.

"St Augustine noted this around the 4th century, and the Victorians understood it quite

clearly. Respected scientists like William James and Mark Baldwin accepted it, and Charles Darwin observed it in his 13 month-old son, and reported it in *Diary of an Infant*.

So, why was such writing ignored?

"It doesn't fit the paradigm," he shrugs "so science ignored it."

Lorenz comes from a family who realize that values of risk-taking research, and whose achievement forced science to sit up and take notice.

His grandfather was the Austrian Zoologist Dr. Konrad Lorenz, (1903–1989), who shared the 1973 Nobel Prize in Physiology or Medicine, and was the founder and co director of the Comparative Ethology Department in the Max Planck Institute.

Ethology is the study of animal behavior, especially its physiological, ecological, and evolutionary aspects. Dr Lorenz is remembered for his

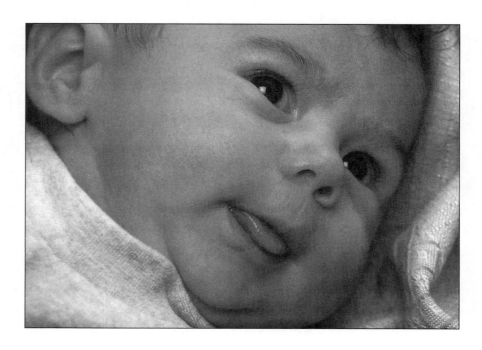

Go On ▶

discovery that auditory and visual stimuli from an animal's parents are needed to induce the young to follow the adult, a phenomenon he called "imprinting." Lorenz's controversial 1966 book *Das sogenannte Böse (On Aggression)* argued that aggressive impulses are basically innate, and drew analogies between humans and animals. He believed human fighting and warfare had genetic origins in lower animal's actions, shown when defending territory.

At the same time that *On Aggression* was hitting the bookshelves, experts in human behavior began to accept that human infants are untouched by emotions, because they lack the necessary representational skills. Parents and pediatricians have long agreed that at two months, babies listen to, and attempt, conversation. Between three and four months, infants become interested in games, and songs, even repeating body movements of adults. They also start looking at their reflection in mirrors, and make silly faces, encouraged by the smiles of appreciative adults, and because their brains produce vast numbers of synapses, the connections from one nerve cell to another, through which information is passed.

However, it was thought that more complex emotions, like jealousy, arrived long after their first footsteps. Riccardo Draghi Lorenz begged to differ. In July he revealed to the International Society of Infant Studies Conference 2000 at Brighton, UK how interactions between parents and infants of 2 to 11 months were videotaped, and as part of a related study, then mothers' reports examined.

Most participants said they first noticed jealousy at about 7-9 months, and a few as early as 4-5 months, but long before their infants' first birthdays, all volunteers had reported several convincing instances of jealousy. Lorenz's methods were straightforward. Moms were encouraged to talk with other adults, and then kiss and cuddle another baby, while their own child's reaction was measured.

"When mothers were talking to adults, three out of the 24 babies became distressed and started to cry. But when the mothers showed love to another baby, 13 out of 24 babies cried, leaving their mothers feeling quite guilty. All but one of the other 11 babies showed some level of jealous reaction." Lorenz explained.

He admitted to the Earth Times that not all physiologists at the conference agreed with his findings, and suggests that it may be another decade before such research is widely accepted. Lorenz believes that science is often about walking on less-traveled pathways.

"If you don't do that then why are you involved in research?"

Development of Food Acceptance Patterns in Early Childhood

by H.A. Guthrie PhD, Rd

ROLE OF GENETIC FACTORS

Reaction to Flavors:

Research at the Monell Chemical Senses Center has shown that newborns have a positive response, as measured by facial expressions, to sweet flavors and a negative response to sour and bitter flavors; responses that may be modified by subsequent learning. The response to salty stimuli is delayed until about four months, at which time infants react positively. Mennella and Beauchamp have also demonstrated that flavors such as chocolate, vanilla, and alcohol in the mother's diet, reflected in the flavor of her milk, influence the sucking reflex and total breast milk intake. It is hypothesized, but as yet not tested, that these infants who have had this early flavor experience are more likely to accept the same or similar flavors in foods. They may also be more receptive to variety in flavors as other foods are introduced later. Formula-fed infants for whom there is little or no flavor variation from one feeding to the next do not have the same early experience of such a range of flavors.

Neophobia:

In general, young infants have a genetically related predisposition to reject new foods. This reaction is known as neophobia —fear of new. A caregiver may find this rejection inconvenient and/or interpret it as a dislike for the food offered and label the infant as a 'fussy eater'. In reality this response is entirely normal and adaptive serving to protect the child should it be offered a food which, if ingested, might lead to adverse consequences including gastrointestinal upset, nausea or even toxicity. Thus, an adult should not expect a child to accept a new food immediately unless it is sweet or salty. Instead, the caregiver should persist in offering the food repeatedly at intervals and anticipate that the child will accept it when it recognizes that the food is not associated with any unpleasant consequences. This changed behavior sometimes referred to as 'conditioned preference' or 'learned safety' may also reflect pleasant outcomes such as satiety or absence of hunger. The change is often quite dramatic but it may require three or four or as many as ten offerings before it occurs. Once an infant has accepted a particular food (e.g. bananas) its acceptance of similar foods (e.g. other fruits such as peaches or pears) is enhanced. The intake of other foods such as vegetables will require the usual number of trials for acceptance. Parents should recognize that in order to overcome neophobia the infant must consume the food not merely taste or smell it. Since omnivores need variety in their diets in order to promote adequate nutrient intake it is important that parents persist in their efforts to teach their children to accept a wide variety of flavors and textures from an early age.

Go On ▶

ENVIRONMENTAL FACTORS:

Positive context:

Research has confirmed that feeding an infant or young child in a positive environmental context, free of distractions such as noise, activity or loss of the mother's attention is more likely to result in food acceptance than when it is offered in a negative or distracting environment. Acceptance is also more likely when the child is comfortable and hungry, but not ravenously so. Children as they experience new eating opportunities learn to associate foods with the context and consequences of eating. Although they do not need to learn to accept sweet and salty foods, their acceptance of other foods is strongly influenced by their experiences, both positive and negative, at the time they first ingest a particular food. It usually takes only one negative association to establish a 'learned food aversion' but many more to establish a 'learned preference'. For older children, coercion to eat a food with either a food or non-food reward frequently has the effect of a negative rather than a positive context.

Go On

Answer questions 9 through 20. Base your answers on the articles "New Studies Suggest Babies Have 'Feelings' Too" and "Development of Food Acceptance Patterns in Early Childhood."

9 According to the information in the articles, which statement best explains an infant's development?

    A. Psychologists believe that infants are capable of little emotion besides expressing pain.

    B. Infants develop strong food preferences and display complex emotions at an early age.

    C. Parents are primarily responsible for infants' ability to accept new foods or display emotions.

    D. Infants are passive and accept anything they are given as long as they are rested and well-fed.

10 Which of the following sentence gives an example of the reaction know as neophobia?

    F. Infants have a natural instinct to fear sweet and bitter flavors.

    G. Infants learn to accept a new food when they are given only that food.

    H. Infants learn to slowly accept pleasant foods and then learn to love them.

    I. Infants may reject a new food because of a natural instinct to protect themselves.

11 READ THINK EXPLAIN   How do both authors support the position that infants are complex beings? Use details and information from the articles to support your answer.

12 Which of the following sentences give an example of imprinting?

    A. A bear cub refuses to eat the food its mother provides.

    B. An infant is born with the strong instinct to protect itself.

    C. A lion cub finds its way to its mother when it hears her roar.

    D. A baby becomes jealous when his mother plays with another child.

13 Which statement best expresses the main idea of the article "Development of Food Acceptance Patterns in Early Childhood?"

    F. Infants who are breast-fed become more accepting of a variety of food.

    G. .Infants who reject sweet flavors need to be given sour and bitter flavors.

    H. Children are often fussy eaters and they should be allowed to eat what they like.

    I. Children's eating habits can be shaped by gradually introducing a variety of foods in a pleasant atmosphere.

14 "Conditioned preference" can best be explained as

    A. a child expecting the gradual introduction of new foods.

    B. a child rejecting any unpleasant tasting or smelling foods.

    C. a child smelling and then tasting small amounts of new foods.

    D. a child accepting new foods that have been introduced gradually

15 According to both articles, who has the most influence over an infant's behavior?

    F. parents

    G. pediatricians

    H. psychologists

    I. researchers

16 What is the effect of gradually introducing a new food to an infant?

    A. The infant will accept the food if it is sweet or bitter from the first taste.

    B. The infant will initially reject the food but if it is given often, he/she may learn to like the food.

    C. The infant either likes or dislikes the food immediately and this preference remains for life.

    D. The infant automatically accepts food as soon as it recognizes that the food will not cause illness.

Go On ▶

How do the views of experts in human behavior differ from the view of parents and pediatricians regarding infant emotions? Use details and information from the first article to support your answer.

_____

_____

_____

_____

_____

_____

_____

_____

18 Which of the following statement's best describes the reaction to the research of Dr. Lorenz regarding infant emotions?

A. Lorenz's research is not yet widely accepted by other physiologists.

B. Most physiologists agree that Lorenz has the answers to infant emotions.

C. This research is accepted because it is associated with his grandfather's research.

D. Most researchers in the field have easily accepted the research done by Dr. Lorenz.

19 How does Dr Lorenz's research on infant jealousy compare to the work of scientists in the past?

F. Dr. Lorenz based his studies on his grandfather's research.

G. Dr. Lorenz found support for his work as far back as the 4th century.

H. Dr. Lorenz's work is original and he has no support from past research.

I. Dr. Lorenz has not yet investigated past research on the topic of infant jealousy.

20 How do infants protect themselves from foods that may cause them to get sick?

A. They seek out sweet and salty tastes that they feel are safe.

B. They often reject unfamiliar food the first time it is offered.

C. They smell the food and taste a little before they will accept it.

D. They have an instinct that guides them to a variety of safe foods.

Part 2
Read the excerpt from "The Authobiography of Malcome X" and the poem "Mother to Son" and answer Numbers 21 through 32.

from
The Autobiography of
Malcolm X

It was because of my letters that I happened to stumble upon starting to acquire some kind of a homemade education.

I became increasingly frustrated at not being able to express what I wanted to convey in letters that I wrote, especially those to Mr. Elijah Muhammad.[1] In the street, I had been the most articulate hustler out there—I had commanded attention when I said something. But now, trying to write simple English, I not only wasn't articulate, I wasn't even functional. How would I sound writing in slang, the way I would say it, something such as, "Look daddy, let me pull your coat about a cat, Elijah Muhammad—."

Many who today hear me somewhere in person, or on television, or those who read something I've said, will think I went to school far beyond the eighth grade. This impression is due entirely to my prison studies.

It had really begun back in the Charlestown Prison, when Bimbi[2] first made me feel envy of his stock of knowledge. Bimbi had always taken charge of any conversation he was in, and I had tried to emulate him. But every book I picked up had few sentences which didn't contain anywhere from one to nearly all of the words that might as well have been Chinese. When I just skipped those words, of course, I really ended up with little idea of what the book said. So I had come to the Norfolk Prison Colony still going through only book-reading motions. Pretty soon, I would have quit even these motions, unless I had received the motivation that I did.

I saw that the best thing I could do was get hold of a dictionary—to study, to learn some words. I was lucky enough to reason also that I should try to improve my penmanship. It was sad. I couldn't even write in a straight line. It was both ideas together that moved me to request a dictionary along with some tablets and pencils from the Norfold Prison Colony school.

I spent two days just riffling uncertainly through the dictionary's pages. I'd never realized so many words existed! I didn't know which words I needed to learn. Finally, just to

[1]**Elijah Muhammad:** the Black Muslims' founder and leader.

[2]**Bimbi:** a fellow inmate he met in 1947, at Charlestown State Prison.

American civil rights leader, Malcom X, speaking in New York City, 1963.

Go On ▶

start some kind of action, I began copying.

In my slow, painstaking, ragged handwriting, I copied into my tablet everything printed on that first page, down to the punctuation marks.

I believe it took me a day. Then, aloud, I read back, to myself, everything I'd written on the tablet. Over and over, aloud, to myself, I read my own handwriting.

I woke up the next morning, thinking about those words— immensely proud to realize that not only had I written so much at one time, but I'd written words that I never knew were in the world. Moreover, with a little effort, I also could remember what many of these words meant. I reviewed the words whose meanings I didn't remember. Funny thing, from the dictionary first page right now, that

"aardvark" springs to my mind. The dictionary had a picture of it, a long-tailed, long-eared, burrowing African mammal, which lives off termites caught by sticking out its tongue as an anteater does for ants.

I was so fascinated that I went on—I copied the dictionary's next page. And the same experience came when I studied that. With every succeeding page, I also learned of people and places and events from history. Actually the dictionary is like a miniature encyclopedia. Finally the dictionary's A section had filled a whole tablet-and I went on into the B's. That was the way I started, copying what eventually became the entire dictionary. It went a lot faster after so much practice helped me to pick up handwriting speed. Between what I wrote in my tablet, and writing letters, during the rest of my time

in prison I would guess I wrote a million words.

I suppose it was inevitable that as my word-base broadened, I could for the first time pick up a book and read and now begin to understand what the book was saying. Anyone who has read a great deal can imagine the new world that opened. Let me tell you something: from then until I left that prison, in every free moment I had, if I was not reading in the library, I was reading on my bunk. You couldn't have gotten me out of books with a wedge. Between Mr. Muhammad's teachings, my correspondence, my visitors— usually Ella and Reginald[3]—and my reading of books, months passed without my even thinking about being imprisoned. In fact, up to then, I never had been so truly free in my life.

[3]**Ella and Reginald:** his sister and brother

⇥ MOTHER TO SON ⇤
by Langston Hughes

Well, son, I'll tell you:

Life for me ain't been no crystal stair.

It's had tacks in it,

And splinters,

And

Boards torn up,

And places with no carpet on the floor—

Bare.

But all the time

I'se been a-climbing on,

And reachin' landin's,

And turnin' corners,

And sometimes goin' in the dark

Where there ain't been no light.

So boy, don't you turn back.

Don't you set down on the steps

'Cause you finds it's kinda hard.

Don't you fall now—

For I'se still goin' honey,

I'se still climbin'

And life for me ain't been no crytal stair.

Go On ▶

Answer questions 21 through 32. Base your answers on the excerpt from "The Autobiography of Malcolm X" and the poem "Mother to Son."

21 What would be another good title for the poem?

    A. Words of Praise

    B. The Steps of Life

    C. Believe in Miracles

    D. Joys of Motherhood

22 Read the following lines from the poem.

> **Well, son, I'll tell you:**
> **Life for me ain't been no crystal stair.**
> **It's had tacks in it,**
> **And splinters,**
> **And**
> **Boards torn up,**
> **And places with no carpet on the floor—**
> **Bare.**

What image does the author convey with these lines? Use details and information from the poem to support your answer.

Go On

23 What is most likely the author's purpose in this poem?

    A. to describe the hardships life has to offer

    B. to inspire a son to persist through life's struggles

    C. to show a close relationship between mother and son

    D. to persuade the reader a son has respect for his mother

24 What comparison does the author use repeatedly throughout the poem?

    F. life's struggles to a staircase

    G. the love of a mother to a staircase

    H. the poverty of life and the problems it causes

    I. the hope of a mother to the struggles of her son

25 READ THINK EXPLAIN

According to his autobiography, what were the effects of Malcolm X not being able to read? Use information and details from the story to support your answer.

_____

_____

_____

_____

_____

_____

_____

_____

_____

_____

_____

_____

_____

_____

Go On ▶

26 What evidence does the author of the poem have that the narrator has not given up her struggle to succeed?

    A. The mother says she has not given up hope for her son.

    B. The mother decided that she would stop at the landing.

    C. The mother tells her son she is continuing to climb the stairs.

    D. The mother tells her son that life will always have hardships.

27 What is similar about Malcolm X and the narrator in "Mother to Son?"

    F. both have been unable to read and write well.

    G. both have served extended sentences in prison.

    H. both have been unfairly treated and misjudged.

    I. both have been determined to overcome obstacles.

28 Read the following sentence from the passage.

    I spent two days just riffling uncertainly through the dictionary's pages.

What does *riffling* mean?

    A. investigating

    B. skimming words

    C. thumbing through

    D. carefully searching

29 What is the theme of both the poem and the autobiography?

    F. Getting an education can solve most of life's problems.

    G. Reading and writing are two important ingredients for success.

    H. When we are unfairly treated, we must find a reason to succeed.

    I. Even though life can be difficult, we should strive to reach our goals.

30 What was the main reason Malcolm X felt so frustrated not being able to read and write?

    A. He wanted to be thought of as a leader within the prison

    B. He had a great desire to read the books in the prison library.

    C. He was jealous of people he knew who could read and write.

    D. He wanted to be able to communicate with Elijah Muhammad.

Go On ▶

31 Read the following sentence from the excerpt.

> **In the street, I had been the most articulate hustler out there—I had commanded attention when I said something.**

What does *articulate* mean?

F. confident

G. expressive

H. faltering

I. proud

32 How does the author use specific language to portray an image of the narrator in the poem? Support your answer with details and information from the poem.

_____

_____

_____

_____

_____

_____

_____

_____

_____

Go On

Read the article "Poverty in the United States" and answer Numbers 41 through 52.

POVERTY in the UNITED STATES

The market system has worked well for most Americans, but we all know that a free market does not provide for the needs of all people. There are some individuals in the United States who are powerless to provide adequately for themselves and their families. Can our nation with its huge budget deficits provide financial support for all people who need help? Some will ask whether society should be responsible for the economic support of its members. They will say instead that is each individual's responsibility to care for oneself and one's family? Even those who agree that society is responsible for the welfare of others disagree over what organizations within society should shoulder the responsibility—the federal government, the states, or the local governments? Or perhaps charieties and other private organizations?

The distribution of income in the United States—and in every other country, for that matter—is unequal. We find poverty in the midst of plenty. Why is this so? Can we (and should we) do anything about it? First, let us see who the poor are.

WHO ARE THE POOR?

According to the U.S. Census Bureau, in 1998 approximately 34.5 million people in the country (or 12.7 percent of the population) were poor. By government definition, the poor are people whose cash income fall below certain set minimums. These minimum income levels, or *poverty levels* (also called *poverty thresholds*) are adjusted from year to year to account for changes in prices. In 1998, the poverty threshold was $8,316 for an individual living alone and $16,655 for a family of four.

The third column of Table 20.1 lists *poverty rates* (percentages of people below the poverty level) for various groups. As the table indicates, certain groups suffer a much higher rate of poverty than the national average.

Members of Some Minority Groups. In 1998 (when 11 percent of the nation's families were classified as poor), the poverty rates for African-American and Hispanic families were 24.7 percent and 24.3 percent respectively. Compare these percentages with the poverty rate for white families that year. You might note that the poverty level of white individuals (10.5) was also much smaller than that of African-American individuals (26.1) and persons of Hispanic origin (25.6).

Table 20.1
POVERTY STATUS OF INDIVIDUALS AND FAMILIES, 1998

Category	Number Below Poverty Level	Poverty Rate
Total Persons	34,476,000	12.7
White	23,454,000	10.5
African American	9,091,000	26.1
Hispanic origin*	8,070,000	25.6
Asian and Pacific Islander	1,360,000	12.5
Age		
Under 18 Years	13,467,000	18.9
18 to 24 years	4,312,000	16.6
25 to 44 years	8,664,000	10.4
45 to 64 years	4,848,000	8.0
65 years and over	3,386,000	10.5
All Families	7,186,000	11.2
White	4,829,000	10.5
African American	1,981,000	24.7
Hispanic origin	1,648,000	24.3
Type of Family		
All Married Couples	2,879,000	6.2
White	2,400,000	5.8
African American	290,000	8.6
Hispanic origin	775,000	17.8
All Female Householders, No Husband Present	3,831,000	33.1
White	2,123,000	27.6
African American	1,557,000	42.8
Hispanic origin	756,000	46.7

*Persons of Hispanic origin may be of any race.

Go On

Family Households Headed by Women in Which There is No Husband Present. Families in which the head of household is a woman and there is no husband present show a significantly high incidence of poverty. In 1998, some 33.1 percent of the families in those circumstances were poor.

The Young. Approximately 40 percent of all individuals living below the poverty level are under the age of 18. As indicated by Table 20.1, the poverty rate was greatest among persons under 18 (18.9 percent) followed by persons 18 to 24 years of age (16.6 percent). In comparison, the poverty rate was lowest among persons 45 to 64 years of age (8.0 percent).

Income Distribution. Some people earn more than others. Market and nonmarket forces affect wage earnings. In addition to wage income, however, many individuals receive all or part of their income from non-wage sources (such as from government payments, interest on savings accounts or bonds, dividends, rents, insurance income payments, and pension funds.) The amount of income that different individuals receive from non-wage sources varies considerably. An individual's total income, therefore, including earnings from wages and non-wage sources.

Measuring Income Distribution. A commonly used measure of *income distribution* (the percentage of total income received by various groups) ranks household earnings from the lowest to the highest incomes. The total number of families is divided into equal fifths, and the total income earned by

Table 20.2
PERCENT OF INCOME RECEIVED BY EACH FIFTH OF FAMILIES

Income Rank	1950	1960	1970	1980	1990	1998
Lowest Fifth	4.5	4.9	5.5	5.3	4.6	3.6
Second Fifth	12.0	12.0	12.0	11.6	10.8	9.0
Middle Fifth	17.4	17.6	17.4	17.5	16.6	15.0
Fourth Fifth	23.5	23.5	23.5	24.0	23.8	23.2
Highest Fifth	42.6	42.0	41.6	41.6	44.3	49.2

each group is tallied. Statisticians then calculate what percentage of the total income for each group total. These percentages are illustrated in Table 20.2.

As we look at Table 20.2, we can see changes income distribution patterns in the United States during the period 1950–1998. For example, the lowest fifth received an increasing percentage of total income during the period 1950–1970, but their relative situation deteriorated after 1970. The second fifth's percentage of total income remained stable from 1950 to 1970, but declined thereafter. The middle fifth's and fourth fifth's shares of total income did not change much over the years, while that of the highest fifth declined slightly during the period 1950-1980 (and has more recently skyrocketed). What can we conclude (from Table 20.2) regarding the equality of income distribution in the United States? First, we might say the obvious—that income is not equally distributed. A second response might be during the period 1950–1970, income distribution tended toward greater equality. But in the period since 1970, the trend has gone toward greater inequality.

Go On

Answer questions 33 through 42. Base your answers on "Poverty in the United States."

33 The phrase *poverty thresholds* can best be explained as

     A. the national average of income of most Americans.

     B. a variable figure that determines the ceiling of income.

     C. the income that determines the poverty status of a family.

     D. the income level below which people are considered poor.

34 How do poverty rates for total persons who are African-American compare to the poverty rates of Hispanics?

     F. The poverty rate of African-Americans is equal to the poverty rate of Hispanics.

     G. The poverty rate of African-Americans is much greater than the poverty rate of Hispanics.

     H. The poverty rate of African-Americans is slightly lower than the poverty rate of Hispanics.

     I. The poverty rate of African-Americans is slightly higher than the poverty rate of Hispanics.

35 READ THINK EXPLAIN   How did income distribution change from 1950 to 1980? Use information and details from the article and the tables to support your answer.

_____

_____

_____

_____

_____

_____

_____

_____

36 What is most likely the author's purpose in this passage?

     A. to convince the reader that poverty is a problem.

     B. to identify who makes up the poor in the United States

     C. to explain the poverty level difference among ethnic groups.

     D. to suggest solutions for the poverty crisis in the United States.

Go On

37 How do statisticians measure income distribution?

    F. They group people by age and then calculate each group's total.

    G. They divide the total number of families into groups and rank them by income.

    H. They group people by family type and age, and then calculate each group's total.

    I. They calculate how many people from each minority group are below the poverty level.

38   What details does the author use to support the idea that different factors affect the poverty status of families? Use details and information from the article to support your answer.

---

39 Which statement best describes the trend of income distribution since 1970?

    A. Inequalities between the lowest fifth and highest fifth of families has become less.

    B. Inequalities between the lowest fifth and highest fifth of families has become greater.

    C. Inequalities between the lowest fifth and highest fifth of families has remained constant.

    D. Inequalities between the middle fifth and lowest fifth of families has remained constant.

40 What information about age is true concerning the poverty status of individuals?

    F. Those 65 years and over have the highest number below the poverty level.

    G. Every age group has an average of 20% of their population below the poverty rate.

    H. Those 18 years and younger have the highest number of people below the poverty level.

    I. Age groups under 54 have an average of 10% of their population below the poverty rate.

41 Which would be the best example of a non-wage source?

    A. Money from a rental property

    B. Overtime pay for weekend work

    C. An annual salary from a steady job

    D. Birthday gifts from a family member

42 After reading the article, what conclusions can you reach regarding the poverty status of families?

    F. Young families have a higher poverty rate than older families.

    G. It is the individual's responsibility to care for his/her own family.

    H. Female led households (with no husband) have a high rate of poverty.

    I. White families have more people below the poverty level than Hispanic families.

Go On ▶

Read the article "Sitting Fit for Everyone" and answer Numbers 43 through 50.

SITTING FIT
for Everyone

By Susan Winter Ward

Public enemy #1 for our bodies ... the simple chair. Or is it how we *use* chairs that's the problem? When I was a kid, my Dad asked me if I could design a chair for people whose knees bent backwards. I'm still working on that one. And since I began doing yoga, I've been working on designing a body for those of us whose knees bend forward many hours a day.

More accurately, what do we do with bodies that ache because we sit, and sit, and sit? We're a society of "chair people". We sit for meals, sit for classes, sit in the car, sit at a desk, sit in meetings and movies. We sit to talk on the telephone and watch TV, sit at computers, on planes, on trains, in waiting rooms. Some of us sit due to the fact that we just have a lazy lifestyle. Do you ever feel that your life has become a series of transitions from one seated location to another?

I don't think our bodies were meant to live that way any more than our knees were meant to bend backwards! Most chairs aren't designed to support our bodies with healthy posture. They cause us to slump, curve our spines, push our heads forward or lean us back onto our tailbones. The worst back problem I ever

had came after sitting in a seminar room for three days of lectures.

Inactivity can cause stiffness, backache, weakness, constipation, poor circulation, mental dullness, nervousness, cramps, and degeneration. Depressing thoughts. Whatever the reason and wherever you sit, it is possible to begin becoming fit, even while sitting in your chair.

Yoga, the 5000-year-old gift of body/mind balance, can be adapted to a seated stretching program that can counteract the inevitable results of too much sitting. Body awareness, better posture, relief from aches and pains, as well as increased flexibility and strengthening, and a deep sense of relaxation can be achieved right where you are... are you sitting down?

Although a consistent yoga program of standing, balancing, lying poses, and inversions is a more complete practice, yoga need not be relegated to the yoga studio or health club. The time commitment of hours per week can sometimes be difficult to fit into a busy schedule. Doing a pose or two hourly throughout the day can give you some of the benefits of a yoga practice and help to relieve the results of sitting too much.

Small efforts while sitting in various daily situations, can contribute greatly to our strength, flexibility, relaxation, increased circulation, stronger respiration, and clarity of mind. Yoga poses adapted to small bites may not have the same intensity as a full yoga class, but the benefits of yoga are readily available to those who nibble on yoga throughout the day.

Those who are physically challenged due to age, illness, or who just can't do poses on the floor, need not miss out on the many benefits of yoga. Those who are physically challenged, confined to wheelchairs or recovering from injury, with their physician's approval, can benefit from their own adaptation of the breathing and gentle seated poses.

Seated yoga can build the strength and flexibility, needed to progress to more and more challenging poses. Breathing, stretching and strengthening can be introduced at a slow pace, gently bringing bodies to new levels of fitness, increasing circulation and bringing in healing "life force" energy.

The Sitting Fit ™ programs on CDRom and ScreenSaver benefit all of us, regardless of our physical condition. Sitting needs to be balanced with moving, breathing and stretching, so try some of these simple poses for a "mini yoga break". You'll feel the difference and return your attention to work refreshed, more relaxed and with a clearer mind.

Go On ▶

SIMPLE EXERCISE YOU CAN DO WHILE SITTING

Breathing

Sit up straight on the edge of your chair, feet flat on the floor directly below your knees. Let your hands rest on your thighs. Take a long, deep breath, and exhale completely.

Inhale deeply again, reaching for the ceiling with the crown of your head, lengthening your spine. Continue breathing with full deep inhalations and complete exhalations for 10 to 20 breaths.

Arms Overhead

As you inhale, bring your arms out to your sides and slowly raise them overhead. Try to keep your elbows straight and bring your arms along side your ears.

Keep lifting your ribs away from your hips, flattening your back, elongating your spine. As you exhale, slide your shoulder blades down your back, dropping your shoulders away from your ears as you reach through your finger tips. Keep breathing deeply for 3 to 5 breaths. Exhale as you lower your arms.

Shoulder Shrugs

Inhaling, bring your shoulders up tightly toward your ears. Roll your shoulders back, pressing your shoulder blades tightly together.

Exhale as you press your shoulders down toward the floor. Inhaling again, bring your shoulders up again, roll them back and press your blades together, and release down. Repeat several times and don't forget to breathe!

Forward Fold

Still sitting on the edge of your chair with your feet hip width apart, inhale as you bring your arms out to your sides.

Reach forward with your chin as you rotate from your hips, exhaling as your bring your chest toward your thighs. Keep you back flat. With you next exhalation, allow yourself to relax, chest on your thighs, arms and head dangling, relaxed. Take 3 to 5 deep, full, relaxing breaths. Inhale as you sit up slowly with a flat back.

Knee Raises

Sitting up straight, inhaling as you raise your right knee up in front of you. Grasp your leg in front of your knee with both hands.

Keep your back flat as you exhale and draw your knee in toward your chest. Hold it there for 3 to 5 breaths. Release as you exhale. Repeat with you left leg.

Answer questions 43 through 50. Base your answers on the article "Sitting Fit for Everyone."

43 What tone does the author use in the first paragraph of the passage?

   A. advisory

   B. humorous

   C. reminiscent

   D. serious

44 The main idea of the passage could best be described in which of the following sentences?

   E. We have become a society of "chair people."

   F. Depression is caused by long periods of inactivity.

   G. Chairs are a serious threat to the well-being of our bodies.

   H. Seated yoga is a practical way to bring the body to fitness.

45 READ THINK EXPLAIN How does the author support the idea that yoga can help to counteract the damage done to our bodies from too much sitting? Use details and information from the article to support your answer.

46 Why did the author include the instructions for how to do the sitting yoga exercises?

    A. The reader probably spends most of the day in a seated position.

    B. The reader may be unable to attend yoga classes at a yoga center.

    C. A reader is more likely to start an exercise program if instructions are provided.

    D. The author wanted to make the reader aware that many different exercises exists.

47 READ THINK EXPLAIN   What are some of the causes of the inactivity in our society? Use information and details from the article to support your answer.

_____

_____

_____

_____

_____

_____

_____

48 Read the following sentence from the article.

    Do you ever feel your life has become a series of transitions from one seated location to another?

What does *transition* mean?

    A. bridges

    B. exercises

    C. shifts

    D. thoughts

Go On ▶

49 What advice would the author give to someone who was unable to attend regular yoga classes?

F. Begin another form of exercise as quickly as possible.

G. Try to stand and move around as much as possible during the day.

H. Begin an adapted yoga program by doing various exercises while seated.

I. Try to attend yoga classes at least once a week until you have more time.

50 Imagine you are interested in getting the physical education department in your school to start a yoga class? What reasons would you give for starting the class. Use information and details from the article to support your answer.

_____

_____

_____

_____

_____

_____

_____

_____

_____

_____

_____

_____

STOP

Index

A

Adjectives in descriptive writing, 81
Adjective suffixes, 36
Analysis
    charts in, 80
    diagrams in, 62
    of primary source information,
      139–156
    in reading, 84, 86, 104, 123, 143, 181,
      204
Antonyms, 38
Argument/support, 83
Author, point of view of, 99–118
Author's purpose, 99–118

B

Bulleted lists, 83

C

Captions, drawing conclusions from, 41
Cause
    defined, 177
    signal words for, 179
Cause–and–effect relationships, 38, 80
    implied, 180
    recognizing, 177–196
    transition words in, 81
Characters, 202–203
    comparison and contrast of, 58
Charts
    in analyzing main idea and details,
      80, 84
    reading, 40–41, 74
Chronological order, 88
Climax in plot, 199–200
Comparison, 57
    signal words for, 60
Comparison and contrast, 57–78, 124
    examples of, 58
    in organization, 80–81
    Venn diagrams showing, 60–61
Conclusions, drawing, 40–41, 157–176
Concrete nouns in descriptive writing,
    81
Conflict in plot, 199–200
Context clues, 33, 42, 43, 143
Contrast, 38, 57
    signal words for, 60

D

Degree order, 83
Descriptive writing
    author's purpose in, 101
    organization in, 80
    transition words in, 81
Details, 77–98
Diagrams
    in analyzing text, 62
    in answering questions, 61
Directly stated main idea, 79

E

Effect
    defined, 177
    signal words for, 179
Evaluation, 123
Examination, 181
Examples, 38
Explanation, 38
Exposition in plot, 199–200
Expository writing, author's purpose
    in, 101

F

Fiction
    point of view in, 102
Flashbacks, 83
Foreshadowing, 83

G

Generalizations, 159–160
Graphic organizers, 205
    charts as, 80, 84
    diagrams as, 61, 62, 200
    graphs as, 40–41
    Venn diagram as, 60–61, 63
Graphs, reading, 40–41

I

Implied main idea, 79
Inferences, 32, 40, 43
Information
    gathering, analyzing and
      evaluating, 119–138
    primary source, 139–156
    secondary source, 141
    synthesizing, 120, 157–176
Information sources, 121

L

Library reference materials, 121

M

Main idea, 77–98
    comparison and contrast of,
      58
    directly stated, 79
    identifying, 62
    implied, 79

N

Narrative writing, 197–217
    author's purpose in, 101
    characters in, 202–203
    plot in, 199–201
    setting in, 201–202
    theme in, 203

Nonfiction, point of view in, 102
Noun suffixes
    for people, 35
    for places or things, 35
Number-related prefixes, 33

O

Organization, patterns of, 77–98
    argument/support, 83
    bulleted lists, 83
    cause and effect, 80, 81
    comparison and contrast, 80–81
    degree order, 83
    descriptive, 80, 81
    flashbacks, 83
    foreshadowing, 83
    problem/solution, 80–81
    question/answer, 80
    spatial order, 83
    time-order, 80–81

P

Persuasive appeal, 99–118
Persuasive writing
    author's purpose in, 101
    point of view in, 102
Plot, 199–201
    climax in, 199–200
    conflict in, 199–200
    exposition in, 199–200
    resolution in, 199–200
    rising action in, 199–200
    turning point in, 199–200
Plot map, 200–201
Point of view, 99–118
    comparison and contrast of, 58
Position-related prefixes, 34
Prediction in reading, 62, 84, 86, 104,
    123, 143, 144, 161, 181, 204
Prefixes, 33–35
    number-related, 33
    position-related, 34
    time-related, 34
Primary source information, analysis
    of, 139–156
Problem/solution organization, 80
    transition words in, 81
Purpose, setting, for reading, 42

Q

Question/answer organization, 80

R

Reading
    charts, 40–41
    context clues in, 33, 42, 43, 143
    graphs, 40-41
    inferences in, 32, 40-41, 43
    predictions in, 62, 84, 86, 104, 123,
      143, 144, 161, 181, 204

Acknowledgments

"DNA Detectives." Reprinted with permission of *Best Friends* magazine, Best Friends Animal Sanctuary. Article by Julie Richard. Pages 1–3.

"Diablo Country" by Art Buchwald. Reprinted with permission of Penguin Putnam Inc. Pages 7–8.

"Nuclear Engery" from *Environmental Science* by Martin Schachter. Copyright © 1999 Amsco School Publications, Inc. Pages 9–10.

Excerpt from "Marigolds" by Eugenia Collier. Originally printed in *NEGRO DIGEST,* November 1969. Reprinted by permission of the author. Page 14.

"World is Skating on Thin Ice." Copyright © 2000 Natural Life. Printed by Permission of Worldwatch Institute (http://www.worldwatch.org). Pages 17–18.

"The Boom of the 1880s" from *California Then and Now* by Abraham Hoffman. Copyright © 1996 by Amsco School Publications, Inc. Pages 22–23.

"Oranges" from *New and Selected Poems* by Gary Soto. Reprinted with permission from Chronicle Books. Page 26.

"The Babylonian Empire" and "Growth of a New Economic Order" from *Global History* by Henry Brun, Lillian Forman, and Herbert Brodsky. Copyright © 2000 by Amsco School Publications, Inc. Pages 43, 48.

"An Organic Farmer's Secret" by Robert E. Sullivan. *Earth Times* News Service © 2000 The Earth Times. Reprinted by permission. Page 44.

"Music on the Brain" by Michael D. Lemonick. *Time* magazine June 5, 2000 © Time Inc. Reprinted by permission. Page 53.

"Columbus and the Moon" from *A Reader For Developing Writers.* Copyright © 1990 by McGraw-Hill, Inc. Page 62.

"Speech of Chief Seattle." *Seattle Sunday Star,* October 29, 1887. Page 65.

"Three Styles of Farming" from *Global Geography* by Milton Finkelstein, James Flanagan, and Norman L. Lunger. Copyright © 1999 by Amsco School Publications, Inc. Pages 68–69.

"The New Colossus" by Emma Lazarus. Page 73.

"A Nation of Immigrants" from *Global History* by Henry Brun, Lillian Forman, and Herbert Brodsky. Copyright © 2000 by Amsco School Publications, Inc. Page 74.

"Three Passions I Have Lived For," an excerpt from *Autobiography* by Bertrand Russell. Page 84.

"The Southwest Tradition" from *DesertUSA.com.* Copyright © 2001 Digital West Media Inc. All rights reserved. Page 87.

"Critters Vex People as Habitats Collide" by Andrew Alderson. October 9, 2000. *London Daily Telegraph.* Reprinted by permission. Pages 90–91.

"Animal Reaction: Pets suffer from allergies too—sometimes to humans" by Lisa Gutierrez. From *The Kansas City Star.* Reprinted by permission. Pages 94–96.

"Alabama Centinnial" by Naomi Long Madgett. Reprinted by permission of Lotus Press. Page 104.

Excerpt from "A Thousand Days: John F Kennedy in the White House" by Arthur Schlesinger. Copyright © 1965 by Arthur M. Schlesinger, Jr. Reprinted by permission of Houghton Mifflin Co. Page 107.

"Martin Luther King, Jr." from *Enjoying American History* by Henry Abraham and Irwin Pfeffer. Copyright © 1998 Amsco School Publications, Inc. Page 108.

"The New Enemies of Journalism" by Charles Kuralt. From *Life on the Road.* Copyright © 1990 Putnam Inc. All rights reserved. Pages 111–112.

"Death of Privacy" by Christine Varney. From *Newsweek* December 2000-February 2001, Special Edition © 2000 Newsweek, Inc. All rights reserved. Reprinted by permission. Pages 114–115.

"Natural Fossil Fuels" and "The Carboniferous Era (345–280mybp)" by Steve Thackery, UK. Reprinted by permission. Page 123.

"Sea Turtles" and "Conservation—Threats to Sea Turtle Survival" from *Marine Science* by Thomas F. Greene. Copyright © 1998 Amsco School Publications, Inc. Pages 126–127.

"Pushing the Envelope" From *Smithsonian* Magazine October 1997, Copyright © 1997 Smithsonian Institution. Pages 130–132.

"China" from *Global History* by Henry Brun, Lillian Forman, and Herbert Brodsky. Copyright © 2000 by Amsco School Publications, Inc. Pages 135–136.

"Does Modern Society Make Us Fat?" by Tracy Boyd © The Detroit News, February 15, 2000. Reprinted by permission. Pages 143–144.

"Nature's Classroom" from *Wildlife Conservation* magazine. February 2001. Copyright 2001 by Gary Turbak. Pages 147–148.

"The Lifestyle Rx" From *Consumer Reports* magazine October 2000. Copyright © 2000 Consumer's Union. Pages 151–153.

"Recycle and Reuse." Excerpt from *Design or a Livable Planet* by John Naar. © 1998 Harper and Row. Page 161.

"What Makes a Safe Driver?" from *Transportation—America's Lifeline,* 1997 Edition. Used with permission of the publisher. Pages 164–166.

"The Motion Picture Industry" from *California Then and Now* by Abraham Hoffman. Copyright © 1996 by Amsco School Publications, Inc. Pages 169–170.

"Teens and Sleep" from *KidsHealth* (http://KidsHealth.org). Copyright © 2001 The Nemours Foundation. Used with permission. Pages 173–174.

"Silent Spring" from *Marine Science* by Thomas F. Greene. Copyright © 1998 Amsco School Publications, Inc. Page 181.

"Women Win the Right to Vote!" *Historical Gazette,* volume 3, number 5. © Bridget E. Smith, Historical Gazette, 1995–2001. Used by permission. All rights reserved. Pages 184–186.

Excerpt from "Leiningen Versus the Ants" by Carl Stephenson. Pages 189–190.

"The Paper Chase" by Fenella Saunders. (http://www.Discover.com) Posted 12/9/98. Pages 193–194.

"Celebration of Grandfathers" by Rudolfo Anaya. Copyright © 1983 by Rudolfo Anaya. First published in *New Mexico Magazine,* March 1983. Page 204.

"Lost Sister" from *Picture Bride* by Cathy Song. Copyright © 1983 Yale University Press. Reprinted by permission of publisher. Page 206–207.

Excerpt from "With All Flags Flying" by Anne Tyler. Reprinted with permission of Knopf Inc. Page 210–211.

"The Blanket" by Floyd Dell. Page 214–215.

"Jackie Robinson" from *Enjoying American History* by Henry Abraham and Irwin Pfeffer. Copyright © 1998 Amsco School Publications, Inc. Page 221.

Photo and Art Credits